The Homemaker's Cookbook

Edited by MARION HOWELLS

Cover photography by Roger Phillips

This edition first published 1979 by Octopus Books Limited
59 Grosvenor Street, London W1

© Octopus Books Limited 1971

ISBN 0 7064 1083 1

Produced by Mandarin Publishers Limited
22a Westlands Road, Quarry Bay, Hong Kong

Printed in Hong Kong

Contents

Weights and measures

To get consistently good results when cooking it is necessary to weigh or measure the ingredients very accurately. All recipes in this book are based on the Imperial weights and measures with American equivalents given in parenthesis. Dry ingredients are given in ounces or spoonfuls and the British Standard Institute measuring spoon has been used to ensure accurate measurements.

All spoons should be filled level. This is most important.

Metric measures

When the Metric system comes into operation, although many people will continue to use their well tried recipe books the new weights will be in grams instead of ounces and kilograms instead of pounds.

The exact conversion would not be practicable from the cook's point of view, and we have therefore given a working equivalent.

Imperial oz.	Metric grams	Working Equivalent grams
1	28·35	25
2	56·7	50
4	113·4	100
8	226·8	200
12	340·2	300
1·0 lb.	453	400
1·1 lb.	½ Kilo	
2·2 lb.	1 Kilo	

Liquid measures

	millilitres	millilitres
¼ pint (1 gill)	142 ml	150 ml
½ pint	284 ml	300 ml
1 pint	568 ml	600 ml
1¾ pints	994 ml	1 litre

Linear measures for cake tins

1 inch	2½ cm
2 inch	5 cm
3 inch	7½ cm
6 inch	15 cm

The B.S.I. measuring jug is used to measure liquids. The one illustrated holds 10 fluid oz. or ½ pint. A larger one holding 1 pint or 20 fluid oz. is also available.

The standard measuring cup shown on this page measures up to 250 millilitres; this is equivalent to quarter of a litre.

NOTE: The American 1 pint is 16 fluid ounces. The standard American cup measure is 8 fluid ounces.

When measuring a liquid ingredient, the cup should be on a level surface.

For those who wish to adopt the Metric system of measuring, we give above the exact conversion and also the agreed working equivalent.

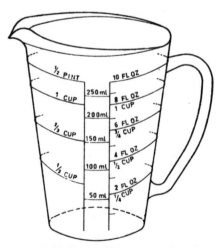

Standard Imperial ½-pint measure

Oven temperatures

When you buy a gas or electric cooker the manufacturer will provide you with a chart giving his recommendations for the oven settings. There is often a slight variance between different makes of cookers and also between gas and electric temperatures. The chart which follows, therefore, can only be a guide but if you follow it carefully, whatever type of cooker you use, you will not go far wrong.

	Mark	Temperature ° Fahrenheit
Very cool or very slow	¼—1	225°—275°
Cool or slow	1—2	275°—300°
Very moderate	3—4	325°—350°
Moderate	4—5	350°—375°
Moderately hot	5—6	375°—400°
Hot	7—8	425°—450°
Very hot	8—10	450°—500°

Temperature conversion

Measurements of heat used in Britain at present are given in degrees Fahrenheit or Centigrade. When the metrication programme has reached a more advanced stage, it is possible that a change will be made.

The unit at present known as the degree Centigrade will be replaced by degrees Celsius. The reason is to avoid confusion with a unit in some other countries having the same name, but used to denote fractions of a right angle.

IN THIS BOOK DEGREES FAHRENHEIT ARE USED THROUGHOUT
—but for future reference we give a conversion chart.

	Fahrenheit	Celsius
Very cool or very slow	275 F.	135 C.
Cool or slow	300 F.	149 C.
Very moderate	325 F.	163 C.
Moderate	350 F.	177 C.
Moderately hot	375 F.	190 C.
Fairly hot	400 F.	204 C.
Hot	425 F.	218 C.
Very hot	450 F.	238 C.

Appetizers

In this section we give a tempting selection of hors d'oeuvre, canapés, savouries and dips.

Hors d'oeuvre make a tasty, colourful beginning. They should have a distinct, sharp taste to clear the palate for the next course. They should be light, so that the appetite for the next course is not dulled.

Canapés are savoury pieces, generally bite-sized, to offer with drinks. They are small rounds, squares, triangles or fingers of fresh bread, toast or crisply fried bread, or savoury biscuits. They're topped, simply, with a pâté or spread, or they can have an irresistible selection of good things to top them. The word 'canapés' is derived from the French, meaning 'sofa'; it was considered the small bases acted as a 'seat' for the delicacies which topped them.

Savouries are another popular accompaniment to party drinks; these are savoury bites such as Angels on Horseback.

Hors d'Oeuvre

A selection of any of the following would look appetizing and colourful.

Sliced continental sausages: salami, liver sausage, etc.

Vegetables, both fresh and canned: artichoke hearts, beans, asparagus, tiny champignons (mushrooms), mixed vegetables, cauliflower, carrot, broccoli, beetroot, etc. When using fresh vegetables, cook them lightly, drain well, toss in a little French dressing.

Fish of all types: smoked salmon, herrings made into roll mops, oysters—fresh and smoked—crab, prawns, lobster, etc.

Salads of various types: potato, mushroom, etc.

Chicken Liver Pâté

This superb Chicken Liver Pâté makes the perfect first course for a dinner party; or use it as a spread, on small toast squares, to serve with drinks.

1½ teaspoons gelatine	¼ teaspoon thyme
2 tablespoons cold water	1 bayleaf
¼ pint (½ cup) chicken stock	2 tablespoons dry sherry
1 lb. chicken livers	4 tablespoons cream
2 tablespoons brandy	2 tablespoons chopped parsley
2 oz. (¼ cup) butter	salt, pepper
2 small onions	3 oz. (good ¼ cup) butter, extra
4 rashers bacon	

Soften gelatine in cold water, add to boiling stock, stir until dissolved. Pour into a lightly oiled mould or loaf tin, refrigerate until set.

Chop chicken livers roughly, place in basin with brandy and marinate 1½ hours. Drain livers, heat 1 oz. (2 tablespoons) butter in frying pan, add livers and sauté just long enough to brown on all sides.

In separate pan, melt remaining butter and cook the chopped onion, chopped bacon, thyme and bayleaf. Add the semi-cooked chicken livers, cook further 5 minutes. Remove from heat, remove bayleaf.

Blend mixture until smooth in electric blender or pound to a paste, then rub through sieve. Stir in any brandy left from marinade, sherry, cream, parsley, and salt and pepper to taste. Melt extra butter and fold through. Spread over gelatine in mould, pressing mixture in gently and evenly; refrigerate until firm. Unmould on to serving plate. Serve with triangles of toast.

Serves 4 to 5.

Liver Pâté

1 lb. calves liver	3 dessertspoons medium cream
2 oz. (¼ cup) butter	
4 oz. belly of pork	1 beaten egg
1 tablespoon parsley	salt, black pepper
pinch thyme	2 oz. chicken livers
1 clove garlic	1½ tablespoons brandy
lemon juice	4 oz. streaky bacon
	4 bay leaves

Brown liver in butter, put through a mincer with the pork. Add finely chopped parsley, thyme, crushed garlic, lemon juice to taste, cream, egg and seasoning.

Trim chicken livers and fry in remaining butter. Remove from the pan, add brandy and flame. Stir up the sediment and add to the liver mixture.

Line a terrine with the bacon rashers, half fill with the liver mixture, spread chicken livers on top and cover with remaining liver. Fold ends of bacon over the top and add the bay leaves.

Cover tightly with the lid or buttered foil and

stand in a baking tin with about ½ in. water.

Cook in a very moderate oven, Mark 3, 325°F., for 2 hours.

Put a light weight on top while cooling and serve when completely cold with hot toast.

Brandied Liverwurst Pâté

2 oz. (¼ cup) butter
1 lb. liverwurst
2 tablespoons chopped parsley
½ teaspoon dried thyme
pinch nutmeg
2 teaspoons grated onion
2 tablespoons medium cream
2 tablespoons brandy

Beat together butter and liverwurst until smooth. Add remaining ingredients, beat again. Place in a greased mould, refrigerate several hours or overnight.

Serves 5 to 6.

Ham Rolls

4 oz. (⅔ cup) rice
1 bay leaf
pinch saffron
1 tablespoon oil
2 oz. onion (½ small onion)
2 oz. apple (½ apple)
1 oz. (2 tablespoons) butter
1½ teaspoons curry powder
4 tablespoons single (light) cream
grated rind of 1 lemon
2 tablespoons lemon juice
1 oz. (2 tablespoons) chopped ham
1 tablespoon chopped red pepper
8 slices ham

Cook the rice with bay leaf and saffron, drain, rinse and add the oil. Sauté the peeled and chopped onion and apple in the butter for 5 minutes. Remove from heat, add cream, lemon rind, lemon juice, ham and red pepper. Season carefully and set aside in a cool place for 1 hour. Roll in slices of ham and garnish with black olives and red pepper.

Serves 8.

Smoked Haddock Pâté

¼ lb. cooked smoked haddock
4 oz. (½ cup) butter
1½ tablespoons finely chopped onion or shallot
¼ teaspoon freshly ground pepper
1 teaspoon lemon juice
¼ teaspoon curry powder
chopped parsley

Skin and bone fish. Pound butter and fish together until well blended. Add onion or shallot, pepper, lemon juice and curry powder, beat well. Sprinkle with a little chopped parsley.

Serves 4.

Tchinin

A tasty fish-flavoured hors d'oeuvre.

7 oz. can sardines
5 hard boiled eggs
2 tablespoons mayonnaise
1 tablespoon lemon juice
1 teaspoon Worcestershire sauce
salt, pepper
2 tablespoons whipped cream

Drain oil from sardines and remove bones. Chop eggs roughly. Emulsify all the ingredients except the cream. Correct the seasoning then add cream. Put the mixture into a forcing bag and decorate the lettuce hearts, dust with paprika and sprinkle with finely chopped nuts or chives.

Serves 5 to 6.

Avocado Creams

2 avocado pears
1 tablespoon wine vinegar
4 anchovies very finely chopped
1 teaspoon very finely chopped onion
2 teaspoons sugar
salt, cayenne
1 teaspoon paprika
¼ pint (½ cup) whipped cream

Remove the stone and flesh from the pears and mash the flesh to a soft cream. Add all the other ingredients, mix well and correct the seasoning. Pile back into the avocado cases and garnish with lemon.

Serves 4.

Mushrooms à la Grecque

2 tablespoons oil
juice of 1 lemon
2 tablespoons tomato purée
bouquet garni
1 clove garlic
pepper, salt
8 oz. (2 cups) button mushrooms

Put the oil, lemon juice, tomato purée, bouquet garni and crushed garlic into a small pan, cover and cook for a few minutes. Season with pepper and salt. Wash mushrooms, drain and add to sauce. Cover and cook for 7 minutes. Serve cold.

Serves 4.

Cauliflower with Aioli

1 cauliflower
2 cloves garlic
2 egg yolks
½ pint (1 cup) oil

Divide the cauliflower into small sprigs. Pound the garlic, stir in the egg yolks. Add the oil very gradually at first, as if for mayonnaise. When all the oil has been added, put the aioli into a bowl standing on a flat dish. Arrange the sprigs of cauliflower round.

Savoury Pancakes

2 eggs	approx. 1 pint (1¾ cups)
1 oz. (2 tablespoons)	milk
butter	4 oz. (1 cup) grated
8 oz. (2 cups) plain	cheese (Cheddar or
flour	similar)
salt, pepper	parsley
1 teaspoon dry mustard	

Separate eggs, melt butter. Sift together dry ingredients. Make well in centre, add egg-yolks and melted butter to flour mixture. Gradually add milk, stirring constantly until mixture is smooth. Lastly fold in stiffly beaten egg-whites.

Heat a little oil in small frying pan. Pour sufficient batter into frying pan to make thin pancakes, cook over medium heat until lightly browned, turn and cook other side. Turn on to a board, spread with desired filling and roll up. Put on to dish and keep hot while rest of pancakes are being cooked. Sprinkle with cheese and put under grill to brown. Serve garnished with parsley.

Makes 10 to 12 pancakes.

A choice of 3 fillings is given below. If the main course is to be fish, meat or poultry, you can choose a filling for the pancake entrée that will contrast with the main dish.

Red Salmon

7½ oz. can red salmon	1 teaspoon curry
2 dessertspoons	powder
chopped mint	½ teaspoon sugar
4 oz. (½ cup or 1	2 dessertspoons lemon
package) cream	juice
cheese	salt, pepper
2 oz. (½ cup) grated	
cheese (Cheddar or	
similar)	

Drain salmon and remove bones. Combine salmon with remaining ingredients; mix well. Season to taste with salt and pepper.

Asparagus

10 oz. can green	2 oz. (½ cup) grated
asparagus tips	cheese (Cheddar or
2 oz. (¼ cup) butter	similar)
2 oz. (½ cup) flour	4 rashers bacon
2 egg-yolks	salt, pepper
2 sticks finely chopped	
celery	

Drain asparagus, make liquid up to ¾ pint (1 cup) with water. Melt butter in saucepan, stir in flour, cook few minutes. Gradually add reserved liquid. Bring to boil, stirring; simmer 3 minutes. Remove from heat, add egg-yolks, celery, grated cheese and asparagus.

Chop bacon, cook in frying pan until crisp, add to asparagus mixture. Season to taste.

Chicken

½ lb. cooked chicken	2 egg-yolks
3 oz. (1 cup) mushrooms	2 teaspoons curry
1 stick celery	powder
2 medium potatoes	2 tablespoons port wine
1 oz. (2 tablespoons)	1½ teaspoons salt
butter	pinch pepper
¼ pint (½ cup) milk	½ teaspoon nutmeg
2 chives or spring	
onions chopped	

Finely chop chicken meat, mushrooms and celery. Rub peeled boiled potatoes through sieve.

Melt butter in saucepan, sauté mushrooms until soft. Add sieved potato and milk, stir over low heat until mixture is heated and thoroughly combined. Remove from heat, add chopped chives or spring onions, celery, egg-yolks and chicken. Stir in curry powder and wine. Season to taste with salt, pepper and nutmeg; mix well.

Serves 6.

Stuffed Peaches

Use 2 large ripe peaches or 4 halves of canned peaches.

6 oz. (¾ cup) cream	1 oz. (2 tablespoons)
cheese	walnuts
1 oz. (2 tablespoons)	endive
seedless raisins	watercress
(plumped in boiling	
water)	

Mix the cheese, raisins and chopped nuts and shape into 12 small balls. If the mixture is too soft refrigerate for a short while before shaping.

Arrange the peaches on a little endive, put 3 balls of cheese in each and garnish with watercress.

Serves 4.

A tempting selection of canapés; use any of these toppings; smoked salmon with scrambled eggs; lettuce, camembert cheese, sliced radish; asparagus and rare roast beef; prawns, shrimps, lettuce, mayonnaise (see page 121); lettuce, sardines, lemon; creamed blue cheese with stuffed olives; smoked salmon, asparagus, cucumber; liver pâté, beetroot, gherkins; egg slices with anchovies; cucumber, prawns, mayonnaise (see page 121); cucumber, rare roast beef and cocktail onions.

Grilled Chicken Livers

2 oz. (¼ cup) butter
1 lb. chicken livers

2 oz. (½ cup) fine dry
 breadcrumbs

Sauce

1 oz. (2 tablespoons)
 butter
1 tablespoon prepared
 mustard
2 tablespoons tomato
 paste

2 tablespoons water
1 dessertspoon grated
 onion
pinch cayenne
2 teaspoons
 Worcestershire sauce

Melt butter, dip cleaned chicken livers into butter, then coat firmly with breadcrumbs. Thread on to 3 or 4 skewers. Place on greased grilling tray and grill about 3 minutes on each side or until chicken livers are tender. Serve with sauce for spooning over or dripping.
Serves 3 to 4.

Sauce Melt butter in saucepan, add remaining ingredients, stir over heat until boiling.

NOTE: In their uncooked state, chicken livers are very tender; if too thick skewers are used, the livers may break. The fine bamboo skewers are ideal. They can be bought in some speciality shops, or shops which sell oriental goods.

Dutch Bitterballs

3 oz. (½ cup) chopped
 raw veal
1 teaspoon gelatine
1 oz. (2 tablespoons)
 butter
2 tablespoons flour
3 oz. (½ cup) chopped
 ham
1 oz. (¼ cup) grated
 cheese (Cheddar or
 similar)

1 teaspoon chopped
 parsley
salt, pepper
nutmeg
dried breadcrumbs
1 egg
oil

Cover veal with water and simmer until tender. Drain, reserve ½ pint (1 cup) stock. Dissolve gelatine in hot veal stock.
Melt butter, add flour, cook 1 minute. Remove from heat. Gradually add stock. Return to heat, bring to boil, simmer until smooth and thickened, stirring constantly. Add chopped veal and ham, grated cheese and parsley. Season well, turn into bowl, refrigerate overnight.
Using teaspoon, form mixture into small balls. Roll in dried breadcrumbs, dip in beaten egg, roll again in breadcrumbs to give firm coating. Deep fry in hot oil—till golden, drain on absorbent paper.
These are the famous Dutch savoury snack and drink accompaniment. They are traditionally served with a mild mustard, into which the balls are dipped before eating. It is the mustard accompaniment which gives them their name.
Makes approx. 2 dozen.

Crunchy Cheese Croutons

1½ oz. (3 tablespoons)
 butter
2 oz. (½ cup) Cheddar
 cheese

2 tablespoons chopped
 parsley
salt, pepper
French bread

Combine butter, grated cheese and parsley in bowl; blend well until creamy and smooth. Season to taste. Place slices of French bread on baking tray; cover surface with cheese mixture. Bake in very hot oven, Mark 8, 450°F., 8 to 10 minutes or until lightly golden brown and crisp.
Sufficient covering for approx. 12 slices of French bread.

NOTE: For a more crunchy top, press tops of croutons in finely chopped nuts before baking.
These are a quick-and-easy, delightfully savoury snack to eat just as they are, hot from the oven. Or serve them as an accompaniment to soup or grills.

Ham Savouries

3 teaspoons gelatine
8 oz. cooked ham
2 oz. (¼ cup) butter
2 oz. (½ cup) flour
½ pint (1 cup) milk
1½ tablespoons chopped
 parsley

pinch dry mustard
pinch nutmeg
salt, pepper
beaten egg
breadcrumbs

Soften gelatine in 1½ tablespoons water. Mince or chop ham finely. Melt butter, add flour and cook, stirring, 1 minute. Remove from heat, gradually add milk. Return to heat, cook until thickened, stirring constantly.
Dissolve gelatine over hot water. Add ham, parsley and gelatine to sauce, add mustard and nutmeg; season to taste. Spread on tray, refrigerate until set.
Form into balls, about the size of large walnut. Dip in beaten egg, then in breadcrumbs; do this twice. Deep fry until golden brown.
Makes approx. 3½ dozen.

Cheese Twists

4 oz. (½ cup or 1 stick)
 butter
6 oz. (1½ cups) plain
 flour

7 oz. (2 cups) grated
 Cheddar cheese
1 egg
salt

Rub butter into sifted flour. Add ⅔ of the grated cheese, stir in egg; mix well. Roll out dough to

⅛ in. thickness on floured board. Cut out ¼ in. × 4½ in. strips. Twist 2 strips together, place on greased oven tray, sprinkle with remaining cheese. Bake in hot oven, Mark 7, 425°F., 10 to 12 minutes or until golden brown. Sprinkle with salt while still hot. Loosen and allow to cool on trays. Makes approx. 5 dozen.

Savoury Bread Cases

| sliced bread | melted butter |

To Make Cases Remove crust from bread slices. If using one-day-old bread, brush slices lightly with melted butter; for fresh bread, this is not necessary. Press into deep, greased patty pans. Bake in moderate oven, Mark 4, 350°F., approximately 20 minutes or until golden and crisp.

Spoon hot filling in just before serving, or they can be filled 30 minutes ahead, then reheated in moderate oven, Mark 4, 350°F., 5 to 7 minutes; they can also be made days ahead and stored, unfilled, in air-tight tin.

Fillings

Basic Sauce

| 1 oz. (2 tablespoons) butter | ½ pint (1 cup) milk |
| 2 tablespoons flour | salt, pepper |

Melt butter in saucepan, stir in flour, cook 1 minute. Remove from heat, gradually add milk, blend well. Return to heat, bring to boil, reduce heat, simmer until smooth and thickened, stirring constantly. Season well.

Canned salmon, seasoned with lemon juice, with chopped parsley added, can be mixed into the basic sauce; or stir in drained asparagus pieces with chopped hard-boiled eggs and a little curry powder; or drained whole kernel corn, little grated cheese, chopped parsley makes a good combination.

Makes enough filling for approx. 12.

Little Italian Pizzas

Quick Pizza Dough

| ½ lb. (2 cups) self-raising (all purpose) flour | 1 oz. (2 tablespoons) butter |
| pinch salt | about 6 fl. oz. milk oil |

Sift dry ingredients into basin, rub in butter. Add milk nearly all at once, keeping a little back to be used only if dough seems too dry. Knead lightly on floured board and roll out thinly. Cut into squares or rounds, place on oiled tray. Brush dough over lightly with oil. Bake in hot oven, Mark 7, 425°F., 5 to 8 minutes. Remove from oven. Arrange toppings on partly cooked scone dough,

return to oven and continue cooking until golden brown (approximately further 10 to 15 minutes). For flavour and colour sprinkle a little chopped parsley on top of each pizza after cooking.

Ideas for Toppings

1. Rounds of salami, slices of tomato, salt, pepper, cheese slices, and, if desired, sliced stuffed olives.
2. Bacon and onion chopped finely and cooked lightly, slices of tomato, salt, pepper, grated cheese.

Stuffed Eggs

Eggs, hard-boiled and halved, with yolks removed and combined with savoury ingredients, make a delicious hot weather snack. Serve on a bed of crisp lettuce, or with sticks of young celery or asparagus spears.

To make stuffed eggs, hard-boil eggs, cool and shell. Cut in halves lengthwise, remove yolks. Rub yolks through sieve, using wooden spoon, then mix in any of the following well-blended combinations and spoon or pipe back into egg-halves. Quantities given are sufficient for 6 eggs.

1 can sardines, drained and mashed, 1 teaspoon chopped capers, 1 teaspoon lemon juice, salt, pepper.

2 tablespoons finely chopped ham, 2 chopped gherkins, salt, pepper. Add sufficient mayonnaise (see page 121) to make a creamy mixture.

2 tablespoons pâté, 1 tablespoon chopped parsley, salt and pepper.

2 tablespoons cream cheese, 1 teaspoon anchovy paste, salt and pepper. Add mayonnaise (see page 121) to make a creamy mixture.

1 small can tuna, 1 teaspoon prepared mustard, salt and pepper, mayonnaise (see page 121) to bind. Decorate platter with black olives.

1 small can anchovies. Chop finely, add to eggs with sufficient mayonnaise (see page 121) to bind.

Devils on Horseback

prunes	small rounds of bread
port wine	oil
short ends of bacon rashers	

Stone prunes, soak overnight in port wine. Prunes can be stuffed with a little chutney. Roll each prune in slice of bacon, secure with small wooden stick. Grill gently, turning once. Serve on round of bread which has been fried in oil or hot bacon fat until crisp.

Hot Crab Savouries

½ oz. (1 tablespoon) butter
1½ tablespoons flour
¼ pint (½ cup) chicken stock
7½ to 8 oz. can crab meat
2 tablespoons chopped mushrooms
2 tablespoons mayonnaise (see page 121)
2 tablespoons heavy cream
1 dessertspoon chopped parsley
salt, pepper
seasoned flour
oil for deep drying

Melt butter, blend in flour, cook 1 minute. Remove from heat, blend in chicken stock; return to heat and cook, stirring, until sauce boils and thickens. Drain crab well, sauté mushrooms in a little butter, add to sauce with mayonnaise, cream, parsley, salt and pepper. Refrigerate mixture until firm; roll into balls, toss in seasoned flour.
    Fry in hot deep oil until golden brown.
    Makes approx. 1½ dozen.

Savoury Celery Stick

celery sticks, approx. 2½ in. long
4 oz. (1 packet or ½ cup) cream cheese
1 tablespoon chopped gherkin
2 slices ham (about 3 oz.)
salt, pepper

Wash celery sticks, cut into required length. Beat cheese in bowl until smooth. Stir in chopped gherkin and finely chopped ham; blend well. Season to taste with salt and pepper. Fill cheese mixture into celery sticks.
    Two ounces blue cheese can replace 2 oz. of the cream cheese in above ingredients.

Garlic Crisps

3 oz. (⅜ cup) butter
2 cloves garlic
12 slices bread
3 to 4 oz. (about 1 cup) grated Parmesan cheese

Place butter and crushed garlic in saucepan; heat gently, stirring, until butter has melted. Remove from heat, let stand several hours so butter absorbs the full garlic flavour. Remove crusts from bread. Brush bread slices generously with garlic butter on one side, sprinkle generously with grated cheese. Cut bread into fingers or triangles (or, with sharp cutter, cut out 2 in. rounds of bread before brushing with butter). Place on lightly greased baking tray, bake in moderate oven, Mark 4, 350°F., 15 to 20 minutes.
    Makes approx. 12 circles or approx. 4 dozen triangles or fingers.

Hot Steak Titbits

1 lb. rump steak
1 green pepper
1 onion
2 cloves garlic
8 tablespoons oil
8 tablespoons wine vinegar or white vinegar
¼ pint (½ cup) water
¼ pint (½ cup) red wine
1 teaspoon salt
½ teaspoon mixed spice
2 oz. (¼ cup) butter

Cut steak into 1 in. squares. Combine in a bowl sliced pepper and onion, add crushed garlic with remaining ingredients, except butter. Marinate steak in mixture. Leave in refrigerator several hours or overnight. Drain, reserve liquid and vegetables.
    Melt butter in frying pan, add meat. Sauté quickly until well done. Add onions, green pepper, and 8 tablespoons of reserved liquid. Sauté further 2 to 3 minutes.
    Serve hot, in a bowl, accompanied by cocktail sticks and toast squares.
    Serves 4 to 5.

Crab Tartlets

8 oz. shortcrust pastry (made with 2 cups flour)
2 oz. gruyère cheese
4 oz. can crab meat
¼ pint (½ cup) sour cream
1 tablespoon mayonnaise (see page 121)
approx. ¼ pint (½ cup) heavy cream
2 eggs
1 tablespoon finely chopped parsley
½ teaspoon salt
pepper

Roll out pastry to ¼ in. thickness, cut into rounds with 2½ in. cutter; line 24 tartlet tins. Dice cheese very finely, flake crab meat. Put into pastry cases.
    Combine sour cream with mayonnaise, add cream to measure ½ pint (1 cup) of liquid. Blend in lightly beaten egg, chopped parsley and seasoning. Pour into pastry shells. Bake in moderately hot oven, Mark 5, 375°F., 25 minutes.
    Makes 2 dozen tartlets.

DIPS

Creamy mixtures, almost endless in their variety. Serve them with a surround of small cracker biscuits; or have crisp sticks of celery or young carrot, or potato chips for dunking. Dips can also be used as savoury spreads for canapés.

Cheese Dip

½ small red pepper
4 to 6 stuffed olives
2 to 3 gherkins
1 teaspoon capers

8 oz. (1 cup) cottage cheese
salt, cayenne pepper

Slice red pepper very thinly, slice olives thinly, chop capers and gherkins.

Mix all ingredients together, season carefully, chill and leave to stand for at least 1 hour before use.

Serve with biscuits, crisp bread or potato crisps.

Cheese and Cucumber Dip

4 oz. (1 package or ½ cup) cream cheese
1½ tablespoons sour cream
1½ tablespoons grated onion

3 tablespoons finely chopped cucumber
¼ teaspoon salt, pinch pepper

Blend all ingredients in a small bowl.
Makes approx. ¾ pint.

Avocado Dip

1 large, ripe avocado
4 oz. (1 package or ½ cup) cream cheese
1 tablespoon mayonnaise (see page 121)

1 tablespoon lemon juice
salt, pepper
1 teaspoon grated onion

Cut avocado in half, remove stone, scoop all the flesh into a bowl, add the softened cheese and mayonnaise. Blend together well. Add lemon juice salt, pepper and grated onion, mix well. Use as a dip or savoury spread for toast and biscuits.

Asparagus Dip

1 small can asparagus pieces
4 oz. (1 package or ½ cup) cream cheese

salt, pepper
lemon juice

Drain asparagus, reserve liquid, mash asparagus pieces with a fork. Place cream cheese in a basin, beat until smooth and softened, then gradually beat in asparagus pulp, mixing to a soft consistency; add a little asparagus liquid, if necessary. Season with salt, pepper, flavour with lemon juice.
Makes approx. ½ pint.

Brandied Blue Dip

4 oz. Danish blue cheese
½ oz. (1 tablespoon) butter
2 tablespoons mayonnaise (see page 121)
1 egg-yolk

1 tablespoon brandy
1 tablespoon light cream or milk
½ clove garlic

Cream cheese and butter in bowl until smooth. Add mayonnaise, egg-yolk, brandy and cream or milk. Blend well to make a soft consistency. Add crushed garlic.
Makes approx. ¾ pint.

Tuna Dip

7½ oz. can tuna
2 hard boiled eggs
2 oz. (¼ cup) softened butter
1 dessertspoon chopped parsley

1 teaspoon chopped chives or spring onion (scallions)
salt, pepper
lemon juice

Drain tuna, rub through fine sieve or blend in electric blender with eggs until well combined and smooth. Add softened butter, parsley, chives or spring onion. Blend on low speed or mix until well combined. Season to taste with salt, pepper and a little lemon juice.
Makes approx. ½ pint.

Devilled Ham Dip

1 teaspoon gelatine
8 tablespoons tomato juice
6 oz. liverwurst
1 small can devilled ham paste

1 very small onion
1 teaspoon lemon juice
salt, pepper

Soften gelatine in tomato juice, stir over very low heat until gelatine dissolves. Blend liverwurst, ham paste, finely chopped onion, lemon juice, salt and pepper together in a basin; gradually stir in tomato juice mixture. Spoon into small bowl, refrigerate until required.

Serve with triangles of toast.
Makes approx. ¾ pint.

Soups

Hot Soups

The family will hurry home for these hot, hearty soups. A small bowl or cup of soup is a good start to a meal; a generous steaming mug of soup, served with hot cheese or bacon sandwiches, is a satisfying meal in itself.

French Onion Soup

2 large onions
1 oz. (2 tablespoons) butter
pinch sugar
1 dessertspoon flour
3 pints (6 cups) beef or chicken stock
salt, pepper
French bread
grated cheese

Peel onions, cut into thick slices. Heat butter in pan (you may need a little more butter); add onions and sugar and cook, stirring, until golden and transparent; they should not be dark in colour. Stir in flour, gradually stir in stock. Season to taste with salt and pepper. Cover, cook gently 20 minutes. Spoon into hot bowls.

Take some slices of French bread, toast them, and sprinkle well with grated cheese. Place under grill until cheese melts and is golden. Put one toasted cheese slice on top of each bowl of steaming soup.

Or place a toasted round of French bread in base of soup plate, sprinkle with grated cheese, and gradually pour in soup. As toast floats to top, sprinkle with extra grated cheese.

(For easier eating, some people prefer to cut the crusts from toast before putting into bowl.)

On a cold winter's night, put 1 dessertspoon of brandy into each bowl before pouring in the hot onion soup.

Serves 6 to 8.

Scotch Broth

2 carrots
2 onions
2 leeks
3 sticks celery
4 oz. ($\frac{2}{3}$ cup) barley
bouquet garni
1½ lb. neck of mutton
2 quarts of water or stock
chopped parsley
salt, pepper

Prepare vegetables, chop finely. Wash barley, put into pot with vegetables, bouquet garni, meat and stock or water. Bring slowly to the boil, skim well, then reduce heat, simmer, covered, 2 to 3 hours. Remove bones from meat, chop meat, return to saucepan, add chopped parsley; season to taste.

Serves 8.

Celery Soup with Rice

2 oz. ham
1 small onion
½ oz. (1 tablespoon) butter
¼ lb. (1 cup) finely chopped celery
2 tablespoons rice
3 pints (6 cups) water
4 chicken stock cubes
salt, pepper
chopped parsley

Cut ham in strips, finely chop onion. Melt butter, fry ham and onion 2 minutes. Add celery and rice, fry further 2 minutes. Add water, crumbled stock cubes and seasonings; stir well. Cover, cook approximately 20 minutes, stirring occasionally. Serve sprinkled with chopped parsley.

Serves 6 to 8.

Lentil Soup

6 oz. (1 cup) dried lentils
2½ pints (5 cups) beef stock
ham or bacon bones
2 potatoes
1 oz. (2 tablespoons) butter
1 tablespoon flour
freshly ground black pepper

Wash lentils and drain. Cover with cold water and leave to stand at least 2 hours. Strain. Place in a large saucepan, with stock and bones, cover, bring to boil, reduce heat and simmer for half an hour, or until lentils are tender. Add potatoes and simmer a further 20 minutes. Cream together butter and flour gradually mix into soup, then cook for a few minutes longer. Add pepper to taste. Serve with lots of hot buttered toast, or hot rolls.

Serves 6.

French Onion Soup—so easy to make, so very good to eat. Hot cheese-toast can top each serving.

Pea Soup

½ lb. (1¼ cups) split peas
1 chopped onion
1 carrot
few bacon pieces and
   ham bones

2½ pints (5 cups) stock
   or water
salt, pepper

Wash peas well. Put into saucepan with onion, carrot, bacon bones and pieces and stock or water. Bring slowly to boil, skim well. Cover, cook gently until peas are tender (about 2 hours). Rub through coarse sieve, return to saucepan; taste, and season if necessary. A little finely chopped mint can be added to the soup before serving.

Top with small croutons or sippets made by sautéing small cubes of bread in bacon fat, butter or hot oil until golden; drain well before using.

Serves 6.

Curried Pea Soup

1 lb. quick-frozen peas
hot water
2 oz. (¼ cup) butter
2 tablespoons flour
3 chicken stock cubes

2 pints (4 cups) water
1 to 2 dessertspoons
   curry powder
scant ½ pint (¾ cup) milk
salt, pepper

Cover peas with hot water, bring to boil, boil until tender. Drain. Rub through a fine sieve or purée in electric blender.

Melt butter in saucepan, stir in flour, mix well. Cook over low heat 2 minutes. Remove from heat, gradually add chicken stock (made with stock cubes and water). Return to heat, simmer 2 minutes stirring constantly.

Stir puréed peas, curry powder, and milk into sauce. Season with salt and pepper. Bring to boil, stirring, reduce heat, simmer 2 minutes.

Serves 6 to 8.

Minestrone

½ lb. (1¼ cups) haricot
   beans*
1 clove garlic
1 onion
6 shallots
3 sticks celery
2 carrots
2 potatoes
1 dessertspoon oil
1 teaspoon chopped
   parsley

¾ teaspoon basil
1 tablespoon tomato
   paste
1 cup elbow macaroni
2 pints (4 cups) chicken
   stock
salt, pepper
extra parsley
grated parmesan cheese

* Green beans could be used instead of haricot, but would not require overnight soaking.

Soak beans overnight in cold water; drain. Boil in salted water about 1 hour or until tender; drain and reserve.

Prepare vegetables: crush garlic, chop onion and shallots, peel, seed, and chop tomatoes, chop celery and 1 carrot, slice the other carrot, peel and chop potatoes.

Heat oil in large saucepan, sauté garlic, onion, shallots, parsley and basil until lightly browned. Add tomato paste and cook, stirring, 5 minutes. Add tomatoes, celery, carrots, potatoes and stock. Bring to the boil; reduce heat, simmer gently 45 minutes to 1 hour or until vegetables are tender; add the beans. Add macaroni and cook 10 minutes or until tender.

Season to taste with salt and pepper. Serve sprinkled with chopped parsley and grated parmesan.

Serves 6 to 8.

Chinese Long Soup

½ lb. lean pork
8 chives or spring
   onions
¼ head cabbage
1 tablespoon oil
3 pints (6 cups) chicken
   stock

1½ tablespoons soy
   sauce
salt
4 oz. (1 cup) egg noodles
4 tablespoons finely
   chopped chives or
   spring onions

Cut pork in shreds. Wash chives and cabbage, slice finely. Heat oil in large saucepan, add pork and cabbage, fry quickly a few minutes, stirring constantly. Add stock and seasonings. Bring slowly to boil, reduce heat, add chives, simmer 10 to 15 minutes.

Meanwhile, cook noodles until tender in boiling salted water (5 to 6 minutes); drain well. To serve, place a spoonful of noodles in the base of each soup bowl. Pour over the hot soup, sprinkle a few extra chopped chives on top.

Serves 8.

Cream of Cauliflower Soup

¼ large cauliflower
1 pint (1¾ cups) milk
1 pint (1¾ cups) water
2 oz. (¼ cup) butter
1½ oz. (3 tablespoons)
   flour

1 chicken stock cube
½ teaspoon nutmeg
salt, pepper
2 to 3 tablespoons
   medium cream

Trim cauliflower, cut into large flowerets. Wash well. Place in saucepan with milk and water. Bring to boil, reduce heat, simmer slowly, covered, until just tender. Remove from heat; drain, reserve liquid. Melt butter in saucepan, stir in flour, cook 1 minute. Remove from heat, gradually stir in reserved liquid. Return to heat, bring to boil, stirring; stir until smooth and thickened. Reduce heat, stir in crumbled stock cube, nutmeg and salt and pepper to taste. Stir in cream. Cut cauliflower into small flowerets, return to soup. Heat through gently.

Serves 4 to 6.

Crab Chowder

1 pint (2 cups) fish or chicken stock	1 large potato
6½ oz. can crab meat	1 teaspoon Worcestershire sauce
½ pint (1 cup) milk	salt, pepper
½ oz. (1 tablespoon) butter	¼ pint (½ cup) medium cream
1 large chopped onion	3 oz. (⅔ cup) grated firm cheese (Cheddar or similar)
2 oz. bacon	chopped parsley
1½ tablespoons flour	

Combine in saucepan the stock, liquor from the can of crab, and milk. Bring to boil; remove from heat. Melt butter in separate saucepan; add onion and chopped bacon, brown lightly. Stir in flour, cook 1 minute. Gradually add hot stock. Bring to boil, stirring; simmer 5 minutes. Peel and cut potato into small cubes; cover and simmer further 20 minutes.

Season to taste with Worcestershire sauce, salt and pepper. Add crab meat, flaked into large pieces. Just before serving, pour in cream, heat through gently. Top each serving with grated cheese and parsley.

Serves 4 to 6.

Cream of Asparagus

2 oz. (¼ cup) butter	3 chicken stock cubes
1 medium onion	10 oz. can asparagus spears
2 sticks celery	¼ pint (½ cup) medium cream
1½ oz. (3 tablespoons) flour	salt, pepper
1½ pints (3 cups) boiling water	

Melt butter in pan, fry chopped onion and celery until soft but not brown. Stir in flour, cook 1 minute. Remove from heat, gradually stir in water, in which stock cubes have been dissolved. Return to heat, bring to boil, stirring. Add asparagus and liquor from can. Simmer for 30 to 40 minutes.

Purée in blender or rub through a sieve, return to pan, reheat gently. Add cream; season with salt and pepper, if necessary.

Serves 4 to 6.

Potato and Marjoram Soup

2 potatoes	¼ pint (½ cup) water, extra
½ pint (1 cup) water	¼ pint (½ cup) milk, extra
½ pint (1 cup) milk	salt
1 oz. (2 tablespoons) butter	chopped marjoram
1 tablespoon flour	

Peel potatoes, cut into small pieces. Simmer uncovered in combined water and milk until soft. When completely soft, purée or rub through a sieve with the liquid.

In another pan, melt butter, stir in flour, cook 1 minute. Remove from heat. Gradually add ¼ pint (½ cup) milk and ¼ pint (½ cup) water. Return to heat. Bring to boil, simmer until smooth and thickened, stirring constantly. Add potato purée and finely chopped marjoram. Reheat gently.

Serves 4.

Mulligatawny Soup

3 oz. (⅜ cup) butter	1 lb. uncooked chicken
1 onion	4 oz. (⅔ cup) lentils
2 teaspoons garam masala	2 tablespoons flour
2 cloves	3 to 4 tablespoons tomato purée
2 bayleaves	4 pints (8 cups) stock
2 teaspoons curry powder	3 oz. (1 cup) cooked rice

Garam masala is a mixture of spices obtainable from some speciality or continental shops. If not available add ⅛ teaspoon cumin and ⅛ teaspoon cardamom with the other spices.

Melt butter, fry chopped onion until golden, add spices and cook 1 minute. Add chicken, fry 5 minutes. Add remaining ingredients, bring to boil, reduce heat and simmer, covered 1½ to 2 hours. After 30 minutes of cooking remove chicken, allow to cool, cut meat into dice. Set aside.

At serving time, strain soup through a sieve, reheat. Put a little diced chicken and a little boiled rice in base of each serving dish, pour over the hot soup.

Serves 6.

Shrimp Soup

1 lb. potatoes	2 egg-yolks
2 oz. (½ cup) leek (white part only)	¼ pint (½ cup) medium cream
2 pints (4 cups) fish stock (or milk)	2 to 3 oz. (½ cup) shrimps
little chopped fennel	croutons
1 oz. (2 tablespoons) butter	salt

Peel and quarter potatoes, slice the leek and put into a pan with the stock and fennel. Cover and simmer 20 minutes. Rub through a sieve, return to the pan and bring slowly to boiling point stirring in the butter in small pieces.

Mix the egg-yolks and cream, add 3 to 4 tablespoons of the soup then stir into the rest of the soup. Add the shrimps, season carefully and reheat without boiling.

Serve with croutons.

Serves 5 to 6.

Cold Soups

These are superb soups you'll be proud to serve. They're light, subtly flavoured—the perfect start to a summer meal.

Tomato Soup

10½ oz. can condensed tomato soup
¾ pint (1½ cups) chicken stock
1 medium onion
pinch of dill or oregano
1 dessertspoon tomato paste
¼ pint (½ cup) medium cream
chopped parsley

Place tomato soup, chicken stock, chopped onion, dill and tomato paste into saucepan, heat gently, stirring constantly, until soup begins to boil; remove from heat, strain through sieve; stir in cream. Refrigerate. Garnish with chopped parsley.
Serves 4 to 6.

Fresh Tomato Soup

3 lb. ripe tomatoes
juice of 1 orange
juice of ½ lemon
sugar
black pepper
salt
brown bread and butter

Scald the tomatoes, skin, cut in half and remove seeds. Strain through a fine strainer pressing gently to extract all juice.

Sieve the flesh of the tomatoes, mix with the tomato juice, orange and lemon juice. Add sugar; pepper and salt to taste. If too thick, dilute with a little white wine and water.

Serve very cold with rolls of brown bread and butter.

A little grated orange rind mixed with the butter before spreading on the bread, gives a distinctive touch.
Serves 5 to 6.

Cold Curry Soup

6 spring onions
1 oz. (2 tablespoons) butter
2 teaspoons curry powder
2 tablespoons flour
2 pints (4 cups) vegetable or chicken stock
1 piece lemon rind
salt, pepper
1 egg-yolk
2 tablespoons medium cream
chopped chives

Chop spring onions, cook gently in butter until golden brown; add curry powder, cook another 5 minutes. Stir in flour; add stock and lemon rind. Bring to the boil, reduce heat, simmer 15 minutes, stirring occasionally.

Purée or rub through a sieve. Return to saucepan, season to taste. Add 2 tablespoons of hot soup

to egg-yolk and cream combined, then add this slowly to the soup, beating constantly. Reheat without boiling until soup thickens. Cool, then refrigerate. Serve topped with chopped chives.
Serves 4 to 6.

Gazpacho

¾ lb. ripe tomatoes
1 small cucumber
1 small onion
½ green pepper
2 sticks celery
1 small clove garlic
½ pint (1 cup) tomato juice
2½ tablespoons oil
1½ tablespoons wine vinegar
salt, pepper
few drops tabasco sauce

Prepare and coarsely cube all vegetables; reserve about ¼ of vegetable mixture to use for garnish. Place remaining vegetables in blender with tomato juice, oil, vinegar, salt, pepper and tabasco sauce; blend 40 seconds on high speed. Pour into bowl, refrigerate. Place vegetable mixture reserved for garnish into blender. Blend 10 seconds on low speed. Spoon into soup bowls, pour chilled puréed mixture on top.
Serves 4 to 5.

Vichyssoise

4 leeks
1 medium onion
2 oz. (¼ cup) butter
5 medium potatoes
2 pints (4 cups) chicken stock
1 tablespoon salt
¾ pint (1½ cups) milk
½ pint (1 cup) medium cream
chopped chives or parsley

Slice leeks and onions and fry in butter until just turning golden. Add peeled and sliced potatoes, chicken stock and salt. Bring to boil; reduce heat, cook 35 to 40 minutes; cool. Place about half the cooled mixture in blender, blend on high speed 1 minute, repeat with remaining half. Pour mixture back into saucepan, add milk and half the cream.

Season to taste, bring to boil; cool. Put quarter of mixture into blender. Blend on high speed 30 seconds. Repeat until all mixture is blended. When cold, stir in remaining cream; refrigerate.

Serve sprinkled with chopped chives or parsley.
Serves 8.

Superbly flavoured cold soups for hot days. 1. Tomato Soup; 2. Borsch; 3. Vichyssoise; 4. Cream of Broccoli (also in tureen); 5. Gazpacho; 6. Curry.

Green Vichyssoise

6 oz. (1 cup) peeled and chopped raw potato
4 chopped spring onions (scallions) (green tops included)
¾ pint (1½ cups) chicken stock
¼ lb. (½ cup) fresh or frozen green peas
salt
¼ pint (½ cup) medium cream
extra cream for topping

Simmer vegetables with stock and salt for 10 minutes, or until barely is tender. Rub through sieve or purée in electric blender. Return to saucepan, add cream, heat gently without boiling. Cool, then refrigerate. Top each serving with a spoonful of whipped cream.

Serves 4.

Iced Cucumber Soup

3 cucumbers
1 leek (white part only)
1 oz. (2 tablespoons) butter
1 bayleaf
1 dessertspoon flour
¾ pint (1½ cups) chicken stock
1 teaspoon salt
¼ pint (½ cup) medium cream
juice ½ lemon
salt, pepper
1 teaspoon finely chopped mint
sour cream or whipped cream

Peel and halve 2 cucumbers, remove seeds, cut into ½ in. dice, slice leek. Melt butter in saucepan, add cucumber, leek and bayleaf; sauté 10 minutes until tender but not brown. Stir in flour, cook over low heat 1 minute; gradually add chicken stock. Cook, stirring constantly until thickened. Add salt, simmer gently 30 minutes. Remove from heat, cool.

Rub through fine sieve or blend in electric blender; refrigerate. Peel, seed and grate remaining cucumber, add to soup with medium cream and lemon juice, mix well. Adjust seasoning with salt and pepper, stir in mint; refrigerate. Serve icy cold, topped with a spoonful of sour cream or whipped cream.

Serves 6.

Cream of Broccoli Soup

1 onion
1 carrot
1 stick celery
salt, pepper
9 oz. packet frozen broccoli
1 clove garlic
½ pint (1 cup) chicken stock
¼ pint (½ cup) medium cream

Peel and chop onion and carrot and place in small saucepan, with chopped celery. Add ¼ pint (1 cup) boiling water and a good pinch of salt. Cover,

cook until tender; set aside. Cook frozen broccoli in boiling water until tender. Drain and cool.

Purée drained broccoli with vegetables and liquid in which vegetables were cooked, crushed garlic and chicken stock in electric blender, or rub through a fine sieve. Stir in cream, season to taste. Refrigerate until well chilled. If desired, top each serving with a little whipped cream.

Serves 4 to 5.

Iced Avocado Soup

2 large ripe avocados
little lemon juice
2 10½ oz. cans beef consommé or consommé madrilene
¼ pint (½ cup) sour cream
salt, pepper
1 teaspoon grated onion
chopped parsley

Halve avocados, scoop out flesh. Mash with lemon juice, or purée in electric blender approximately 12 seconds on low speed. Warm soup slightly, remove from heat, combine with avocado and sour cream. Season with salt, pepper and onion; refrigerate.

Top each serving with a little parsley.

Serves 6 to 8.

Cream of Carrot Soup

4 carrots
1 onion
1 stick celery
1½ pints (3 cups) chicken stock
salt, pepper
1½ oz. (½ cup) cooked rice
¼ pint (½ cup) medium cream

Slice carrots, onion and celery; place in saucepan with half the stock. Bring to boil; reduce heat, cover, simmer 15 minutes. Remove from heat, add salt, pepper and rice. Purée in electric blender or rub through a fine sieve. Beat in remaining stock and cream; chill. Garnish each serving with a little chopped parsley.

Serves 4 to 6.

Cold Borsch

1 lb. fresh beetroot
1 small onion
1½ pints (3 cups) chicken stock
1 tablespoon sugar
1 teaspoon salt
1 tablespoon lemon juice
sour cream

Peel beetroot and onion, cut into ½ in. dice; cover and cook in chicken stock until tender. Drain the vegetables, reserving the liquid. Cool a little. Place vegetables with a little liquid into electric blender, or rub through a fine seive. Add remaining liquid, sugar, salt and lemon juice to the vegetable purée. Refrigerate until well chilled. Top each serving with a spoonful of sour cream.

Serves 6 to 8.

Eggs

Eggs are one of the few foods we can eat, in one form or the other, each day—and enjoy them every time. Omelets, souffles, vegetarian curries—eggs play an essential part in all types of sweet and savoury dishes.

When buying eggs it is obviously wise to obtain the freshest possible. The water trial is a reliable test for freshness. To make this test, place the egg in sufficient cold water to cover it. Fresh eggs will lie flat in water. Slightly stale eggs will tilt a little. They can be used for frying or scrambling without ill effect. Stale eggs will sit upright in water.

Eggs should be stored in refrigerator or cool cupboard, with ends pointing down; when the yolk rises, the air space protects it from touching the shell. If storing in cupboard, ensure there is good circulation of air. Eggshells are porous and should not be washed before storing, because this removes the fine covering film. They tend to absorb strong odours, and should not be stored near strong-smelling foods.

Storage of left-over eggs

Yolks Store in refrigerator, covered with cold water.
Whites or *Whole Eggs out of shell* Store in covered container in refrigerator.

Basic Cooking Methods

Eggs are coagulated by heat, and are best cooked slowly at low temperature. High cooking temperatures toughen coagulated protein contained in eggs, and over-cooking results in a tough, dry dish or, if any liquid has been added, curdling.

There are five basic ways of cooking eggs—boiling, poaching, steaming, baking, frying.

1. Place eggs in saucepan, add cold water to cover them by 1 in. Bring rapidly to boil. Start timing from when water boils. (Cooking times are given below.) Once water boils, reduce heat to simmering, cook for required time.

2. Bring to the boil sufficient water to cover eggs. Gently spoon eggs into saucepan. Keep at full heat until water boils again and start timing from this moment. Reduce heat to simmering for rest of cooking.

For this method it is important the eggs should be at room temperature before lowering into water, otherwise the shell could crack. A simple way to bring them quickly to room temperature is to hold eggs for a few minutes under warm running water.

3. For hard-boiled eggs use Methods 1 or 2. Cook eggs for 8 to 10 minutes. Do not over-cook eggs or the smell can be unpleasant. When eggs are cooked, run cold water over them. Crack each shell gently. Eggs will shell easier if cracked and peeled from broad end.

Cooking Times

Times given are for a standard-sized 2 to 2½ oz. egg. Adjust cooking times slightly for smaller or larger eggs.
Soft—3 minutes.
Medium—4 minutes.
Hard—8 to 10 minutes.

Boiled Eggs

There are several methods of boiling eggs—we set them out below. You might like to try each method to see which one gives the best results for your family's taste.

In each case, choose a saucepan of suitable size. Don't have a big saucepan if you're cooking only one or two eggs, but don't overcrowd a number of eggs into a small saucepan.

Coddled Eggs

This cooks the eggs with a soft white, and is the method recommended for young children or invalids. Lower eggs into boiling water, as for Boiled Eggs, Method 2. Remove saucepan from heat, cover, and allow eggs to stand in hot water for 8 to 10 minutes. If a slightly firmer white is required, let egg boil for 1 minute only before removing from heat and covering to let stand.

Fried Eggs

Butter or bacon fat adds a rich flavour when used to fry eggs, or they can be cooked without fat in non-stick pans. Here's how to get best results from both methods.

1. Melt small amount of butter or bacon fat in frying pan. Break eggs into pan one at a time—or break into saucer first, then slip into the melted butter. Cook slowly, basting yolk occasionally with the butter. Remove from pan with a flat perforated spoon.

If you like fried eggs to be perfectly round use egg-rings, or plain pastry cutters. These are quite cheap from hardware stores or kitchen sections of departmental stores.

Place egg-rings in hot butter, then turn over so that both sides are well greased—this will keep eggs from sticking to the rings. Use tongs or a fork for turning rings. Or use rings with non-stick coating.

Break an egg carefully into each ring. Baste the yolk occasionally until cooked. Remove rings before lifting eggs from pan with egg-slice. If rings stick, run a knife carefully around inside of ring to separate it from egg.

2. For health reasons—or because it saves time in the busy breakfast period—many people prefer to fry eggs in a non-stick pan, without butter. Just brushing the pan with butter will make all the difference to flavour and finished result. Without butter the white is apt to cook long before the yolk, and the white of the finished egg can be tough and somewhat indigestible.

However, if you prefer to fry eggs without fat, here's how to get the best results. Break eggs into pan, then quickly sprinkle about 3 tablespoons of hot water around eggs. Cover with lid. Cook gently about 3 minutes. This will partially steam the egg-yolk and hasten cooking time.

Poached Eggs

Place approximately 1 in. of water in frying pan of suitable size. Add ½ teaspoon salt or 1 dessertspoon lemon juice to help eggs set and add flavour. Bring water to simmering point only; fast-boiling water tends to break up egg-whites.

Gently break in eggs. Hold eggs as close as possible to surface of water; this will help prevent them breaking, as they might if dropped from a height of a few inches. Occasionally, spoon some of the hot water over yolks. Simmer gently until cooked.

Cooking time will vary according to whether you like a soft or firmly poached egg, but it is around 3 to 5 minutes. Lift carefully with egg-slice, hold above pan for a few seconds to drain well.

Steamed Eggs　This is a variation of the poached egg. Take a shallow pan with lid. Half-fill it with water, bring to the boil. Break eggs into the boiling water. Then place close-fitting lid on top, remove pan from heat. Let stand for 3½ to 4 minutes.

Baked Eggs

Also known as *Eggs en Cocotte*. Grease one small ramekin or 'cocotte' dish per person. Break an egg into each dish, season with salt and pepper; spoon cream over to cover egg. Bake in moderate oven, Mark 4, 350°F., 15 minutes, or until egg has set.

Some finely chopped cheese can be sprinkled into the dish before adding the egg and cream, and extra grated cheese sprinkled on the cream before baking.

Scrambled Eggs

Allow 2 to 3 eggs per person. Add 1 tablespoon of water or milk or cream for each egg; water will make the scrambled eggs lighter in texture but milk or cream gives more flavour. Season with salt and pepper. Beat together lightly.

Melt ½ oz. (1 tablespoon) butter in pan, add egg mixture; cook, stirring, until eggs are just set; don't have the heat too high, or eggs will be tough. Spoon on to hot toast.

Some grated cheese, chopped chives or spring onions, curry powder, chopped parsley, canned whole kernel corn can be mixed in with the beaten eggs.

Creamy Scrambled Eggs

2 oz. (1 package or ½ cup) cream cheese	salt, pepper
1 oz. (2 tablespoons) butter	2 tablespoons finely chopped spring onions (scallions)
2 tablespoons medium cream	
3 eggs	

Combine cream cheese, butter and cream in frying pan, stir over low heat until creamy. Break eggs into mixture, cook gently until egg whites are barely set, add salt, pepper and spring onions, stir mixture well with a fork until eggs are cooked. Serve on hot buttered toast.

Serves 2.

Omelets—mixed and cooked in minutes—make a delicious light meal.

26 *Eggs*

Omelets

An omelet is quick to make, inexpensive, and most versatile. Plain, or with varying fillings, it can be served for breakfast, lunch, or a light main course for dinner. And sweet dessert omelets make a perfect light ending to a meal.

Flavourings, such as those for scrambled eggs, can be mixed into the savoury omelet. Asparagus; chopped, cooked bacon; fried tomato slices; chopped, cooked chicken; sautéed mushrooms, are other popular fillings or additions.

The Omelet Pan

It is best to keep a special pan just for omelets. A new omelet pan should be 'seasoned' before use. To do this, pour oil into the pan to cover the base and come a little way up sides. Warm this slowly over heat, and turn or gently shake pan occasionally so that the oil coats the sides. When the pan and oil are hot, remove from heat and allow to cool. Do this once more, and let the oil stand in the pan overnight. Next day, warm the pan and oil again, pour off the oil and wipe the pan dry. The pan is now ready for the cooking of omelets.

If possible, do not wash the omelet pan after use. Simply rub it clean with paper towelling or a clean cloth. This helps prevent omelets sticking to the pan. If you have to wash the pan, then season it again with oil, as above, before using it again.

Types of Omelet

There are three basic types of omelet—the classic French omelet, the Spanish omelet and the Soufflé, or 'puffy' omelet.

French Omelet

| 3 eggs | 1 dessertspoon water |
| salt, pepper | ½ oz. (1 tablespoon) butter |

Break eggs into bowl, season with salt and pepper; add water. Beat eggs briskly with fork until well mixed. Heat pan, add butter; it should sizzle and foam almost immediately. Pour in egg mixture, and, using a fork, draw the eggs from the side of the pan into the centre; do this quickly, shaking

the pan constantly. Continue lifting the eggs with a fork until all the liquid is cooked. With spatula or fork fold omelet and roll on to warmed serving plate. Serve immediately.

Serves 1.

Spanish Omelet

Unlike the French or Soufflé omelet, the Spanish omelet is not folded or rolled, but is served flat. When the omelet is golden brown underneath, turn with spatula and cook the other side until just set, or place under grill to set the top; do not over-cook, or the omelet will toughen.

| 2 oz. (¼ cup) butter | 4 eggs |
| 2 oz. (½ cup) finely diced mixed vegetables | salt, pepper |

Heat 1 oz. (2 tablespoons) butter in saucepan, add vegetables, sauté over gentle heat until tender but not brown. Break eggs into bowl, beat lightly with fork, season with salt and pepper, add cooked vegetables. Melt remaining butter in large omelet pan, when sizzling pour in egg mixture. Stir gently to distribute mixture evenly, then allow to set over low heat. When golden underneath, turn with spatula and allow to set on other side, or place under grill to set top. Serve immediately.

Serves 2.

Vegetables can include chopped cooked onions; tomatoes; cooked green peas; cooked potatoes; a light touch of crushed garlic and chopped parsley can also be added.

Soufflé Omelet

The soufflé (or 'puffy') omelet, as its name indicates, puffs up like a small soufflé while cooking. After base of omelet is cooked, the pan is placed under grill or into moderate oven, Mark 5, 375°F., for a few minutes to set top lightly.

4 eggs	1 tablespoon milk
½ teaspoon salt	½ oz. (1 tablespoon) butter
pinch pepper	

Separate eggs, beat yolks until thick. Add salt, pepper and milk. Beat egg-whites until soft peaks form. Fold whites into yolks.

Heat pan, add butter, turn pan to allow butter to flow evenly over base and around sides of pan. Spread egg mixture evenly into pan, cook over medium heat until omelet puffs and under-part is lightly golden. Bake in moderate oven, Mark 5, 375°F., 5 minutes or place under hot grill until top is firm and springs back when pressed lightly with fingertips. Fold over, serve immediately.

Serves 2.

For a savoury topping, sprinkle finely grated cheese over before placing under grill.

Dessert Omelets

These are a version of the soufflé omelet; omit salt and pepper from the soufflé omelet recipe, add ¼ teaspoon sugar per egg before mixing omelet.

Individual dessert omelets can be made with 2 eggs in 6 in. pan.

Here are some suggested fillings:

Apricot Spoon hot, sieved apricot jam over half of omelet, turn on to warm serving plate. A spoonful of rum can be added to the jam when heating, or a little rum can be warmed in a separate saucepan, poured over the omelet and set aflame. Serve a bowl of whipped cream separately.

Strawberries and Cream Sweeten sliced fresh strawberries to taste, or use warmed canned strawberries. Fill omelet with 1 dessertspoon berries for each egg used. Fold over, decorate with whole fresh strawberries, or another spoonful of the canned strawberries. Serve with cream.

Caramel Cream Do not fold omelet. Spread with fresh or canned peach slices marinaded in brandy or rum. Spread sour cream over, sprinkle with castor sugar. Place, unfolded, under grill just long enough to set cream and lightly caramelize the sugar.

Sweet French Omelet For a sweet French omelet, add a small pinch salt and 1 dessertspoon sugar to the eggs before beating together; omit the pepper. Make the omelet, and after folding sprinkle with an extra dessertspoon of sugar; place under very hot grill for a few minutes or until sugar melts and glazes the omelet. Place on warmed serving plate. Alternately, fill with a sweet filling as for Soufflé Omelet.

Egg and Bacon Pie

Cheese Pastry

6 oz. (1½ cups) plain flour	3 oz. (⅜ cup) butter
½ teaspoon salt	3 oz. (¾ cup) grated firm Cheddar cheese
1 teaspoon baking powder	approx. 1 tablespoon water

Filling

1 oz. (2 tablespoons) butter	½ teaspoon dry mustard
3 onions	3 eggs
4 to 6 rashers bacon	1 pint (2 cups) milk
1 teaspoon salt	1 dessertspoon chopped parsley
¼ teaspoon pepper	

Pastry Sift flour, salt and baking powder into basin. Rub in butter, add grated cheese. Mix to dry dough with a little water. Knead lightly on floured board. Roll pastry out to line base and sides of 11 in. × 7 in. or deep pie plate.

Filling Melt butter in saucepan, add sliced onions and chopped bacon; fry 4 minutes. Add salt, pepper and mustard, mix thoroughly. Beat eggs in basin, add warmed milk, drained onion-and-bacon mixture, and parsley. Spoon mixture into pastry case. Bake in moderate oven, Mark 4, 350°F., 35 to 40 minutes or until pie has set and browned.

Serves 6.

Quiche Lorraine

Pastry

4 oz. (½ cup or 1 stick) butter	4 oz. (1 cup) plain flour
4 oz. (1 package or ½ cup) cream cheese	

Filling

6 oz. gruyère cheese	2 to 3 tablespoons thin cream
4 rashers bacon	¼ teaspoon nutmeg
1 small onion	salt, pepper
3 eggs	

Pastry Cream butter and cheese together. Add sifted flour, and blend with a fork. Wrap in waxed paper, refrigerate for 1 hour. Roll out to fit 8 or 9 in. pie plate. Refrigerate while preparing filling.

Filling Slice cheese thinly (or use packaged cheese slices), cut into 2 in. strips. Cut bacon into small pieces, fry until crisp, drain. Arrange alternate layers of bacon and cheese in pie case; sprinkle with chopped onion. Beat eggs lightly, combine with cream and seasonings, pour over bacon and cheese.

Bake in hot oven, Mark 7, 425°F. for 10 minutes, reduce heat to moderate, Mark 4, 350°F., cook further 30 minutes or until set.

Serves 6.

Malayan Egg Curry

1½ lb. onions	1 teaspoon turmeric
1 or 2 small green chillies	1 tablespoon curry powder
1 clove garlic	1 teaspoon salt
¾ pint (1½ cups) chicken stock	6 hard boiled eggs

Slice onions, green chillies and garlic. Combine all ingredients, except salt and eggs in saucepan, simmer uncovered 30 minutes. Halve eggs, add with salt to curry mixture, heat well, serve over hot boiled rice.

Serves 4.

Egg Nog

1 egg	1 tablespoon rum
1 tablespoon sugar	½ pint (1 cup) milk
1 tablespoon brandy	grated nutmeg

Whisk all ingredients together, except nutmeg, until well blended. Pour into glass and sprinkle top with nutmeg.

Serves 1.

Indian Egg Curry

4 medium onions	2 teaspoons cumin
2 cloves garlic	2 teaspoons paprika
4 medium tomatoes	1 teaspoon salt
4 oz. (½ cup or 1 stick) butter	¼ teaspoon chilli powder
2 teaspoons coriander	2 teaspoons garam masala*
1 teaspoon turmeric	6 hard boiled eggs
1 teaspoon ground ginger	*See note on page 21

Slice two onions, finely chop remaining onions and garlic. Peel and chop tomatoes. Heat butter in a saucepan, add sliced onion, sauté until golden brown, add remaining onion, garlic and tomatoes, sauté 3 minutes. Add remaining ingredients, except garam masala and eggs, simmer uncovered, until some of the liquid has evaporated (approximately 30 minutes), stir occasionally.

Halve eggs, add with garam masala to curry mixture, heat well, serve over hot boiled rice.

Serves 4.

Cheese Soufflé—tall, tempting, feather-light in texture. The soufflé mixture can be refrigerated—even frozen—in advance.

Soufflés

In the past, soufflés have been temperamental—you had to mix, cook, serve them without a moment's delay. But these special recipes allow you to prepare the mixture well ahead of time, refrigerate it overnight—or even freeze it for up to five days—and when baked it will rise as tall and as tempting as ever before.

Preparing the Dish

Each recipe in this section will make one large or four individual soufflés. For large soufflé, 7 in. (approximately 2½ pint capacity) soufflé dish is used; individual soufflé dishes have about ½ pint capacity. Grease dish or dishes; tie collar of greased greaseproof paper or aluminium foil round outside of dish; this will help soufflé to rise straight.

Cheese Soufflé

4 eggs	pepper
4 oz. (½ cup or 1 stick) butter	¼ teaspoon dry mustard
4 tablespoons plain flour	1½ gills (½ cup) milk
1 teaspoon salt	4 oz. Cheddar cheese

Separate eggs; allow to stand, covered, while preparing sauce. Melt butter in top part of double saucepan over hot water; remove from heat, stir in flour and seasonings, stirring until smooth and free from lumps. Stir in milk all at once, return to heat; stir over hot water until smooth and thick. Remove from heat; stir in grated cheese while still hot, stirring until melted. Allow to cool slightly. Beat egg-yolks until pale and fluffy, gradually stir into cheese mixture, using thin-edged metal spoon or rubber spatula.

Using clean bowl and beaters, beat egg-whites until short, moist peaks form. Add half the whites to sauce, folding through carefully with flat spatula; then fold in remaining whites. (Adding whites in two portions like this makes it easier to fold them through the mixture; it also makes sure you do not over-beat mixture; thus breaking down the aeration). Pour soufflé mixture over back of spoon or over spatula into prepared dish. This prevents mixture dropping hard on to base of dish, so bursting some of the air bubbles. Fill soufflé dish to within ½ in. of top. Place on oven tray.

Serve cooked soufflé with a green salad.

Directions for Baking

To bake at once   Bake in moderate oven, Mark 4, 350°F. Allow 40 to 45 minutes for one large soufflé; 25 to 30 minutes for individual soufflés.
To refrigerate overnight (or up to 24 hours) Refrigerate uncovered. Next day, place in moderate oven, Mark 4, 350°F. Allow 55 to 60 minutes cooking time for large soufflé; 30 minutes for individual soufflés.
To freeze   Cover top of soufflé dish, or dishes, with plastic food wrap or aluminium foil; this will prevent hard skin forming on top of mixture during freezing time. When ready to bake, remove plastic wrap or foil. Soufflés can go direct from freezer to oven; do it this way. Place soufflés in cold, unlit oven; then light oven and set temperature at moderate. Mark 4, 350°F. Allow approximately 60 minutes cooking time for large soufflés; approximately 40 minutes cooking time for individual soufflés.

Crab and Chive Soufflé

4 eggs	1½ gills (½ cup) milk
4 oz. (½ cup or 1 stick) butter	6½ oz. crab meat
4 tablespoons plain flour	2 tablespoons chopped chives or spring onions (scallions) (including green tops)
1 teaspoon salt	
¼ teaspoon mustard	

Separate eggs; allow to stand, covered, while preparing sauce. Melt butter in top part of double saucepan over hot water; remove from heat, stir in flour and seasonings, stirring until smooth and free from lumps. Stir in milk all at once, return to heat; stir over hot water until smooth and thick. Remove from heat; stir in crab and chives. Allow to cool slightly.

Then proceed as for Cheese Soufflé. Baking times are the same as for Cheese Soufflé.

Vanilla Soufflé

4 eggs	½ teaspoon salt
4 oz. (½ cup or 1 stick) butter	1½ gills (½ cup) milk
4 tablespoons plain flour	1 tablespoon castor (superfine) sugar
	1 teaspoon vanilla

Separate eggs, allow to stand, covered, while preparing sauce. Melt butter in top part of double saucepan over hot water; remove from heat, stir in flour and salt, stirring until smooth and free from lumps. Stir in milk, all at once, add sugar; return to heat; stir over hot water until smooth and thick. Remove from heat, allow to cool slightly, stir in vanilla.

Then proceed as for Cheese Soufflé. Baking times are the same as for Cheese Soufflé.

Chocolate Soufflé

4 eggs
4 oz. (½ cup or 1 stick) butter
4 tablespoons plain flour
½ teaspoon salt
1½ gills (½ cup) milk
6 oz. (6 squares) plain chocolate
2 oz. (¼ cup) castor (superfine) sugar

Separate eggs; allow to stand, covered, while preparing sauce. Melt butter in top part of double saucepan over hot water; remove from heat, stir in flour and salt, stirring until smooth and free from lumps. Stir in milk all at once, return to heat; stir over hot water until smooth and thick. Remove from heat; stir in grated chocolate and sugar while still hot, stirring until dissolved.

Then proceed as for Cheese Soufflé. Baking times are the same as for Cheese Soufflé.

Other Hot Soufflés

The following two soufflés—Chestnut and Apricot cannot be refrigerated or frozen. They should be mixed, baked and served at once.

Apricot Soufflé

4 oz. (1 cup) dried apricots
4 egg-whites
2 oz. (¼ cup) castor (superfine) sugar
extra castor (superfine) sugar

Place apricots in bowl, cover with hot water, leave until well plumped; then purée in electric blender or rub through sieve. Place egg-whites and 1 tablespoon of the sugar in large mixing bowl, beat until thick and of meringue consistency. Gradually beat in remaining sugar and apricot purée. Grease soufflé or ovenproof dish, dust lightly with extra castor sugar. Pour in soufflé mixture gently so air bubbles will not be broken down (a good way to do this is to pour it over back of spoon). Bake in moderate oven, Mark 4, 350°F., 30 minutes.

Chestnut Soufflé

1 large can (about 1 lb.) unsweetened chestnut purée
6 oz. (¾ cup or 1½ sticks) butter
5½ oz. (⅔ cup) castor (superfine) sugar
1 teaspoon vanilla
8 egg-yolks
6 egg-whites
extra castor (superfine) sugar

Prepare 8 in. soufflé dish, by greasing and dusting lightly with extra sugar; place a greased paper collar around outside of dish, secure firmly with string.

Rub chestnut purée through sieve, place in saucepan with butter and sugar. Stir constantly over low heat until butter is melted and sugar dissolved; add vanilla. Remove from heat, cool slightly. Beat egg-yolks until thick and creamy, gradually add chestnut mixture, beating constantly. Beat egg-whites until soft peaks form. Lightly fold half the egg-whites into chestnut mixture, then remaining egg-whites. Pour mixture carefully into prepared dish, sprinkle top lightly with extra castor sugar. Bake in moderate oven, Mark 4, 350°F. 50 to 60 minutes. Serve at once with cream.

NOTE: There are two types of canned chestnuts; one is puréed chestnuts flavoured with sugar, glucose and vanilla. The other is pure chestnuts puréed; this is the type to use for this recipe. Check ingredients on can.

Cold Soufflés

The cold soufflé can be made in endless variations. Simply prepared, it stands above the rim of the dish in distinguished imitation of the baked soufflé.

Lemon Soufflé

3 eggs
4 oz. (½ cup) castor (superfine) sugar
grated rind and juice 3 lemons
1½ dessertspoons gelatine
5 tablespoons water
½ pint (1 cup) whipping cream

Prepare a 6 in. soufflé case or straight-sided container, by tying double band of greased greaseproof paper round dish on the outside with string, extending paper 2 in. above the edge.

Separate eggs. Place yolks, sugar, lemon juice and rind in the top of double saucepan, cook over hot water, stirring constantly, until mixture thickens slightly, approximately 10 minutes.

Soak gelatine in the water, dissolve over hot water, add to slightly cooled custard mixture. Allow to cool, stirring occasionally to prevent mixture setting at the bottom. When mixture is beginning to set, fold in gently the whipped cream and stiffly beaten egg-whites. Pour into prepared soufflé dish, refrigerate until set. Decorate with whipped cream and a sprinkling of grated lemon rind.

Orange Soufflé

As for Lemon Soufflé, but substitute the grated rind of 2 oranges and the juice of 1 orange for the lemon rind and juice.

Cheese

There are so many varieties in cheeses, it is difficult to imagine that they all begin in much the same fashion. Most cheese is made from cows' milk, although cheese can be made from the milk of any milk-giving animal. Simply defined, cheese is the solid portion of milk separated from the whey. The many different cheeses which result from this similar beginning are the product of variations in the manufacture and curing of each variety.

A wide variety of cheese is available. Apart from that made in this country cheese is imported from France and many other countries.

Cheese can be divided broadly into three categories, hard, medium and soft. Below are some of the most popular.

French Cheeses

Brie　One of the world's great cheeses. A creamy, flat round cheese of delicate flavour. It does not keep very well, and should be served at room temperature.

Camembert　At its best when soft and served at room temperature. Also available from Denmark, Sweden and Ireland.

Port Salut　A soft creamy cheese, full of little holes and of good flavour.

Roquefort　Made from ewe's milk, has a creamy but crumbly texture and a rich pungent flavour.

Tome or Grape Cheese　Has a white buttery texture, mild in flavour and the outside is covered closely with grape pips taken from the wine press.

English Cheeses

Caerphilly　A medium hard cheese made in Wales. White in colour and with a mild flavour.

Cheddar　Close textured, ranging from semi-soft to firm, creamy in colour and has a unique nutty flavour. It is much used in cooking. This cheese is also imported from Australia, New Zealand and Canada. In America it is usually considered best crumbly, pungent and well-aged.

Cheshire　Stronger in flavour than Cheddar and more crumbly. It can be white or a rich golden colour, or, in America, blue.

Cottage Cheese　A crumbly, low caloried cheese, generally served in salads.

Double Gloucester　Very smooth in texture and similar to Cheddar in flavour.

Dunlop　A Scottish cheese similar to Cheddar.

Lancashire　White in colour and with a rather strong flavour. Its loose texture makes it ideal for crumbling over soups and hot-pots and it toasts well.

Leicester　Deep in colour with a mild flavour, often served with fresh fruit.

Stilton　A rich blue veined cheese. White Stilton is a younger version, milder in flavour.

Wensleydale　Semi creamy-textured cheese, white and slightly veined with green. Often served with apple pie.

Italian Cheeses

Bel Paese　A soft cheese, full of flavour.

Gorgonzola　A strong cheese veined with blue.

Mozzarella　Has a mild flavour and usually sold in pear shaped bags. Excellent for pizzas.

Parmesan　A very hard pungent cheese used only for cooking.

Provolone　Firm, smoked cheese cured while hung from ceiling.

Ricotta　Soft, unsalted and unripened cheese. Extremely perishable but used extensively in Italian cooking.

Neapolitan Pizza has a topping of quick-melting Mozzarella cheese; it's an excellent supper dish, and popular with all teenagers.

Swiss Cheeses

Gruyère A firm pale yellow cheese with large holes, often mixed with Parmesan for cooking.

Emmenthal A little softer than Gruyère with large and irregular holes. An all-purpose cheese.

Swiss Cheese The American name for Emmenthal.

Dutch Cheeses

Edam A round decorative cheese with red skin, mild in flavour, primarily for appetisers or snacks.

Gouda Mild flavour, golden in colour with a white skin. Richer in butterfat than Edam.

Danish Cheeses

Crema Danica Soft white dessert cheese, high in butterfat.

Danish Blue Has a creamy texture and a well developed piquant flavour.

Samsoe From the island of Samsoe—pale yellow in colour with a few large shiny holes and has a mild nutty flavour.

American Cheeses

American Pasteurized, golden cheese mild in flavour.

Coon New York State Cheddar.

Liederkranz Soft, pungent cheese resembles a mild Limburger (creamy, smelly).

Muenster Mild, semifirm with small holes.

Cream or Mild Cheeses

Demi-sel A soft milk cheese.

Petit Gervaise and Petit Suisse Made from cream.

Cooking with Cheese

When cheese is to be melted during the cooking process, make sure it is grated, or the pieces cut in similar size, so they will melt evenly at the same time. In all cheese cookery, it is important to remember cheese must be cooked slowly, over gentle heat. If cooked too quickly, the protein in cheese toughens, and the cheese becomes stringy.

Keeping Qualities and Storage

The moisture content of cheese—whether it is a hard cheese or soft—is a guide to its keeping quality. Very hard cheese, such as parmesan has excellent keeping quality. Parmesan can be bought grated in packets. If this is to be kept, once the packet has been opened, transfer it to a screw-top jar; this will ensure that it keeps fresh and retains its flavour. Wrap firm cheeses, such as cheddar, in plastic food wrap or aluminium foil, and store in a cool place, or refrigerate. For best flavour, let cheese return to room temperature before using.

Soft cheeses, such as cream or cottage cheese, have a high moisture content. Wrap them well in plastic food wrap or aluminium foil, or place in plastic food container, and keep refrigerated. They should be used within 3 or 4 days of purchase and again with the exception of cream or cottage cheese should be served at room temperature.

Cheese-Topped Vegetable Pie

Rice Pie Shell

1 oz. (2 tablespoons) butter	6 oz. (2 cups) cooked rice
1 small onion	1 egg

Filling

1 oz. (2 tablespoons) butter	1 carrot
4 small zucchini (courgettes)	1 teaspoon salt
2 onions	$\frac{1}{4}$ teaspoon pepper
3 sticks celery	1 teaspoon curry powder
$\frac{1}{4}$ lb. (2 cups) mushrooms	

Cheese Sauce

2 oz. ($\frac{1}{4}$ cup) butter	4 oz. (1 cup) grated cheese
4 tablespoons flour	2 tablespoons medium cream
$\frac{1}{2}$ teaspoon salt	
pinch pepper	
$\frac{1}{2}$ teaspoon dry mustard	1 dessertspoon chopped parsley
$1\frac{1}{2}$ gills ($\frac{1}{2}$ cup) milk	

Pie Case Melt butter in saucepan, sauté chopped onion. Add to rice; mix well. Beat egg, stir into rice mixture. Press into 8 in. pie plate, covering base and sides.

Filling Melt butter in saucepan, add sliced

zucchini, chopped onion, sliced celery, halved mushrooms and thinly sliced carrot; sauté 3 minutes. Add salt, pepper and curry powder; mix thoroughly. Place vegetables into rice case. Pour sauce over vegetables, bake in moderate oven, Mark 4, 350°F. for 35 to 40 minutes.

Cheese Sauce   Melt butter in saucepan, stir in flour, and cook 1 minute; remove from heat. Add salt, pepper, mustard and milk; blend well. Return to heat, stirring constantly until mixture boils and thickens. Stir in grated cheese, cream and parsley.

Serves 5 to 6.

Neapolitan Pizza

Yeast Dough

4 tablespoons milk	½ teaspoon salt
½ oz. (1 package)	½ teaspoon sugar
compressed yeast	1 oz. (2 tablespoons)
1 egg	butter
6 oz. (1½ cups) plain	
flour	

Filling

1 dessertspoon oil	salt, pepper
14 oz. can tomatoes	2 oz. salami
1 clove garlic	8 oz. mozzarella cheese
2 small cans (2½ oz.)	sliced olives
tomato paste (¼ cup	1 teaspoon basil or
tomato purée)	oregano
1 teaspoon sugar	chopped parsley

Yeast Dough   Warm milk, add crumbled yeast, stir until dissolved, add beaten egg. Add yeast mixture to well in centre of sifted dry ingredients, blend well. Cream butter, work into the dough. Cover bowl, stand in warm place 40 minutes, or until doubled in bulk.

Press dough into oiled 9 in. pie plate, or pizza pan, brush dough lightly with oil. Arrange filling ingredients except olives over dough, and bake in hot oven, Mark 7, 425°F. for 15 to 20 minutes, or until golden brown. Sprinkle with sliced black or green olives.

Filling   Heat oil in saucepan, add undrained can of tomatoes, crushed garlic, tomato paste, sugar, salt and pepper, simmer uncovered until mixture is thick, and some of the liquid has evaporated; cool.

Spread over dough, top with slices of salami and Mozzarella cheese. Sprinkle with basil or oregano and parsley.

Ham and Cheese Squares

½ lb. (2 cups) self-raising (all-purpose) flour	¾ gill (6 tablespoons) milk
½ teaspoon salt	3 tablespoons mayonnaise (see page 121)
2 oz. (¼ cup) butter	

Filling

½ lb. smoked ham sausage	2 tablespoons chopped parsley
1 onion chopped	salt, pepper
4 oz. (1 cup) grated cheddar cheese	milk
¼ teaspoon dry mustard	extra grated cheese

Sift flour and salt into basin, rub in butter. Combine milk and mayonnaise, cut into dry ingredients with knife until all liquid is absorbed. Turn on to floured board and knead lightly. Divide in half, roll out one portion to fit base of greased 11 in. × 7 in. tin.

Sprinkle over chopped ham sausage. Combine onion, cheese, mustard and parsley, season to taste and sprinkle over ham. Roll out remaining pastry and place over filling. Glaze with milk and sprinkle with extra grated cheese. Bake in hot oven, Mark 7, 425°F. for 20 minutes. Cut into squares while still warm.

Makes approx. 15 squares.

Swiss Cheese Tart

Pastry

7 oz. (1¾ cups) plain flour	4 oz. (1 cup) grated cheese (preferably parmesan and gruyère mixed)
pinch salt	
pinch paprika	
5 oz. (good ½ cup) butter	1 egg
	egg-white for glazing

Filling

1 teaspoon cornflour	2 egg-yolks
1 teaspoon flour	4 tablespoons sour
1½ gills (½ cup) milk	cream
4 oz. (1 cup) grated cheese (preferably parmesan and gruyère mixed)	salt
	paprika

Pastry   Sift dry ingredients, rub in the butter. Add grated cheese, mix to a dry dough with beaten egg; chill 30 minutes.

Roll out, line 8 in. pie plate. Brush surface of pastry with a little beaten egg-white.

Filling   Blend flours with cold milk. Add cheese, egg-yolks, cream, salt and paprika. Beat together spoon into pie case. Bake in moderate oven, Mark 4, 350°F., 40 minutes to 1 hour.

Fish

Fish should be a permanent part of the weekly family menu, not only for its high protein value, but for its good taste and the interesting variety it can add to family and party meals.

Sole Véronique

1½ to 2 lb. sole filleted	1½ oz. (3 tablespoons)
½ small onion	butter
1 bayleaf	1½ oz. (3 tablespoons)
few peppercorns	flour
juice ½ lemon	1 pint (2 cups) milk
water	salt, pepper
	½ lb. white grapes

Fold fillets or roll up and secure with small wooden sticks. Place fillets in greased ovenproof dish. Put in sliced onion, bayleaf, peppercorns and lemon juice, add sufficient water to half-cover fillets. Cover with greased paper, poach in moderate oven, Mark 4, 350°F. for 15 to 20 minutes or until cooked.

Transfer fish to hot serving dish; keep warm. Reserve ¼ pint (½ cup) liquid in which fish was cooked. Melt butter in saucepan, add flour, cook 1 minute. Remove from heat, gradually add milk and reserved liquid which has been reduced to half the quantity by fast boiling. Return to heat, bring to boil, simmer until smooth and thickened, stirring constantly. Season to taste with salt and pepper; spoon over fish. Simmer peeled grapes in a little boiling water few minutes; drain. Arrange grapes at side of dish. Serve immediately.

Serves 4.

Sole and Asparagus with Wine Sauce

1 lb. sole fillets	1 small can asparagus
approx. ¼ pint (½ cup)	tips
white wine	

Sauce

1½ oz. (3 tablespoons)	1½ gills (scant cup) milk
butter	salt, pepper
2 tablespoons flour	

Place skinned and boned fillets in ovenproof dish. Pour wine over, fish should be barely covered, poach in moderately hot oven, Mark 4, 350°F. for 20 minutes. Drain, reserve liquid for sauce. Place poached fillets on to warm individual dishes, arrange on top few drained asparagus tips, which have heated in their own liquor. Spoon sauce over.

Sauce Melt butter in saucepan. Stir in flour, cook 1 minute. Remove from heat, gradually add milk and ½ gill (4 tablespoons) of reserved liquid from fish. Return to heat, bring to boil; reduce heat, simmer until smooth and thickened, stirring constantly. Season to taste with salt and pepper.

Serves 4 as an entrée.

Trout in Butter Sauce with Almonds

4 cleaned trout	freshly ground pepper
salt	2 oz. (¼ cup) toasted
flour	almonds
4 oz. (½ cup or 1 stick)	parsley
butter	lemon slices
1 teaspoon lemon juice	

Select trout from 8 in. to 10 in. long; sprinkle inside and outside with salt, toss in flour. Heat half the butter in heavy frying pan, put in fish, cook until well browned on both sides.

Transfer to hot serving dish; keep warm. Add remaining butter to pan with lemon juice, pepper and toasted almonds; simmer a few minutes; pour over fish.

Serve immediately, garnished with lemon slices and parsley.

Serves 4.

Fish Meunière

1½ lb. fillets of white	1½ tablespoons lemon
fish	juice
seasoned flour	chopped parsley
4 oz. (½ cup or 1 stick)	
butter	

Skin the fillets if this has not been done by the fishmonger, toss lightly in seasoned flour. Melt ¾ of the butter in pan, fry fillets until brown on both sides; remove. Melt remaining butter in pan; add lemon juice, spoon over fish, sprinkle with parsley.

Serves 4.

Trout with Almonds is served with lemon-flavoured hot butter sauce. This method of cooking can also be used for other fish, in place of trout.

Sole Bonne Femme

2 oz. (¼ cup) butter	2 tablespoons chopped
1 large onion	parsley
4 oz. mushrooms	½ pint (1 cup) dry white
1½ lb. sole fillets	wine
salt, pepper	

Sauce

2 oz. (¼ cup) butter	6 tablespoons light
1 oz. (2 tablespoons)	cream
flour	salt, pepper
1 egg-yolk	

Melt butter in shallow pan. Add chopped onions and half the sliced mushrooms. Arrange fish fillets over vegetables, season with salt and pepper. Spread remaining sliced mushrooms over fish, sprinkle with parsley; pour wine over. Cover fillets with piece of greaseproof paper the size of pan, with small hole in centre. Bring to boil, cover pan, reduce heat, simmer 10 to 15 minutes. Using large spatula, remove fish and vegetables to warm serving dish, reserving liquid. Keep fish warm.

Sauce Melt butter in saucepan. Stir in flour, cook 1 minute. Remove from heat, gradually stir in reserved liquid; return to heat. Bring to boil, stirring; reduce heat, simmer until smooth and thickened, stirring constantly. Combine beaten egg-yolk and cream, stir into sauce; re-heat few seconds, stirring, season to taste with salt and pepper, if necessary. Spoon over fish.

Serves 4.

Fish Fillets Florentine

1 lb. spinach	salt, pepper
1 oz. (2 tablespoons)	nutmeg
butter	1 tablespoon lemon
2 tablespoons water	juice
1 to 1½ lb. fresh or	lemon slices
quick-frozen	chopped parsley
flounder fillets	

Mornay Sauce

1 oz. (2 tablespoons)	Parmesan cheese
butter	1 oz. (¼ cup) grated firm
2 tablespoons flour	Cheddar cheese
½ pint (1 cup) milk	salt, pepper
1 oz. (¼ cup) grated	nutmeg

Wash spinach, chop and place in saucepan with butter and water. Steam gently over low heat until spinach is just wilted (approximately 2 minutes). Place drained spinach in greased, shallow oven-proof dish. Arrange thawed fish fillets on top, sprinkle with salt, pepper and nutmeg, pour over lemon juice. Cover with greased aluminium foil and bake in moderate oven, Mark 4, 350°F. 20 to 30 minutes or until fish is tender.

Remove foil and spoon over hot Mornay Sauce. Serve as entrée or main course, garnish with lemon slices and chopped parsley.

Mornay Sauce Melt butter in saucepan, add flour, cook 1 minute. Remove from heat, gradually add milk. Return to heat, bring to boil, stirring; simmer until smooth and thickened, stirring constantly.

Remove from heat, add grated cheese and seasonings, stir until cheese has completely melted.

Serves 4 to 6.

Sole Bercy

1½ lb. sole fillets (or	salt, pepper
other fillets)	juice ½ lemon
½ pint (1 cup) fish stock	2 tablespoons chopped
2 small shallots,	parsley
chopped	4 to 5 tablespoons
½ pint (1 cup) white	medium cream
wine	1 tablespoon dry
3 oz. (⅜ cup) butter	breadcrumbs

Place fillets in buttered shallow ovenproof dish, add stock; cover with sheet of greaseproof paper, poach in moderate oven, Mark 4, 350°F. 10 to 15 minutes or until tender. Sauté shallots in ½ oz. (1 tablespoon) butter. Add wine, bring to boil; boil over high heat until liquid is reduced by half. Strain liquid from fish into saucepan with shallots and wine; add salt, pepper, lemon juice and chopped parsley. Bring to boil, add remainder of butter, stir until melted.

Remove from heat, stir in cream. Spoon sauce over fish fillets, sprinkle with breadcrumbs. Place under hot grill or in hot oven, Mark 7, 425°F. until top is lightly brown.

Serves 4.

Grilled Whitefish or Mullet

1 medium sized	1 lemon
whitefish or mullet	1 to 2 oz. (about ¼ cup)
salt, pepper	melted butter

NOTE: Use this quantity for each serving.
Wash and dry fish, make several slashes across each side. Rub well with salt and pepper, sprinkle with lemon juice; insert slices of lemon in slashes on one side. Brush with melted butter, cook under pre-heated grill, allowing 7 to 10 minutes for each side, depending on size of fish. Turn fish once, brush liberally with melted butter.

Serve at once with lemon wedges.

Butter-Fried Whitefish

6 fillets whitefish,   seasoned flour
   mullet or bream   butter

Egg Butter

3 oz. (⅜ cup) butter   parsley
2 hard boiled eggs

Lemony Butter

3 oz. (⅜ cup) butter   lemon slices
lemon juice to taste   parsley

Skin and bone fillets, if not done by fishmonger, dip in seasoned flour. Melt butter in frying pan; fry fillets until cooked on one side, turn and cook on the other side. Serve with Egg Butter or Lemony Butter, or with Sauce Remoulade. (See page 149.)
   Serves 6.
Egg Butter Melt butter in pan. Add finely chopped eggs. Pour over fish and garnish with parsley.
Lemony Butter Melt butter in pan, add lemon juice to taste. Pour over fish, garnish with lemon slices, and fried parsley sprigs. Or lemon slices can be sautéed in hot butter and used as garnish.

Baked Fresh Haddock

1 fresh haddock (2½ to 3 lb.)

Stuffing

4 tablespoons soft   1 large orange
   white breadcrumbs   1 egg
2 tablespoons chopped   salt, pepper
   herbs (parsley,   extra orange juice if
   thyme, marjoram)   needed
2 tablespoons finely   1½ oz. (3 tablespoons)
   chopped onion   butter

Put the breadcrumbs into a basin with the herbs and season well. Soften the onion in the butter for a few minutes without colouring then add to the mixture with the grated rind and juice of the orange. Bind with the egg and add a little extra orange juice if too dry.
   Stuff the fish with this mixture and sew up securely. Put into a buttered dish, brush well with melted butter and bake in a moderate oven, Mark 4, 350°F., for about 40 minutes. Serve with wedges of orange.
   Serves 4.

Sautéed Whitefish or Mullet with Capers

1 lb. Whitefish or   1 dessertspoon grated
   mullet (filleted)   lemon rind
salt, pepper   2 tablespoons capers,
lemon juice   drained
flour   1 tablespoon chopped
2 oz. (¼ cup) butter   parsley
1 tablespoon lemon
   juice, extra

Rub fillets with salt and pepper, sprinkle with lemon juice; roll in flour. Melt half the butter in frying-pan, add fish, fry until golden brown on both sides.
   Transfer cooked fillets to hot dish. Wipe out pan, add remaining butter. Cook until light brown, add extra lemon juice and rind, capers and parsley. Pour over fish.
   Serves 2.

Baked Minted Whitefish or Mullet

1 medium sized   2 or 3 sprigs of mint
   whitefish or mullet   lemon juice
1 lemon   butter
salt, pepper

NOTE: Use this quantity for each serving.
Wash and dry fish. Rub body cavity with lemon, sprinkle with salt and pepper; place mint sprigs inside. Cut 3 gashes on each side of fish, insert small slices of lemon. Sprinkle over a little more lemon juice and about 1 teaspoon of grated lemon rind. Sprinkle with salt and pepper, dot with butter, wrap in greased aluminium foil.
   Bake in moderate oven, Mark 4, 350°F. 30 minutes; serve with lemon slices.

Whiting with Noodles

6 oz. (1 cup) ribbon   4 oz. (½ cup or 1
   noodles   package) cream
1 oz. (2 tablespoons)   cheese
   butter   lemon juice
4 fillets whiting   4 oz. mushrooms
salt, pepper   4 oz. (1 cup) cooked
                                 peas
                              2 oz. prawns (shrimp)

Cook the noodles in boiling salted water. Butter the grid of the grill, arrange the fish on the grid, season and spread with the cream cheese, sprinkle with lemon juice. Cook for about 8 minutes.
   Cook the mushrooms in a little milk or water with salt, pepper and lemon juice. Drain, mix with the strained noodles, add peas and prawns. Toss all in a little butter and put into a hot serving dish. Arrange the fish on top. Serve hot.
   Serves 4.

Escabache

1½ to 2 lb. thick fillet of cod or haddock	1 egg
seasoned flour	2 tablespoons milk
	oil for frying

Vegetable Pickle

½ lb. small carrots	1 small red pepper
½ lb. small turnips	1 to 1½ pints (2 to 3
2 sticks celery	cups) white wine
½ lb. small white onions	vinegar
	2 oz. (¼ cup) sugar
1 small green pepper	1 teaspoon celery seed

Dressing

4 tablespoons salad oil	2 tablespoons dry white wine
2 tablespoons white wine vinegar	½ teaspoon dry mustard
salt, pepper	

Prepare fish and cut into large bite-size pieces. Coat with seasoned flour, brush with beaten egg and milk, coat again with flour. Fry in hot oil till well browned then drain on absorbent paper and place in serving dish.

To make the pickle—prepare carrot, turnip and celery and cut into 2 in. lengths. Peel onions and keep whole. Remove pith and seeds from the peppers, cut into strips. Put carrot, turnip and onion into pan and just cover with vinegar. Add sugar and celery seed and bring to the boil, reduce heat and simmer 15 minutes. Add celery and peppers and a little more vinegar if required. Cook for 3 minutes, then drain off the vinegar.

To make the dressing—mix all ingredients well together, pour over vegetables, toss lightly and pour all over the fish.
Serves 5 to 6.

Sweet and Sour Fish

2 lb. cod or other thick fish fillets	1 pint prawns (shrimp)
½ pint (1 cup) chicken stock	2 medium onions
	4 sticks celery
1 tablespoon tomato paste	3 to 4 chives
	1 red pepper
1 tablespoon soy sauce	cornflour
3 tablespoons white wine	oil for frying
	salt, pepper
1 teaspoon ground ginger	

Cut fish into bite-size pieces. Mix half the stock, tomato paste, soy sauce, wine and ginger. Place fish and prawns in this marinade and leave for 1 hour.

Peel and slice onions, chop celery and chives, remove seeds from the pepper and cut into thin strips.

Drain the fish and reserve the marinade.

Coat the fish and prawns with cornflour and fry in hot oil until golden. Keep hot. Fry onion until transparent, add celery, chives and peppers and cook for 3 minutes. Add fish, pour the sauce over, reheat, stirring well and serve with fluffy rice.

For the Sauce Blend 1 dessertspoon cornflour with remaining stock, add to reserved marinade, stir over low heat until boiling and correct seasoning.
Serves 6.

Indian Curried Fish

2 lb. fish fillets	1 teaspoon turmeric
juice 1 large lemon	2 teaspoons curry powder
salt, pepper	oil for deep frying

Wash fish fillets, dry well. Cut into 2 or 3 pieces, according to size. Sprinkle on both sides with lemon juice, salt and pepper, place into a dish with remaining lemon juice. Allow to stand for a few minutes, then sprinkle with turmeric and curry powder. Move fish around in this mixture to coat well.

Fry in hot, deep oil a few minutes until cooked. Delicious with fried rice.
Serves 4.

Haddock Kedgeree

3 oz. (½ cup) rice	salt, pepper
1 lb. smoked haddock	1 dessertspoon lemon juice
2 hard-boiled eggs	
3 oz. (⅜ cup) butter	2 tablespoons chopped parsley

Cook rice in large quantity of boiling water until tender, 12 to 15 minutes; drain. Poach fish until tender. Shell and chop eggs.

Melt butter in saucepan, add boned, flaked fish and rice. Season to taste with salt and pepper. Stir in chopped eggs, heat thoroughly. Add lemon juice and half the parsley; reserve remainder for garnish.

Serves 4 as an entrée, or 3 as main dish.
Salmon Kedgeree Substitute 7½ oz. can of salmon for the haddock; drain and add with rice, to melted butter in pan, as above.

Escabache—golden-fried fish pieces topped with a colourful vegetable pickle—makes an excellent buffet or barbecue dish; nice, too, for a light summer meal.

Fish Mornay

1 lb. fillet of cod or haddock	2 tablespoons flour
¼ pint (½ cup) milk	salt, pepper
¼ pint (½ cup) water	2 oz. (½ cup) grated cheese (parmesan or cheddar)
1 bayleaf	
1 small onion	2 tablespoons bread-crumbs
few shrimps	
1½ oz. (3 tablespoons) butter	1 oz. (2 tablespoons) butter extra

Wipe the fish. Combine milk, water, bayleaf and half the chopped onion in saucepan. Poach fish in this liquid until tender, drain, reserving liquid. Flake fish coarsely. Remove bayleaf from liquid. Combine fish and shrimps.

Melt butter in saucepan, sauté remaining chopped onion for 1 minute, stir in flour, cook 1 minute. Remove from heat. Gradually add reserved liquid. Return to heat, stir until sauce boils and thickens; cook 5 minutes, stirring constantly. Season to taste, stir in cheese, leaving approximately 2 tablespoons for topping. Fold in fish mixture, spoon mixture into greased ovenproof dish. Sprinkle with mixture of breadcrumbs and remaining cheese. Dot with extra butter; brown under hot grill or in oven, Mark 7, 425°F. Serve with hot rice.

Serves 4 to 5 as an entrée or 3 as a main dish.

Salmon Mornay Make up Mornay Sauce, as for Fish Mornay, omitting the fish and shrimps. Add 1 large can salmon, with bones removed, to the sauce, stir in 1 teaspoon lemon juice. Then spoon into casserole, top with breadcrumbs and cheese, dot with butter and brown.

Salmon Croquettes

7½ oz. can salmon	1 dessertspoon lemon juice
8 oz. (1½ cups) mashed potato	1 egg-yolk
1 teaspoon curry powder	salt, pepper
1 small onion	2 eggs for glazing
1 dessertspoon chopped parsley	dry breadcrumbs
	oil for frying

Drain salmon, remove bones and flake. In a bowl combine salmon, potato, curry powder, onion, parsley and lemon juice; add egg-yolk, salt and pepper, mix thoroughly. Refrigerate until firm. Mould mixture into croquette shapes approximately 1 in. thick by 2 in. long.

Dip in beaten eggs, press breadcrumbs on firmly. Refrigerate 1 hour. Fry in hot oil until golden brown, drain on absorbent paper.

Makes approx. 1 dozen.

Tuna Mousse

1 tablespoon gelatine	1 tablespoon French dressing (see page 121)
2 tablespoons water	
2 6½ oz. cans tuna	2 oz. (½ cup) diced cucumber
4 oz. (½ cup or 1 stick) softened butter	4 to 5 finely chopped spring onions or chives (scallions)
1 egg-white	
1 tablespoon lemon juice	¼ pint (½ cup) whipping cream
salt, pepper	

Cucumber Sauce

2 teaspoons finely chopped chives	2 finely chopped spring onions (scallions)
1 oz. (¼ cup) finely diced cucumber	salt, pepper
¼ pint (½ cup) sour cream	

Soften gelatine in the water, dissolve over boiling water. Place tuna in bowl with liquid from cans, and beat well. Fish can be beaten in an electric mixer. Gradually beat in softened butter. Then add egg-white, lemon juice, pepper, salt and dressing; beat thoroughly.

Fold in dissolved gelatine, cucumber, spring onions and chives. Whip cream until thick, and fold into tuna mixture. Pour mixture into oiled mould, refrigerate until firm. Unmould; serve with Cucumber Sauce and a green salad.

Serves 4 to 5.

Cucumber Sauce Combine all ingredients, mix thoroughly.

Grilled Cutlets of Hake or Cod

3 to 4 oz. (about ½ cup) butter	1 oz. (¼ cup) grated Parmesan cheese
4 steaks of hake or cod	3 oz. (½ cup) blanched almonds
salt, pepper	
4 oz. small button mushrooms	

Brush the fish on one side with butter and season lightly with salt and pepper. Put under a hot grill and cook until golden brown. Turn over, brush with butter, season lightly and sprinkle with cheese. Continue cooking until brown and tender. Meanwhile, fry the almonds and mushrooms in the remaining butter.

Put the fish on to a hot serving dish and arrange the nuts and mushrooms round. Garnish with tomato slices and sprigs of parsley.

Serves 4.

Fish Cocktail

1 lb. fish fillets
1 large onion
white vinegar
juice 2 lemons
2 oz. (½ cup) cooked
  green peas

mayonnaise (see page
  121)
salt, pepper
lettuce
¼ red pepper
¼ green pepper

Prepare the fish, cut into small pieces. Peel onion, cut into thin slices. Put the fish and onion into glass or china bowl, pour over enough white vinegar to cover, stir in lemon juice. Cover, let stand to marinate overnight. Next day drain liquid from fish.

Combine fish and onion with peas and enough mayonnaise to hold mixture together; season to taste. Shred a little lettuce into the bottom of four cocktail glasses and place spoonful of the fish mixture on top. Sprinkle over the finely chopped or sliced peppers.

Serves 4.

NOTE: The fish in this cocktail is not actually cooked; the acid action of the vinegar and lemon juice, as the fish stands overnight, simulates the cooking process.

Halibut Portuguese

Sauce

1 tablespoon oil
1 small onion
¼ green pepper
4 tomatoes
⅓ pint (5 tablespoons)
  white wine
12 stuffed olives

2 steaks halibut
  (1¼ to 1½ lb.)
1 tablespoon flour
salt, pepper
1 tablespoon oil
2 oz. (¼ cup) butter

To make the sauce—heat oil in small pan, add finely chopped onion and cook until transparent, add thinly sliced pepper and cook a few minutes. Skin, quarter and remove pips from tomatoes, slice and put with onion and peppers. Add wine and olives. Cut fish steaks in half and coat with seasoned flour. Heat oil and butter in frying pan, put in the fish and cook on both sides until golden brown and tender.

To serve—reheat the sauce and pour a little into serving dish. Arrange the fish on top and serve the rest of the sauce separately.

Serves 4.

Cod's Roe Pâté

6 oz. smoked cod's roe
4 slices white bread
½ small onion

1 clove garlic
6 tablespoons oil
juice of 1 lemon
chopped parsley

Put cod's roe into a mortar or basin. Trim crusts from bread, soak the bread in water then squeeze well and put with the roe. Pound to a smooth paste. Add grated onion and crushed garlic. Gradually stir in oil and lemon juice alternately until mixture is smooth. Put through a blender or rub through a fine sieve.

Put into a bowl and sprinkle with parsley. Chill, and serve with hot toast.

Serves 4.

Soused Herring

4 herrings
black pepper, salt
1 teaspoon chopped
  tarragon

2 teaspoons finely
  chopped shallot
1 bay leaf
vinegar

Clean and scale herrings, split down the front and remove backbone.

Sprinkle each with salt, pepper, tarragon and shallot. Roll up and put into a fireproof dish. Place a small piece of bay leaf on each.

Cover with equal parts of vinegar and water and bake in a moderate oven, Mark 3, 350°F. for ¾ to 1 hour.

Leave to get quite cold then serve in the liquor.

Serves 4.

Mackerel with Cider Sauce

4 mackerel
¼ pint (½ cup) cider
2 tablespoons tarragon
  vinegar
1 bay leaf

juice of ½ lemon
bouquet garni
salt, pepper
lemon or orange for
  garnish

Remove heads of fish, clean and remove backbone. Put into a fireproof dish with cider, vinegar, bay leaf, lemon juice and bouquet garni. Sprinkle lightly with salt and pepper. Cover and cook in a moderate oven, Mark 4, 350°F. for 25 to 30 minutes.

Cider Sauce

1 oz. (2 tablespoons)
  butter
1½ oz. (scant ¼ cup)
  sugar

1 lb. cooking apples
¼ pint (½ cup) cider

Melt the butter, add sugar, peeled and sliced apples and cider. Simmer until reduced to a thick purée. Beat until smooth.

Garnish the fish with slices or 'butterflies' of orange or lemon and serve with the sauce.

To Cook Fresh Lobster

Most people prefer to buy lobsters already cooked although there is quite a difference between freshly caught lobster cooked at home to exactly the right degree and the cooked lobster bought in shops, but it is often the killing of the fish that deters the inexperienced. There are two methods. The lobster may be plunged into a large pan of fast boiling water or court-bouillon—but if the latter is used, the minimum amount of vinegar should be used or the colour of the shell will be spoiled.

Simmer the fish for 10 to 15 minutes to the pound, then put into cold water to cool quickly. Ideally, use part court-bouillon and part sea water.

It is considered by some to be more humane to put the lobster into cold water and bring it gradually to boiling point.

A lobster should be heavy in weight in proportion to its size and the smaller hen lobsters are more tender and delicate in flavour. A good 2 lb. lobster will yield about ¾ lb. meat.

Lobster Mayonnaise

2 small lobsters, cooked	salt, pepper
½ pint (1 cup) mayonnaise (see page 121)	2 tablespoons finely chopped parsley
2 to 3 tablespoons heavy cream	juice ½ lemon
	lemon wedges

Split lobsters in half. Remove meat from lobster shells, cut in large dice. Combine mayonnaise, whipped cream, salt, pepper, parsley and lemon juice; mix well. Combine most of the mayonnaise with the diced lobster. Mix thoroughly, fill into lobster shells. Spoon over remaining mayonnaise mixture. Serve with lemon wedges.
Serves 4.

Lobster Thermidor

2 1½ lb. lobsters, cooked	2 spring onions (scallions) or chives
½ pint (1 cup) milk	
1 small onion	¼ pint (½ cup) white wine
few cloves	
1 bayleaf	¼ pint (½ cup) medium cream
1 oz. (2 tablespoons) butter	salt, pepper
2 tablespoons plain flour	½ teaspoon prepared mustard
extra 1 oz. (2 tablespoons) butter	4 oz. (1 cup) gruyère cheese

Cut lobsters in half; remove meat, reserve shells, combine milk with sliced onion, cloves and bayleaf. Bring to boil; strain, reserve liquid. Melt butter in pan, stir in flour and cook a few minutes without browning. Gradually stir in hot milk. Cook, stirring, until mixture boils and thickens; set aside. Melt extra butter in pan, add spring onion, chopped, and cook a few minutes. Add wine, reduce over high heat to half quantity; add the white sauce and cream. Season to taste with salt, pepper and mustard. Cook gently, stirring, about 5 to 8 minutes.

Stir in ¾ of the grated cheese. Stir until melted, add chopped lobster meat. Fill mixture into lobster shells, sprinkle with remaining cheese, and brown under hot grill, or in hot oven, Mark 7, 425°F.

Lobster Newburg

2 1½ lb. lobsters, cooked	¼ pint (½ cup) medium cream
2 oz. (¼ cup) butter	salt, pepper
3 tablespoons brandy	2 egg-yolks
¼ pint (½ cup) madeira	

Cut lobsters in half; remove flesh, cut into pieces. Melt butter in pan, add lobster meat, and sauté a few minutes; add brandy, set alight. Allow flame to die out, add madeira. Simmer a few minutes, then add cream, reserving 2 tablespoons. Simmer until reduced slightly. Season with salt and pepper, remove from heat and add beaten egg-yolks mixed with reserved cream. Heat gently, stirring, until mixture thickens slightly (do not allow to boil). Serve with triangles of hot buttered toast.
Serves 4.

Prawn Cocktail

1 to 1½ pints prawns	lemon slices
lettuce	

Cocktail Sauce

2 tablespoons tomato sauce	few drops tabasco sauce
1 dessertspoon Worcestershire sauce	salt to taste
	½ teaspoon mustard
1 dessertspoon white vinegar	2 tablespoons lightly whipped cream

Shell prawns, reserving 6 large ones for garnishing. Shred lettuce; arrange layer of lettuce in each serving dish. Top with prawns, spoon over cocktail sauce. Garnish side of each dish with lemon slice and reserved prawns.
Cocktail Sauce Combine all ingredients except whipped cream, mix well. Fold in whipped cream.
Serves 6.

Prawn Cocktail, topped with a well-seasoned sauce, makes an excellent first course.

Curried Prawns (Shrimp)

1 pint (2 cups) chicken stock	pepper
4 oz. (¾ cup) coconut	pinch cinnamon
3 onions	½ teaspoon salt
4 sticks celery	6 peppercorns
1 apple	2 bayleaves
3 tomatoes	½ pint (1 cup) white wine
2 tablespoons oil	juice ½ lemon
1 tablespoon curry powder	1 tablespoon red currant jelly
½ teaspoon ground ginger	1 dessertspoon cornflour (cornstarch)
½ teaspoon turmeric	3 tablespoons water
¼ teaspoon cayenne	1 pint prawns (shrimp)

Bring stock to boil, pour over coconut, cover and stand for 15 minutes. Then drain, reserving liquid. Slice onions and celery, dice apple, chop tomatoes.

Heat oil, fry onions until lightly brown. Add celery, apple and tomatoes, cook further 5 minutes. Add curry powder, spices, salt, peppercorns and bayleaves. Pour on reserved coconut stock and wine. Cover, simmer 45 minutes. Sieve curry sauce, pressing as much of the vegetables through as possible. Add lemon juice and red currant jelly.

Blend cornflour with water, add to sauce. Bring to boil, stirring constantly; boil 2 minutes. Add shelled prawns, heat through. Serve with hot rice.
Serves 4.

Oysters Natural

'Nature' oysters are an expensive delicacy. Most people prefer to eat them uncooked.

'Sauce' oysters are smaller and less expensive.

Oysters should be closed when purchased; the liquid should be clear and have no unpleasant odour. They are seasonal from September to April.

In most of the recipes given below, canned or bottled oysters are used but fresh ones can of course be substituted if preferred.

A can or bottle of oysters usually contains about 12 oysters.

To serve oysters 'au naturel'—open them only just before they are required, serve in the deep half of the shell, embedded in crushed ice and accompanied by wedges of lemon, cayenne pepper and brown bread and butter.

Oyster Savoury

1 clove garlic	salt, pepper
1½ oz. (3 tablespoons) butter	1 jar or can oysters
4 tablespoons fresh breadcrumbs	4 rashers streaky bacon

Crush the garlic with a little salt and cook for 1 to 2 minutes in the butter. Add breadcrumbs, salt and pepper and brown lightly. Drain the oysters, put into a shallow fireproof dish and cover with the breadcrumbs. Arrange thin strips of bacon on top and put into a hot oven, Mark 7, 425°F. until crisp and brown.
Serves 4 as an appetizer.

Fried Oysters

1 jar or can of oysters	breadcrumbs
1 egg	seasoned flour
1 dessertspoon milk	oil

Beat egg with milk. Dip oysters in seasoned flour, egg mixture, then in breadcrumbs. Drop into hot oil and cook for few minutes until golden brown; drain well. Garnish with fried parsley and serve with tartare sauce (see page 149).

Fried Parsley

Choose good-sized sprigs of parsley. Wash and dry thoroughly. (If the parsley is at all damp, the oil will splutter.) Place sprigs in frying-basket, lower slowly into hot oil. When sizzling noise from parsley ceases, remove basket and drain parsley on absorbent paper. If parsley is fried too long it will lose its colour.

Oyster Cocktail

1 jar or can of oysters	1 dessertspoon Worcestershire sauce
4 tablespoons tomato sauce	1 teaspoon white wine vinegar
1 tablespoon lemon juice	

Arrange oysters in 4 small, stemmed glasses. Combine all remaining ingredients, spoon over oysters. Serve with lemon wedges.

Scalloped Oysters

Fine white breadcrumbs	½ pint (1 cup) white sauce (see page 146)
1 jar oysters	butter
2 sticks celery	parsley
pepper, salt, mace	brown bread and butter

Put a layer of breadcrumbs into a buttered gratin dish. Drain the oysters and arrange on top. Add the finely chopped celery and season with pepper, salt and a pinch mace. Pour over the white sauce and sprinkle with more breadcrumbs. Dot with butter. Bake in a hot oven, Mark 7, 425°F. for 15 to 20 minutes. Garnish with parsley and serve with brown bread and butter.
Serves 4.

Scallops

These are usually prepared for cooking by the fishmonger, and sold shelled and washed. They are highly perishable and should be eaten the day they are purchased. The beard and any black part should be removed and the scallops well washed until free from grit. Always ask for the deep shell as these are more convenient for most methods of serving. Generally allow 1 or 2 scallops per person.

In America the small bays or cape scallops are more tender and delicate than the larger sea scallops. One pound or 1 pint sautéed or fried serves 4 where 1 lb. of sea scallops would serve 3.

Fried Scallops

4 tablespoons lemon juice	2 eggs
1 tablespoon oil	2 oz. (½ cup) dry bread-
1 teaspoon salt	crumbs
½ teaspoon paprika	2 tablespoons grated
2 tablespoons finely	parmesan cheese
chopped parsley	oil for frying
8 scallops	lemon wedges

Combine lemon juice, oil, salt, paprika and parsley in bowl. Add scallops, let stand 1 hour; turn several times while marinating; drain. Beat eggs well. Toss breadcrumbs with grated cheese. Dip each scallop first in beaten eggs, then in crumb mixture. Deep fry in hot oil 4 minutes, or until golden brown. Drain on absorbent paper, serve immediately; garnish with lemon wedges.

Serves 4.

Scallops in Cream Sauce

4 to 6 scallops	salt, pepper
½ pint (1 cup) dry	1 teaspoon curry
white wine	powder
2 oz. (¼ cup) butter	2 tablespoons flour
3 to 4 chives	3 to 4 tablespoons
2 oz. mushrooms	medium cream
2 teaspoons chopped	fresh breadcrumbs
parsley	extra butter

Remove scallops from shells. Bring wine to boil in saucepan, drop in scallops; reduce heat, simmer 3 minutes. Set aside, reserving liquid. Melt butter in separate saucepan, add chopped chives and sliced mushrooms; sauté 5 minutes. Then add parsley, salt and pepper. Remove from heat, stir in combined curry powder and flour, cook a few minutes; off heat, gradually add ½ pint (1 cup) of the liquid in which scallops were cooked. Return to heat, stir sauce until it boils and thickens. Add scallops and cream to pan.

Spoon into greased scallop shells or small dishes. Melt a little butter in saucepan, add breadcrumbs, sauté ½ minute. Sprinkle breadcrumbs over filled dishes. Brown 5 to 8 minutes in moder-

ately hot oven, Mark 4, 350°F., or under moderate grill.

Serves 4.

To Prepare Mussels

Mussels must be absolutely fresh with the shells tightly closed and need to be thoroughly washed and scrubbed before being cooked.

Scrape the joint of the shell with a short, strong knife to remove the filament, scraping away any foreign body attached to the shell. As each is prepared, put it into a bowl of cold water and when all are prepared, wash well with the hands, changing the water several times.

Mussels Marinière

1 quart mussels	1 tablespoon chopped
2 shallots	parsley
¼ pint (½ cup) dry white	salt, pepper
wine	3 to 4 tablespoons
2 oz. (¼ cup) butter	medium cream
1½ tablespoons flour	

Prepare mussels as described above. Place in saucepan with finely chopped shallots and white wine. Cover, boil gently 5 to 6 minutes or until mussels open; drain, reserving liquid. Remove one shell from each mussel, leaving the meat attached to the other shell. Divide mussels between two deep soup plates and keep hot.

Reduce liquid in pan by half over high heat. Cream together butter and flour, add to liquid in pan. Simmer until butter has melted, stirring constantly. Add chopped parsley; season to taste with salt and pepper. Stir in cream, heat through. Spoon over mussels.

Serves 2.

Mussels with Lemon

2 quarts mussels	salt, pepper, grated
2½ oz. (5 tablespoons)	nutmeg
butter	juice of 4 lemons
2 oz. (¼ cup) carrot,	½ oz. (1 tablespoon)
finely chopped	flour
1 tablespoon chopped	
shallot	

Wash and clean mussels thoroughly. Put 1 oz. (2 tablespoons) butter into a large pan, add carrot and shallot, salt, pepper and nutmeg to taste. Cook gently until soft. Add lemon juice and mussels, cook quickly, shaking the pan until the shells open. Keep hot. In another pan, brown flour lightly in ½ oz. (1 tablespoon) butter, add strained liquor from mussels and boil for a few minutes. Add rest of butter in small pieces. Serve mussels in half shells and pour the sauce over.

Serves 4.

Meat

Beef

Varies in quality more than other meat. The lean should be bright red with a brownish tinge. A dark colour and dry appearance indicates that the meat has been cut and exposed to the air for some time or that it is from an old animal. The meat should have a marbled appearance, that is, it should contain small flecks of fat. The fat should be creamy in colour—although sometimes it is much more yellow due to certain breeding and feeding.

There are many different ways of cutting a carcass. They vary, not only between one country and another but also in different parts of one country. The cuts given below are the most commonly used. All prime cuts are usually tender and have a good flavour, medium and coarse cuts need slower cooking to produce these qualities.

The recipes which follow include many of the classic beef dishes of the world.

Cuts of Beef

Aitch-Bone   A medium cut from between the top rump and topside or sirloin usually reasonably priced as there is a large proportion of bone. It can be roasted or pot roasted or pickled and boiled.

Bladebone and Chuck   A coarse cut from the shoulder of the animal. It is fairly lean and needs long slow cooking either by stewing, braising or pot roasting.

Brisket   A coarse cut from the breast or belly with a fair amount of bone and fat. It can be roasted slowly, pot roasted, braised or boiled. It is often pickled and boiled.

Clod and Sticking   A coarse cut from the neck end of the animal. It can be used for stewing or is excellent used for gravy beef to make stock for soups, etc.

Entrecote   Prime cut from the top part of the sirloin—an expensive but very tender cut. Usually cut about $\frac{3}{4}$ in. in thickness and is grilled or fried.

Fillet   A prime cut from the undercut of sirloin. Like the entrecôte, it is expensive but generally considered the most tender cut. It can be roasted whole or cut into steaks across the grain of the meat in $\frac{1}{2}$ to 1 in. slices and grilled or fried under the following names—Fillet steak, Fillet mignon, Chateaubriand, Tournedos.

Flank or plate   A coarse cut from the belly of the animal and varies in thickness. Thick flank is suitable for slow roasting, thin flank should be braised, pot roasted or stewed. Short ribs come from the top of the short plate or thin flank and should be similarly cooked. It can be pickled and boiled and makes good stock for soup.

Leg of Mutton Cut or Chunk   A coarse cut from the shoulder of the animal and needs long slow cooking either by roasting, stewing or braising.

Leg and Shin or Shank   These are coarse cuts, the leg is the hind leg, shin or shank is the fore leg. Both contain a large proportion of gristle and connective tissue but are lean and give excellent gravy. It makes good stews and can be cooked quickly in a pressure cooker.

Ribs   These can be top rib, fore rib, or back rib. They are similar and classed as medium cuts. The difference is in the length of the rib bone, the fore rib having the longest bone. They can all be roasted on the bone as standing rib roasts or boned and rolled and can also be used for pot roasting or braising.

Round   A medium somewhat tough cut from the top part of the leg and divided into top side and silverside (top round and bottom round). Both may be slow roasted but silverside (or bottom round) is more suitable for salting or pickling and boiling.

Rump   A medium cut from the tail end of the animal. It is usually cut into steaks but may also be rolled and roasted.

Beef Bourguignonne—rich-tasting beef casserole with wine and mushrooms.

50 *Meat*

Sirloin A prime cut from the lower part of the back next to the rump. It has a short bone and in shape looks like a large mutton chop. The meat on top of the bone is the upper cut, and that under the bone, the under cut, tenderloin, or fillet. It can be roasted on the bone or boned and rolled.

Steaks cut from the upper part of the sirloin are grilled as entrecôte or Porterhouse steaks.

Silverside See Round.

Skirt A coarse cut, a thin lean steak from around the diaphragm. It gives a good rich gravy and is good for pies, puddings and stews.

Wing Rib A prime cut. This is sirloin cut but without the fillet. Suitable for roasting.

Offal or Variety Meats

Oxtail Excellent for stewing or braising or for stock.

Liver Can be fried or braised.

Kidney Used for stewing and in Steak and Kidney Pie and Steak and Kidney Pudding.

Tongue Boiled and pressed and often salted.

Suet Hard internal fat, used in puddings and for suet pastry.

Roast Beef with Red Wine

Wipe the meat and put into a baking dish. Grind some fresh pepper over the top. Dot with about 2 oz. ($\frac{1}{4}$ cup) butter, and put another 2 oz. ($\frac{1}{4}$ cup) butter into the dish with 2 tablespoons red wine or water.

Bake in moderately hot oven, Mark 6, 400°F., 15 minutes, reduce temperature to moderate, Mark 4, 350°F., for remainder of cooking time. Turn roast over once during cooking time. Allow approximately 15 to 20 minutes per lb. and 15 minutes over for cooking time, depending on thickness of roast and whether you like beef rare, medium or well done. When roast is cooked, remove to warm serving plate; let stand 10 minutes to set juices.

Season pan juices with salt and pepper. For a greater amount of gravy, add 1 or 2 tablespoons of red wine and water. Stir over low heat to incorporate all the crusty pieces from the pan. Add the juices which run off the roast while it is standing. Strain, serve over the carved beef slices.

Some cooks add $\frac{1}{2}$ lb. skirt steak, cut very finely, to the baking dish when cooking roast beef. This steak adds excellent flavour to the pan juices.

Horseradish sauce or mustard are traditional accompaniments. So, too, is a light Yorkshire Pudding.

Roast Fillet of Beef

1 whole fillet of beef (2 to 3 lb.)	freshly ground pepper salt
4 oz. ($\frac{1}{2}$ cup) melted butter	little water

Trim any excess fat from meat, sprinkle with pepper. Place in baking dish, pour over melted butter. Roast in hot oven, Mark 7, 425°F., for the first 5 minutes, then reduce heat to moderate, Mark 4, 350°F., continue cooking until done to taste. Allow 10 minutes per lb. for rare meat and 20 minutes per lb. for medium; allow a little longer for well done. Remove cooked fillet to serving dish; keep warm. Boil up pan juices, adding little water, salt and pepper. Slice meat thickly, spoon over pan juices.

Serves 4 to 6.

Beef Wellington

2$\frac{1}{2}$ lb. fillet of beef	2 oz. pâté de foie gras
4 oz. ($\frac{1}{2}$ cup or 1 stick) butter	salt, pepper
1 small onion	1 lb. puff pastry (see page 201-2)
$\frac{1}{4}$ lb. mushrooms	1 egg-yolk

Spread beef with 1 oz. (2 tablespoons) of the softened butter, bake in hot oven, Mark 7, 425°F., 10 to 15 minutes, or until the fillet is browned well all over. Remove from oven, allow to cool completely; reserve pan juices.

Chop onion finely, slice mushrooms. Sauté in 1 oz. (2 tablespoons) butter until tender.

Combine remaining softened butter with the pâté, season lightly with salt and pepper. Spread over top of the beef fillet, top with cooled onion and mushroom mixture.

Roll out puff pastry very thinly. Place beef fillet in centre and wrap pastry round it; press edges neatly and firmly together. Make sure any overlapping edges of pastry are not too thick, or pastry will not rise well and will not cook through. Place pastry-wrapped fillet in baking dish, brush with beaten egg-yolk. Bake in very hot, Mark 8, 450°F., oven 10 minutes; reduce heat to hot, Mark 7, 425°F., cook further 10 to 15 minutes, or until pastry is rich golden brown.

To the reserved pan juices add $\frac{1}{2}$ pint (1 cup) stock (or $\frac{1}{2}$ pint (1 cup) water and 1 crumbled beef-stock cube) and 1 tablespoon red wine. Cook over high heat until sauce is slightly reduced; strain. Cut fillet into thick slices, spoon sauce over.

NOTE: Pâté de foie gras can be bought in small cans, or loose in bulk from delicatessen shops or counters of most large department stores.

Steak with Red Wine

4 thick pieces fillet	salt, pepper
steak	extra 2 oz. ($\frac{1}{4}$ cup)
butter	butter
$\frac{1}{2}$ pint (1 cup) red wine	juice $\frac{1}{2}$ lemon
4 chives	parsley

Sauté steaks in hot butter until cooked according to taste. Meanwhile, combine in saucepan the wine and the finely chopped chives; cook over high heat until reduced by half, add pinch salt, some freshly ground pepper, extra butter, lemon juice, finely chopped parsley, and pan juices from the steaks. Cook over high heat, whisking all the time, until the sauce is hot and bubbling. Arrange steaks on heated serving dish, pour over the wine sauce. Serve with hot baked potato and green salad.

Serves 4.

Steak Diane

10 to 12 oz. fillet steak	little crushed garlic
freshly ground pepper	1 tablespoon
3 oz. ($\frac{3}{8}$ cup) butter	Worcestershire sauce
1 tablespoon chopped	
parsley	

Ask butcher to cut steak 1 in. thick, then pound steak until it is quite thin. Season each side lightly with freshly ground pepper. Put butter into pan; when sizzling, add steak. While cooking on one side, rub garlic into top of steak with wooden spoon; turn steak over. Add Worcestershire sauce to pan, swirl steak round in the pan juices. When cooked to desired doneness, sprinkle with chopped parsley, transfer to heated plate.

A tablespoon of cream can be stirred into the sauce to soften the characteristic 'sharpness' of the sauce.

Serves 2.

Carpetbag Steak

| 1 piece rump steak | 1 jar or can oysters |
| salt, pepper | butter |

Ask butcher to cut the steak about $2\frac{1}{2}$ in. thick, weighing about 2 lb. Make pocket in steak with sharp knife, dust pocket with salt and pepper. Stuff oysters into the pocket (a little lemon juice can be squeezed over them first, if desired); fasten pocket together with small skewers.

Grill steak to desired doneness, or pan-fry in butter. Cut into serving pieces. Transfer to hot dish, season with salt and pepper, dot with butter.

Serves 4 to 5.

Steak Kebabs

2 lb. rump steak	1 green pepper
2 medium onions	4 medium mushrooms
1 red pepper	marinade

Remove fat from meat, cut into $1\frac{1}{2}$ in. cubes. Combine ingredients for marinade, add steak, and stir until well mixed. Cover and refrigerate overnight; stir occasionally to mix thoroughly.

Peel onions, cut in halves; remove centre portion. Wash peppers, slice in half, remove seeds, and cut flesh into $1\frac{1}{2}$ in. squares. Remove stalks from mushrooms and peel if necessary or just wipe.

Thread vegetables and meat on skewers as follows: First, onion, then meat, green pepper, meat, red pepper, meat. Lastly, top with mushroom cap. Cook under heated grill, turning frequently and brushing with remaining marinade or melted butter until done to taste. Serve on hot Saffron Rice, and accompany with broccoli or other green vegetable.

Serves 4.

Soy Sauce Marinade

1 tablespoon oil	pinch mustard
3 tablespoons red wine	pinch ground thyme
1 tablespoon lemon	1 small chopped onion
juice	salt, pepper
1 tablespoon soy sauce	
1 clove crushed garlic	

Combine all ingredients, add the cubed steak, cover, and let stand overnight.

Steak au Poivre

2 tablespoons black	$1\frac{1}{2}$ gills (5 to 6 table-
peppercorns	spoons) dry white
4 pieces rump, sirloin	wine
or fillet steak	1 dessertspoon brandy
2 oz. ($\frac{1}{4}$ cup) butter	or sherry
1 dessertspoon oil	1 dessertspoon butter

Coarsely crush the peppercorns, using rolling pin or mortar and pestle. You may need more peppercorns, depending on size of steaks. Press the crushed pepper into the steak, on both sides, or pound in with flat side of cleaver. Let stand 1 hour to absorb the pepper flavour.

Heat butter and oil in pan, add steaks, cook quickly on both sides to seal in juices. Then cook to desired doneness. Remove steaks to hot serving plates. Stir into pan the wine and brandy. Bring to boil, scraping the pan. Remove from heat, stir in extra butter. Strain over steaks.

Serves 4.

Tournedos

Tournedos are small, uniform slices of fillet, about 1 to 1½ in. thick. There are nearly 500 different versions; each is named according to the individual garnishings which accompany it.

Simple rules for cooking tournedos:

If necessary, trim or shape tournedos into a round, then tie or secure with small cocktail stick.

If they are to be grilled, brush them generously with melted butter or oil.

If they are to be sautéed, add enough butter to cover the base of a heavy pan; when melted, add 1 tablespoon of oil.

Start cooking over high heat, then reduce heat to moderate and cook to desired degree of doneness.

Remove cocktail stick. Serve at once on hot plate, accompanied by the chosen garnishing.

The tournedos is often raised up on the plate by means of a toasted or fried bread round; or hot pilaf rice can be used beneath the steak. These are to absorb the rich steak juices.

Tournedos Chasseur

4 thick slices fillet steak	oil and butter for frying
4 thick slices white bread	

Sauce

¼ pint (½ cup) stock	2 spring onions (scallions) or chives
1 tablespoon tomato paste	salt, pepper
1 oz. (2 tablespoons) butter	1 dessertspoon corn-flour
1 tablespoon oil	2 tablespoons madeira
½ lb. mushrooms	1 tablespoon chopped parsley

Trim steaks, remove crusts from bread, and cut into rounds. Heat some oil and butter in pan, fry bread until crisp and lightly browned on both sides. Keep warm in oven.

Sauté steaks in oil and butter until brown on both sides, lower heat, and continue cooking until done as desired. Remove steaks from pan, season with salt and pepper. Place on top of fried bread, keep warm in oven until sauce is made.

Pour off excess fat from frying pan, pour in stock and tomato paste. Boil rapidly, stirring in all the brownings and pan juices. In another pan heat butter and oil, sauté the sliced mushrooms 5 minutes over low heat. Add finely chopped spring onions, season, and cook further 1 minute; set aside. Blend cornflour with madeira, stir into sauce, boil 1 minute. Add mushroom mixture, cook a few minutes more. Taste and adjust seasonings. Pour sauce over tournedos, sprinkle with chopped parsley.

Serves 4.

Tournedos Nicoise Prepare and cook steaks as above, top with Tomato Concassé (see page 114-15).

Chateaubriand

This is a thick slice of steak cut from choicest part of fillet of beet—the 'eye' of the fillet. It is at its best when underdone, and is cooked in one piece, then sliced for serving.

Here is a simple but delicious way to serve Chateaubriand.

Chateaubriand steak	2 oz. (¼ cup) butter
½ pint (1 cup) dry white wine	pepper
	Sauce Chateaubriand

Steak should weigh about 1½ to 2 lb. Heat butter in pan. Season meat with pepper, add to pan and brown quickly on all sides. Allow approximately 10 minutes cooking time per lb. for rare meat, slightly more for medium-rare. Cooking time, of course, depends on thickness of steak.

When done, remove from pan, keep warm. Drain butter from pan, pour in the wine. Boil rapidly until reduced by ⅔, stirring to collect any pan juices. Also add any juice which may have run from the fillet while being kept hot. This liquid forms the basis of the Sauce Chateaubriand.

To Serve Slice Chateaubriand thickly, place on hot serving dish. Spoon prepared Sauce Chateaubriand over. Serve with Pommes Parisienne.

Sauce Chateaubriand

2 shallots	1 teaspoon chopped fresh tarragon
1 oz. (2 tablespoons) butter	prepared pan juices
1 teaspoon chopped parsley	

Chop shallots finely. Melt half the butter in small saucepan, add shallots. Cook until softened, then add prepared pan juices. Cook few minutes, remove from heat, swirl in remaining butter. Stir gently; as butter melts, the sauce will thicken. Add tarragon and parsley.

Pommes Parisienne

Press potato baller into raw potato, twist, turn, scoop out potato ball. Parboil 3 minutes, drain well. Fry in hot butter, shaking pan occasionally, until golden. Alternatively, the parboiled potato balls can be deep-fried.

Tournedos are small pieces of fillet steak topped with a rich sauce; shown here are Tournedos Nicoise and, at back, Tournedos Chasseur.

Beef Stroganoff

2 lb. rump or fillet steak	1 teaspoon salt
½ lb. mushrooms	pepper
1 onion	1 oz. (2 tablespoons) butter
¼ pint (½ cup) sour cream	

Cut meat into thinnest possible strips, about ½ in. by 2 in. Melt butter in pan and fry chopped onion, add meat, and continue to cook until almost done. Add the sliced mushrooms, and fry until meat is tender. Pour in sour cream, season to taste, and heat through gently.

Serves 5 to 6.

Beef Goulash

1½ lb. topside (round steak)	3 teaspoons paprika
1 onion	2 oz. (½ cup) flour seasoned with salt and pepper
½ red pepper	¾ pint (1¼ cups) water
3 tomatoes	2 beef stock cubes
1 tablespoon oil	salt, pepper

Trim meat, cut into 1 in. cubes, chop onion, seed and slice pepper, peel and chop tomatoes.

Heat oil in large saucepan, add onion and pepper, sauté until tender, add paprika. Toss meat in seasoned flour, add gradually to pan, cook until well browned. Drain off any surplus fat. Add tomatoes and water in which stock cubes have been dissolved, season with salt and pepper, bring to boil, cover, reduce heat, simmer 1½ hours, or until meat is tender.

Serves 4.

Steak Saté

¼ pint (½ cup) oil	1 teaspoon cumin
4 tablespoons soy sauce	2 lb. rump steak
2 large onions	1 tablespoon sesame seeds or coriander
1 clove garlic	
1 dessertspoon lemon juice	

In bowl combine oil, soy sauce, grated onion, crushed garlic, lemon juice and cumin. Cut steak into 1 in. cubes and add to marinade; stir well and marinate approximately 1 hour. Using rolling pin, crush sesame or coriander seeds to a pulp; add to meat and marinade, leave to stand further 1 hour. Thread meat on skewers and grill lightly, turning occasionally and brushing with marinade.

Serves 5 to 6.

Beef Steak Tartare

4 to 6 oz. fillet steak	1 dessertspoon finely chopped or grated onion
1 egg-yolk	1 dessertspoon capers

Scrape or mince meat, removing any fat. Shape into patty shape, top with egg-yolk. Place onion and capers at side of steak (or they can be mixed into the meat). Have a pepper grinder so that fresh pepper can be ground over the meat. Serve with hot buttered toast or pumpernickel bread.

Gherkins, anchovy fillets, horseradish can be additional seasonings.

Serves 1.

NOTE: Steak Tartare also makes a good, unusual appetizer. Combine all the ingredients, spread on buttered toast, top with a little caviar.

Steak Normandy

2 lb. chuck steak	2 tablespoons tomato sauce or purée
1 dessertspoon sugar	2 tablespoons vinegar
2 tablespoons flour	¼ pint (½ cup) stock
3 onions	2 to 3 rashers bacon
1 clove garlic	salt, pepper
1 tablespoon Worcestershire sauce	bouquet garni

Cut steak into 1 in. squares, coat with mixture of combined sugar and flour. Line ovenproof dish with 2 of the peeled and sliced onions, sprinkle with finely chopped garlic. Place meat on top, pour sauces, vinegar and stock over. Let stand several hours. Top with bacon strips (with rind removed) and remaining onion cut into rings. Season with salt and pepper, add bouquet garni. Cover, bake in moderate oven, Mark 4, 350°F., 2 to 2½ hours. Remove cover for last 20 minutes of cooking time to crisp bacon and onion topping.

Serves 4 to 6.

Boeuf à la Bourguignonne

2 to 3 lb. topside (round steak)	½ pint (1 cup) dry red wine
2 oz. (¼ cup) butter	stock
12 baby onions	salt, freshly ground black pepper
2 oz. bacon	bouquet garni
¼ lb. mushrooms	chopped parsley
pinch sugar	
2 teaspoons flour	

Cut meat into large cubes, brown on all sides in heated butter. Remove meat, add onions, diced bacon and quartered mushrooms, to remaining fat together with sugar, brown slowly. Remove vegetables and bacon, sprinkle in flour, cook slowly until brown. Pour wine into flour mixture, bring to boil, stirring constantly. Put in browned meat; add sufficient stock to cover. Season to taste, add bouquet garni.

Cover tightly, cook in slow oven, Mark 2, 300°F., or on top of stove approximately 1 hour. Then add onions, mushrooms and bacon, continue cooking until meat is tender. Thicken, if necessary, with a little blended flour. Sprinkle with chopped parsley before serving.

Serves 6 to 8.

Steak and Kidney Pie

2 sheep's kidneys or piece of ox kidney	½ bayleaf
	2 small onions
1½ lb. stewing steak	½ lb. flaky or puff
1 pint (2 cups) beef stock or water	pastry (see page 201-2)
	egg-yolk for glazing

Skin, core and dice kidneys, cut steak into 1 in. cubes. Put into saucepan. Add stock, just enough to barely cover meat, bayleaf and chopped onions, and simmer, covered, 1 to 1½ hours or until meat is tender. Adjust seasoning. Thicken with a little blended flour. Pour into pie dish.

If you want a rich dark colour in the gravy, add 1 teaspoon soy sauce.

Roll out pastry to an oblong just larger than pie dish. Cut thin strips from ends and fit round moistened edge of dish. Brush pastry rim with water and place remaining pastry on top of pie. Press edges together, trim off excess pastry, using sharp knife. Make 2 slits in centre to allow steam to escape. Glaze with beaten egg-yolk. Stand dish on baking tray, bake in hot oven, Mark 7, 425°F., 10 to 15 minutes. Reduce heat to moderately hot, Mark 5, 375°F., bake further 25 to 30 minutes or until pastry is golden brown.

Serves 4 to 5.

Carbonnade of Beef

3 lb. chuck or round steak	salt, pepper
	pinch each nutmeg and sugar
2 oz. (¼ cup) butter	
2 large onions	6 to 8 pieces bread about 2 in. square (crusts removed) or use slices French bread
2 tablespoons flour	
1 clove garlic	
1 pint (2 cups) beer	
1 pint (2 cups) hot water	
	French mustard
bouquet garni	

Cut meat into large cubes, brown in butter. Set aside; brown sliced onions in pan. Add flour, cook slowly until brown; then add crushed garlic, beer and water. Bring to the boil, add seasonings and herbs. Put in meat, turn into ovenproof casserole. Cover, cook in very moderate oven, Mark 3, 325°F.,

until meat is tender, about 2 hours. Skim off surface fat. Spread bread squares lightly with French mustard and place on top of casserole, pushing bread down to ensure it is well soaked with gravy. Return to oven and cook, uncovered, further 10 to 15 minutes or until bread crisps on top.

Serves 6 to 8.

Boiled Beef with Dumplings

3 to 4 lb. salted silver-side (bottom round)	1 onion, 2 cloves
	5 to 6 small onions
bouquet garni	5 to 6 carrots
6 peppercorns	2 small turnips

Dumplings

8 oz. (2 cups) flour	⅛ teaspoon salt
1 teaspoon baking powder	4 oz. suet
	water

Put meat into a large pan and cover with cold water. Bring slowly to boil, skimming several times. Add bouquet garni, peppercorns and onion stuck with cloves. Half cover, simmer 1¼ hours. Remove bouquet garni and onion and skim again. Add whole onions, carrots cut in quarters and turnips cut in quarters. Simmer until vegetables are just tender.

Meanwhile, prepare dumplings. Sift flour, baking powder and salt. Add suet, shredded or finely chopped and enough water to make a light dough. Divide into small pieces and roll into small balls. Drop into the boiling stock and simmer a further 15 minutes. Serve the meat on a large dish surrounded with vegetables and dumplings.

Serves 6 to 8.

Tangy Sweet Curry

2 lb. chuck steak	powder
4 sticks celery	1 teaspoon salt
1 large onion	1 tablespoon golden syrup (corn syrup)
2 large carrots	
1 cooking apple	juice ½ lemon
2 tablespoons flour	10 oz. can tomato soup
1 dessertspoon curry	½ pint (1 cup) water

Trim steak and cut into 1 in. pieces, place in a large saucepan. Dice celery, peel and chop onion, carrot and apple, add to meat. Blend flour, curry powder and salt with syrup and lemon juice. Add to meat and vegetables with tomato soup and water; mix well. Cover, simmer gently 2 hours or until meat is tender. Serve with hot rice.

Serves 6.

Easy Sukiyaki

1½ lb. braising or chuck steak	2 oz. (¼ cup) sliced beans
¼ pint (½ cup) beef stock	4 oz. mushrooms
1 teaspoon sugar	3 sticks celery
1 tablespoon soy sauce	½ bunch watercress
2 tablespoons sherry	2 tablespoons oil
½ teaspoon salt	1 onion
pepper to taste	1 teaspoon arrowroot, or cornflour

Cut steak into very thin strips. In bowl, combine stock, sugar, soy sauce, sherry, salt and pepper, add meat; marinate 1 hour. Drain well, reserving marinade.

Slice beans, mushrooms, celery and watercress. Heat oil in large deep pan, sauté meat and sliced onion 10 minutes, stirring occasionally. Add prepared vegetables, cook 5 minutes. Blend arrowroot in a little water; add reserved marinade and arrowroot to meat and vegetables, stir well, bring to boil, cook further 3 minutes.

Serves 4.

Kofta Curry

Kofta Meat Balls

1 large onion	2 teaspoons curry powder
1 clove garlic	
1 green pepper	1½ lb. lean minced beef
2 tablespoons finely shredded cabbage	salt
	1 teaspoon lemon juice
pinch ground ginger	flour seasoned with salt and pepper
pinch ground cloves	
	oil for frying

Curry

2 large tomatoes	¼ teaspoon cayenne pepper
2 oz. (¼ cup) butter	
2 onions	pinch cinnamon
1 clove garlic	1 small potato
½ teaspoon ground ginger	15½ oz. can pineapple drained and chopped
½ teaspoon turmeric	½ pint (1 cup) coconut milk (see below)
1 tablespoon curry powder	salt

Meat Balls Mince or finely chop onion, garlic and green pepper. Mix together cabbage, ginger, cloves, curry powder and meat. Season with salt and lemon juice; add minced ingredients. Roll into balls, dust with seasoned flour. Brown balls in hot oil. Drain, put aside.

Curry Skin tomatoes, slice thickly. Heat butter in pan, add sliced onions and crushed garlic,

sauté until light brown in colour. Add ginger, turmeric, curry powder, cayenne and cinnamon. Stir well, cook 3 minutes. Add tomatoes, peeled potato and diced pineapple. Cook gently 5 minutes, stirring constantly. Add coconut milk and salt to taste.

Add meat balls to sauce. Cover, simmer gently 15 to 20 minutes. Do not stir but shake pan lightly from time to time. Serve with hot fluffy rice.

Coconut Milk If fresh coconut is available, grate the flesh of half a coconut, add ½ pint (1 cup) boiling water, cover and leave to stand for 10 minutes.

If desiccated coconut is used, follow the same method, using 3 tablespoons coconut to ½ pint (1 cup) boiling water.

Serves 4 to 5.

Stuffed Vine Leaves

15 oz. can vine leaves (or use fresh cabbage leaves)	2 onions
	2 teaspoons salt
	pepper
1 lb. minced steak	15½ oz. can mushroom soup
3 oz. (½ cup) rice	
2 tablespoons chopped parsley	

Rinse and drain the vine leaves (or blanch the cabbage leaves by cooking gently in boiling water 5 minutes). Combine the meat, rice, parsley, chopped onions, salt and pepper. Place a little in the centre of each leaf and fold into a neat parcel. If the leaves are small, put 2 together.

Arrange in casserole, pour over the mushroom soup. Bake, covered, in moderately slow oven, Mark 3, 325°F., 1½ to 2 hours. Add a little water or stock to casserole, if necessary, during cooking.

Serves 4.

In place of the mushroom soup, a lightly lemon-flavoured tomato sauce can be poured over the stuffed leaves before baking. Then bake, covered, as above.

Lemon-Flavoured Tomato Sauce

1 dessertspoon oil	salt, pepper
1 large onion	2 teaspoons lemon juice
1 clove garlic	½ pint (1 cup) stock
3 tomatoes	

Heat oil, sauté chopped onion and crushed garlic. Add skinned, chopped tomatoes, salt, pepper, lemon juice, and stock; simmer gently 10 minutes.

Golden-crusted Steak and Kidney Pie—an old-fashioned favourite, just as popular today.

Chilli Con Carne

2 tablespoons oil	1 pint (2 cups) water
1 large onion	1 bayleaf
1 large clove garlic	½ teaspoon chilli
1 lb. minced (ground)	powder
steak	good pinch ground basil
1 green pepper	1½ teaspoons salt
14 oz. can whole	pepper
tomatoes	10½ oz. can kidney
	beans

Heat the oil in large saucepan, add chopped onion and crushed garlic, sauté until golden brown. Add minced steak and chopped green pepper, continue cooking until meat changes colour. Add tomatoes, water, bayleaf, chilli powder, basil, salt and pepper, bring to boil; reduce heat, and simmer gently, uncovered, until sauce thickens approximately 1½ hours). Add undrained kidney beans and reheat.

Serves 4.

NOTE: The strength of chilli powders varies greatly. With some brands, ½ teaspoon will be sufficient; with others, which may be milder, slightly more chilli powder can be used. Taste after an hour's cooking; add more chilli powder then, if necessary. Of course, a lot depends on how hot you like your Chilli.

Savoury Meatloaf

2 lb. minced (ground)	1 teaspoon oregano
steak	1 tablespoon salt
2 eggs	½ teaspoon pepper
2 medium onions	
¼ pint (½ cup) tomato	
sauce	

Brown Sauce

1 oz. (2 tablespoons)	1 chicken stock cube
butter	3 to 4 tablespoons
1 oz. (2 tablespoons)	tomato sauce
plain flour	salt, pepper
½ pint (1 cup) boiling	
water	

Combine minced steak, eggs, chopped onions, tomato sauce, oregano, salt and pepper in mixing bowl. Blend well on electric mixer (this gives very fine texture to the meatloaf) or by hand. Form meat mixture into loaf shape. Add a little stock or water if too stiff. Place in greased shallow baking dish. Bake in moderately hot oven, Mark 4, 350°F., 50 minutes, brushing occasionally with pan drippings. Serve hot, sliced, with brown sauce spooned over.

Serves 6.

Brown Sauce Melt butter in pan, stir in flour; cook until brown, stirring occasionally; do not allow flour to burn. Remove from heat, add boiling water in which stock cube has been dissolved, blend well. Return to heat, bring to boil, stirring; reduce heat, cook until smooth and thickened, stirring constantly. Stir in tomato sauce; season to taste with salt and pepper.

Indonesian Meatballs

1 lb. potatoes	1½ teaspoons salt
1 oz. (2 tablespoons)	¼ teaspoon pepper
butter	¼ teaspoon nutmeg
1 small onion	4 spring onions
2 cloves garlic	(scallions) or chives
1 lb. minced (ground)	2 eggs, separated
steak	oil for deep frying

Cook, drain, and mash potatoes. Melt butter in frying pan. Add finely chopped onion and crushed garlic. Simmer 3 to 4 minutes, then add minced steak, season with salt, pepper and nutmeg. Cook, stirring constantly. When meat is half-cooked, add finely chopped spring onions, including green tops. Remove from heat when meat is cooked.

In a bowl combine mashed potatoes with meat mixture and egg-yolks. Form mixture into small balls. Refrigerate 1 hour to firm. Beat egg-whites very lightly with fork in small bowl. Dip meat balls one at a time in egg-whites. Deep-fry in hot oil until golden brown. These can be prepared in advance and reheated for 10 minutes in moderate oven.

Makes approx. 4 dozen.

Garlic Sausage

¼ lb. lean bacon pieces	2 eggs beaten
½ lb. minced (ground)	6 oz. (2 cups) soft
steak	breadcrumbs
¾ lb. sausage meat	1 teaspoon salt
2 cloves garlic crushed	¼ teaspoon pepper

Put bacon pieces through mincer, or chop finely. Combine with remaining ingredients, mix well. Form mixture into thick sausage roll, approximately 8 in. long. Tie firmly in well-floured pudding cloth. Lower carefully into saucepan of boiling water, making sure sausage is well covered. Boil steadily, covered, 2½ hours. Remove from water, drain, and leave in cloth to cool. Refrigerate several hours or overnight. Remove cloth.

Makes approx. 2 lb. sausage.

Glazed Meatloaf

Glaze

½ teaspoon dry mustard
3 to 4 tablespoons
  tomato sauce

1 tablespoon light
  brown sugar

1½ lb. minced (ground)
  steak
3 oz. (1 cup) soft
  breadcrumbs
1 teaspoon salt
pepper
1 medium onion,
  chopped
1 egg, beaten

1 tablespoon
  Worcestershire sauce
2 tablespoons tomato
  sauce
6 oz. can evaporated
  milk
1 dessertspoon dry
  mustard

Combine ingredients for glaze, set aside. Mix together all remaining ingredients (mixture will be rather moist); press into greased 8 in. × 4 in. loaf tin, then turn upside down on to aluminium foil-lined oven tray, leaving tin still over loaf. Bake in moderate oven, Mark 4, 350°F., 15 minutes. Remove from oven, remove loaf tin. Brush meatloaf well with glaze. (Do not replace loaf tin). Return to oven, cook further 50 to 60 minutes.

Equally nice served hot with vegetables or cold with salads; good for sandwiches, too.

Serves 4.

Beef Olives

2 lb. skirt steak
3 oz. (⅜ cup) butter
1 small, finely chopped
  onion
3 oz. (1 cup) fresh
  breadcrumbs
2 tablespoons chopped
  parsley
½ teaspoon dried thyme
salt, pepper
little milk

3 onions diced
3 carrots diced
1 small turnip diced
1 stick of celery diced
¾ pint (1½ cups) beef
  stock
bouquet garni
1 dessertspoon flour
1 dessertspoon butter,
  extra

Cut steak into thin slices about 2½ in. × 5 in.; mince or finely chop the trimmings. Heat 2 oz. (¼ cup) butter in saucepan, sauté chopped onions until transparent, without allowing them to brown.

Mix together the breadcrumbs, herbs, seasonings, minced or chopped meat, and sautéed onion, bind with a little milk. Spread layer of this mixture over each slice of meat. Roll up; tie with thin string. Heat rest of butter in pan, add diced vegetables, cook until golden in colour. Pour over stock; return meat to pan with bouquet garni. Bring to boil, cover. Reduce heat.

Cook gently 1½ to 2 hours or until meat is tender. (Or place in casserole and cook, covered, in moderate oven, Mark 4, 350°F.) Place meat on serving dish, remove string. Mix flour with the extra butter, pour gravy from pan over this mixture, blend together. Return to pan and bring to the boil, stirring. Adjust seasoning, remove bouquet garni. Pour gravy over meat.

Serves 4.

Lamb and Mutton

English, Scotch, Welsh and New Zealand lamb is consistently tender and of good quality. Lamb, being younger, is naturally more tender than mutton and more suitable for the quick methods of cooking, i.e. frying or grilling.

Lamb is pale pink in colour, a little more so than mutton and has less fat. The main cuts of both are given below.

Cuts of Lamb and Mutton

Breast   Usually reasonably priced and can be cooked in several ways—braised, stewed, boiled or boned, stuffed and roasted.

Chops   Cut from the loin. Chump and loin chops come from the end nearest the leg. Suitable for frying or grilling.

Cutlets or neck slices   Cut from the best end of the neck, rib or rack, and may be grilled or fried.

Leg   A prime joint—can be roasted or boiled whole or divided into the fillet end and shank. The fillet end is roasted, the shank end is generally braised, stewed or used in pies. Boneless slices or 'fillets' from the top of the leg are suitable for shashlik and kebabs.

Loin   Roasted whole, boned and rolled or cut into chops.

Neck   Best end—roasted whole or divided into cutlets
Middle   —stewed, braised or boiled
Scrag   —boiled or used for soup and stock.

Saddle   A prime joint—this consists of the double loin starting from the best end of neck to the end of the loin. A choice cut, excellent roasted for dinner parties or special occasions. Can be cut as rack of lamb or crown roast.

Shoulder   A prime joint—roasted whole but large ones are often cut into two or more pieces useful for braising and pot roasting. Small pieces of shoulder meat without bone are used for grilling and for kebabs etc.

Offal

Trotters or feet—generally used in the preparation of brawn or meat moulds because they contain a large amount of gelatine.

Brains—can be simmered in milk and water or milk and added to a white sauce.

Head—used in the preparation of brawn.

Heart—can be stuffed and roasted or braised.

Kidneys—fried or grilled or used in ragouts.

Liver—fried and used in various ways, e.g. for pâté and can be braised or stewed.

Suet—not quite so hard as beef suet but can be used in puddings.

Sweetbreads—come from the pancreas, throat and heart of the animal. They are very easily digested and generally the demand exceeds the supply. Frozen sweetbreads are available.

Tongue—braised or can be boiled and pressed.

Tripe—comes from the stomach of the animal. It needs careful preparation but is very good and nutritious cooked in milk with onions.

Mint Sauce

2 tablespoons chopped fresh mint	1 tablespoon boiling water
1 tablespoon sugar	2 tablespoons vinegar

Wash and dry mint, remove stalks, chop finely. Boil sugar and water 1 minute, add vinegar, pour over mint; stand 15 minutes. Stir well before serving.

Mint sauce is the most suitable accompaniment to most custs of lamb.

Savoury Lamb—a colourful combination of vegetable and simple but subtle seasonings makes this the perfect family or party casserole.

Roast Lamb

Leg, saddle or shoulder of lamb, when roasted, gives substantial helpings for family meals. You can add subtle flavour by scoring the skin lightly in several places and inserting small slivers of garlic, sprigs of rosemary, or pieces of bayleaf. Or rub lamb well, before cooking, with a cut clove of garlic; mix 1 teaspoon of rosemary into 3 table-spoons of softened butter and rub over joint.

To give a delightfully sweet flavour to meat, baste with orange or pineapple juice while cook-ing—you will need about ¼ pint (½ cup). The Greeks use lemon and marjoram to flavour their lamb dishes.

Moderate heat is best for lamb; it ensures thorough, gentle cooking with a minimum of shrinkage. For joints, allow approximately 20 minutes per lb., and 20 minutes over. Joints which have a stuffing will take a little longer.

Some cooks like to stand lamb on a rack in baking dish to cook; some prefer to put directly into the dish, without a rack. If cooking without the rack, make sure any surplus fat is poured off during the cooking—otherwise the meat will 'stew' in the fat instead of being beautifully crisp-skinned.

When meat is cooked, remove from baking dish; pour off fat, leaving about 2 tablespoons in dish; stir in 1½ tablespoons flour. Cook, stirring until mixture 'bubbles' and browns—do not let it burn. Gradually stir in ½ to ¾ pint (1 to 1½ cups) stock; cook, stirring, until gravy boils and thickens. Season to taste.

Savoury Lamb

2 lb. lean lamb	1 tablespoon lemon
4 small onions	juice
flour seasoned with	1 tablespoon
salt and pepper	Worcestershire sauce
3 tablespoons oil	1 dessertspoon dry
15½ oz. can tomato	mustard
soup	salt, pepper
about ¾ pint (1½ cups)	2 carrots
stock	1 swede or turnip
2 tablespoons sherry	4 sticks celery
1 tablespoon light	1 red pepper
brown sugar	1 green pepper

Trim lamb, cut into large pieces; peel and halve onions. Toss lamb in seasoned flour. Heat oil in large saucepan, gradually add lamb, brown well; add onions, sauté until transparent. Add remain-ing ingredients, except for vegetables; cover, sim-mer 1 hour.

Peel and slice carrots and swede, chop celery into large pieces, seed peppers, chop into 1 in. squares. Add prepared vegetables to lamb mixture, cover, simmer further ½ to 1 hour, or until lamb and vegetables are tender.

Serves 4 to 5.

NOTE: 4 oz. (1 cup) cooked haricot beans may be added when stew is cooked, if desired.

Lamb Italienne

2 lb. lean lamb cut	1 teaspoon sugar
from leg	½ pint (1 cup) stock
seasoned flour	2 tablespoons tomato
2 tablespoons oil	purée
1 clove garlic	¼ pint (½ cup) white
2 onions	wine
3 to 4 sticks celery	¼ teaspoon rosemary
1 teaspoon salt	¼ lb. mushrooms
	parsley

Cut the meat into pieces and coat with seasoned flour. Heat oil in saucepan, add meat, crushed garlic, sliced onions, chopped celery and salt and sauté until the meat is well browned. Add sugar, boiling stock, tomato purée, wine and rosemary. Bring to boiling point, cover and simmer slowly for about 1¼ hours. Add sliced mushrooms and cook a further 10 minutes.

Serve hot sprinkled with parsley.

Serves 5 to 6.

Delicious Lamb Stew

2 lb. best end neck	1 parsnip
lamb	1 stick celery
flour seasoned with	1 large cooking apple
salt and pepper	1 pint (2 cups) stock
2 tablespoons oil	1 tablespoon plum jam
2 onions	
2 carrots	

Trim meat and cut into chops. Dredge with seasoned flour and brown in heated oil. Chop onions, slice carrots, parsnip, celery and peeled apple. Add vegetables and apple to frying pan and sauté a few minutes. Stir in plum jam and stock, bring to boil, reduce heat; simmer for 1¼ hours or until tender.

If extra thickening is required, blend a little seasoned flour with water and add to stew, stirring.

Serves 4 to 5.

Crumbled Cutlets

Remove skin and excess fat from each cutlet. Dip in flour, which has been seasoned with salt and pepper; shake off excess flour.

Dip cutlets in egg beaten with a little oil (to help hold crumbs firmly), or brush over with a pastry brush. Then press firmly into breadcrumbs. Repeat process if you like a crisp coating. Refrigerate 1 hour to firm crumbs.

Shallow-fry in hot oil, turning occasionally, until crumbs are golden brown and cutlets cooked through. Make sure oil is hot before adding cutlets, otherwise crumbs will not hold firm but will drop off.

Devilled Chops

1½ lb. best end neck lamb	1 tablespoon lemon juice
10½ oz. can tomato soup	2 tablespoons sherry
1 dessertspoon prepared mustard	1 onion
1 tablespoon light brown sugar	2 to 3 sticks celery
1 tablespoon Worcestershire sauce	1 clove garlic

Trim the meat, divide into chops and put into a greased casserole. Cover, and cook in a moderate oven, Mark 4, 350°F. for 15 minutes.

Meanwhile, put tomato soup into a pan, add mustard, sugar, sauce, lemon juice and sherry. Mix well, add finely chopped onion and celery and crushed garlic and bring to boiling point. Pour off excess fat from the chops, pour the sauce over and cook a further 20 to 25 minutes.
Serves 4.

Sheep's Liver with Onions

1 oz. (2 tablespoons) butter or oil	¼ teaspoon pepper
2 oz. bacon	½ pint (1 cup) stock
1 lb. onions	1 lb. sheep's liver
2 tablespoons flour	parsley
1 teaspoon salt	mashed potato

Heat the butter in a stew pan. Cut the bacon into small pieces and fry till crisp in the butter. Remove to a plate. Add the chopped onions to the fat in the pan and fry, stirring frequently until just brown. Add the flour and seasoning, mix and cook for a minute then add the stock. Add the bacon and the liver—washed, dried and cut into slices. Cover, and simmer for about ½ hour. Serve in a border of mashed potatoes and sprinkle with parsley.
Serves 4 to 5.

Savoury Lamb Stew with Parsley Dumplings

1½ lb. scrag end neck of lamb	salt, pepper
	1 bayleaf
2 pints (4 cups) water	¼ pint (½ cup) tomato sauce
3 carrots	
4 potatoes	1 tablespoon finely chopped parsley
2 onions	2 tablespoons flour

Parsley Dumplings

4 oz. (1 cup) self-raising (all purpose) flour	1 tablespoon finely chopped parsley
1 teaspoon butter	milk
½ teaspoon salt	

Remove meat from bones, cut into approximately 1 in. cubes, discarding any fat. Place in saucepan with bones, cover with water, bring to boil. Reduce heat, cover and simmer 1 hour. Add peeled and diced carrots and potatoes, chopped onions, salt, pepper, bayleaf, tomato sauce and parsley. Bring to boil; reduce heat, simmer further 10 minutes. Remove bones, skim off any surplus fat.

Blend flour with little water, add to saucepan, and cook, stirring, until liquid thickens. Drop dumpling dough by heaped dessertspoonfuls on top of hot bubbling stew. Cover tightly; cook 15 to 20 minutes.
Serves 4.
Parsley Dumplings Sift together flour and salt. Rub in butter, stir in parsley. Add enough milk to make a soft, sticky dough.

Hot Curry

2 lb. boned shoulder of lamb or mutton	1 teaspoon ground black pepper
1 teaspoon ground coriander	½ teaspoon salt
	1 finely chopped onion
1 teaspoon ground cardamom	2 in. piece green ginger
1 teaspoon poppy seeds	2 to 3 cloves garlic
1 teaspoon ground cinnamon	¼ pint (½ cup) yoghurt
	2 oz. (¼ cup) butter
1 teaspoon ground cloves	1 sliced onion
	2 tablespoons slivered almonds

Cut lamb into 1 in. cubes. Combine all spices, seasonings, finely chopped onion, finely chopped ginger, crushed garlic and yoghurt. Place meat in this marinade, leave several hours.

Heat butter, fry sliced onion until golden; remove, reserve for garnish. Fry almonds, remove, reserve for garnish. Add meat and marinade to pan, stir well. Cover and simmer 45 minutes or until meat is tender. Garnish with reserved fried onion rings and almonds.
Serves 4.

Sweet Curry

2 lb. boned shoulder of lamb
¼ pint (½ cup) sour cream
2 teaspoons garam masala*
1 tablespoon curry powder
4 oz. (½ cup or 1 stick) butter

2 tablespoons slivered blanched almonds
1½ oz. (¼ cup) sultanas
2 oz. (½ cup) thinly sliced dried apricots
2 to 3 cloves garlic
2 in. piece finely chopped green ginger
2 large onions
salt, lemon juice

* If not available add ½ teaspoon ground cardamon and ½ teaspoon cumin seeds.

Cut meat into 1 in. cubes. Place in bowl with sour cream, garam masala, curry powder; stir well, leave to marinate several hours.

Heat butter in saucepan, fry almonds until golden, remove and drain. Fry sultanas and apricots until plumped, remove and drain. Fry sliced garlic, ginger and sliced onions until golden. Add meat and marinade, cook 5 minutes on medium heat. Add sultanas and apricots, cover and simmer 45 to 60 minutes, until meat is tender; add salt and lemon juice to taste. Garnish with the almonds.

Serves 4.

Shashlik

1 lb. lamb cut from the leg
2 small onions
1 green pepper

2 medium tomatoes
8 mushrooms
bayleaves
marinade

Marinade

1 clove garlic crushed
3 to 4 tablespoons oil
2 tablespoons lemon juice

salt, pepper
2 tablespoons finely chopped onion

Remove fat from meat, cut into 1½ in. cubes. Combine ingredients for marinade, add lamb, and stir until well mixed. Cover and refrigerate several hours; stir occasionally to mix.

Peel onions, cut in halves, remove centre portion. Wash pepper, slice in half, remove seeds and cut flesh in 1½ in. squares. Wash tomatoes and cut in quarters. Remove stalks from mushrooms, if desired, or leave whole.

Thread meat on to skewers, brush with marinade and, if desired, place a bayleaf at end of skewer. Thread alternate vegetables on separate skewers, brush with marinade. .Cook under heated grill, turning frequently and brushing with remaining marinade or melted butter until done to taste.

Pilaf (see page 93) is a good accompaniment for Shashlik.

Serves 2.

Moussaka

3 medium eggplants or aubergines
salt
2 lb. lean lamb cut from the leg
1 large onion
8 oz. (2 cups) grated parmesan or cheddar cheese
1½ oz. (½ cup) soft breadcrumbs

3 oz. (⅜ cup) butter
1 clove garlic, crushed
15½ oz. can tomatoes
¼ pint (½ cup) white wine
½ teaspoon nutmeg
salt, pepper
oil for frying
melted butter, extra

Sauce

2 oz. (¼ cup) butter
2 oz. (½ cup) flour
½ teaspoon nutmeg

salt, pepper
1 pint (2 cups) milk
1 egg

Cut eggplant into ½ in. slices, sprinkle lightly with salt, stand 20 minutes. Finely chop or mince meat, finely chop onion. Combine cheese with breadcrumbs.

Heat butter, add meat, onion and garlic, sauté until meat changes colour; add drained tomatoes, wine, nutmeg, salt and pepper, cover, simmer 15 minutes, or until meat is tender.

Drain eggplant, pat dry with absorbent paper, deep fry in hot oil until golden brown; drain.

Arrange fried eggplant in base of large greased casserole dish, sprinkle with ⅓ of cheese mixture, top with meat sauce, then white sauce. Sprinkle with remaining cheese mixture, drizzle over extra melted butter. Bake in hot oven, Mark 7, 425°F., 20 minutes or until golden brown.

Serves 4 to 6.

Sauce   Melt butter in saucepan, remove from heat, stir in flour, nutmeg, salt and pepper, stir until smooth, return to heat, cook 1 minute. Remove from heat, gradually add milk, return to heat, stir until sauce boils and thickens. Add beaten egg, beat until smooth.

To serve as an entrée   Cut 3 small eggplants in half lengthways, scoop out centres, leaving ½ in. shell. Sprinkle inside with salt, stand until liquid appears on surface; drain. Brush egg plants inside and out with melted butter, stand on tray in ½ in. cold water. Bake in moderate oven 8 to 10 minutes.

Layer meat sauce, cheese mixture and white sauce into egg plant shells, finish with cheese mixture, drizzle with extra melted butter. Bake in hot oven Mark 7 425°F. 20 minutes, or until golden brown.

Serves 6.

Moussaka can be cooked in a casserole or cooked in the delightfully unusual way shown above, and served as an entrée.

Veal

Veal is the flesh of young calves, specially treated when killed. It should be a faint delicate pink colour and has little fat. Being an immature meat it should be well cooked.

Cuts of Veal

Breast Can be stuffed and roasted or stewed or braised.

Chops Cut from the loin. Chump chops are cut from the bottom end and have a round bone in the centre. Allow one per portion.

Cutlets Cut from the best end of the neck at the top of the loin. Usually grilled, fried or braised. Allow two per portion.

Fillet Usually the most expensive cut. Normally cut from the top of the leg and boned. It can be stuffed and roasted or cut in thin slices to make escalopes. Continental fillet is the under part of the loin. Allow 4 to 6 oz. per portion.

Neck This is a cheaper cut and very good value. It can be stuffed and roasted and is also suitable for stewing, braising or pot roasting. It is often used to make jellied veal and veal moulds. Allow about 1 lb. per portion.

Knuckle or Shank This is the lower part of the leg, often sold separately and is excellent for boiling, stewing and pies.

Leg Usually roasted, frequently boned and stuffed or cut into chops for grilling or frying.

Shoulder Can be roasted on the bone but easier to handle if boned and rolled and is then sometimes referred to as oyster. Portions of shoulder are suitable for pot roasting or braising and small pieces of boneless meat are used for pies, stews and fricassees. Allow 1 lb. per portion with bone.

Offal

Feet—used for calves foot jelly or for stock and soup.

Head—including tongue and brains—may be braised or boiled or used for brawn.

Sweetbreads—see under Lamb—page 62.

Escalopes

Allow 4 to 6 oz. per person.
To prepare Trim escalopes carefully, then place between several thicknesses of greaseproof paper and pound with a mallet or flat blade of heavy knife. Continue pounding until escalopes are about $\frac{1}{8}$ in. thick. This breaks down the fibres of the meat, making it deliciously tender. Place escalopes on flat dish and squeeze over a little lemon juice; let stand about 1 hour, turning frequently, before cooking.

Escalopes Naturel

4 escalopes	2 oz. ($\frac{1}{4}$ cup) butter
salt, pepper	juice $\frac{1}{2}$ lemon
flour	

Sprinkle each escalope with a little salt and pepper; dip in flour, shake off excess. Sauté in heated butter, allowing 4 to 5 minutes for each side, or longer depending on thickness. Arrange drained escalopes on hot serving dish. Add lemon juice to remaining butter, pour over escalopes.
    Serves 4.

Wiener Schnitzel

4 escalopes	2 oz. ($\frac{1}{4}$ cup) melted
flour seasoned with	butter
salt and pepper	1 tablespoon oil
beaten egg	slices of hard boiled egg
fine dry breadcrumbs	rolled anchovy fillets
	lemon wedges

Toss escalopes in seasoned flour, shake off excess, and dip in beaten egg. Then roll in crumbs, pressing these on firmly; refrigerate 30 minutes to set crumbs.
    Heat oil and butter in heavy frying pan, put in escalopes and cook until golden brown on both sides. Allow 4 to 5 minutes cooking time for each side. Drain meat well, arrange on serving dish. Top each with slice of hard boiled egg and rolled anchovy fillet. Serve with lemon wedges.
    Serves 4.

Escalopes with Cream

4 escalopes	salt, pepper
flour seasoned with	chopped parsley
salt and pepper	2 oz. ($\frac{1}{4}$ cup) butter
3 to 4 tablespoons	a little oil
cream	

Dip escalopes in seasoned flour; sauté in heated butter and oil, allowing 4 to 5 minutes cooking time for each side. Transfer to serving dish; keep warm.
    Add cream to pan juices; simmer until mixture is slightly reduced and well blended. Season with

salt and pepper. Spoon over escalopes; sprinkle with chopped parsley.

Serves 4.

Veal Parmesan

3 oz. (1 cup) fresh breadcrumbs
1 teaspoon grated lemon rind
3 oz. (¾ cup) grated Parmesan cheese

4 veal escalopes
flour seasoned with salt and pepper
1 egg
2 oz. (¼ cup) butter
2 tablespoons oil

Mushroom Sauce

1 large onion
¼ lb. mushrooms
1 tablespoon oil

2 × 5 oz. cans (1½ cups) tomato purée
4 tablespoons dry sherry
salt, pepper

Combine breadcrumbs, lemon rind and Parmesan cheese. Pound escalopes, if necessary, until thin. Dip in seasoned flour, then beaten egg; press on crumb mixture. Refrigerate 1 hour.

Heat butter and oil in large frying pan, cook escalopes until golden on each side and cooked through. Remove to hot serving plates. Serve Mushroom Sauce separately.

Serves 4.

Mushroom Sauce Chop onion and mushrooms, sauté in hot oil until tender; add tomato purée, sherry, season with salt and pepper. Simmer, uncovered 5 minutes.

Veal Marengo

2 lb. veal
2 oz. (½ cup) flour seasoned with salt and pepper
1 oz. (2 tablespoons) butter
1 tablespoon oil
1 clove garlic
¼ pint (½ cup) white wine

1 pint (2 cups) boiling water
2 chicken stock cubes
1 tablespoon tomato paste
12 small white onions
2 tomatoes
½ lb. button mushrooms
chopped parsley

Trim and cut meat into serving-size pieces, toss in seasoned flour. Heat butter and oil in large frying pan, fry meat until golden; remove, place in casserole. Fry crushed garlic a few minutes, add remaining flour; cook, stirring occasionally, until lightly browned. Gradually add wine and boiling water, in which chicken stock cubes have been dissolved, bring to boil, stirring; add tomato paste. Reduce heat, simmer gently until reduced by half. Pour over meat, cover, bake in moderate oven, Mark 4, 375°F., 1 hour.

Meanwhile, parboil onions 5 minutes; remove skin from tomatoes and chop coarsely. When meat is tender, add onions, sliced mushrooms and tomatoes; cook further 15 to 20 minutes. Sprinkle with chopped parsley.

Serves 6.

Veal with Blue Cheese

1½ lb. fillet of veal
4 oz. (½ cup or 1 stick) butter
2 oz. blue cheese
flour seasoned with salt and pepper

1 egg
soft breadcrumbs
4 tablespoons oil
lemon wedges

Cut veal into 5 to 6 pieces and pound until very thin. Cream together butter and blue cheese in warmed basin. Spread some of this mixture on one side of each steak; dip steaks in seasoned flour, then beaten egg; press on breadcrumbs. Refrigerate 1 hour.

Heat oil in large frying pan, cook steaks until well browned and cooked through. Dust with chopped parsley, garnish with lemon wedges.

Serves 5 to 6.

Osso Buco

4 tablespoons oil
3 onions
2 carrots
3 sticks celery
3 or 4 veal shanks sawn into 3 in. pieces
seasoning
flour
1 bayleaf
2 cloves garlic

pinch each basil and thyme
piece lemon rind
2 tablespoons tomato paste
¼ pint (½ cup) white wine
¼ pint (½ cup) stock
2 tablespoons finely chopped celery, extra
1 tablespoon grated lemon rind

Heat oil in pan, fry sliced onions gently until soft and turning golden, place in large saucepan. Gently sauté sliced carrots and chopped celery, add to onions. Roll veal shanks in seasoned flour and brown in oil.

Arrange pieces on top of vegetables, standing upright so that marrow won't fall out during cooking. Add bayleaf, crushed garlic, thyme, basil and lemon rind. Mix tomato paste into combined white wine and stock, add seasonings and pour over. Add more stock, if necessary. Bring to boil, cover and simmer gently for approximately 4 hours or until meat is almost falling off bones. Ten minutes before serving, sprinkle with finely chopped celery and lemon rind. Serve with risotto (see page 94).

Serves 4 to 6.

Veal and Mushroom Ragout

1½ lb. veal
2 oz. (¼ cup) butter
2 onions
1 tablespoon paprika
15½ oz. can cream of
   mushroom or cream
   of tomato soup

1 pint (2 cups) boiling
   water
2 chicken stock cubes
salt, pepper
2 green peppers
4 oz. small mushrooms

Cut veal into 1 in. cubes. Melt butter in frying pan, sauté sliced onions and veal until onions are transparent; stir in paprika.

Combine soup and boiling water, in which chicken stock cubes have been dissolved; stir into veal, season to taste; cover, simmer gently approximately 1 hour or until veal is tender.

Add sliced peppers and whole mushrooms, cook gently until mushrooms are tender, about 7 minutes.

Serves 4.

Veal Cordon Bleu

6 veal escalopes
6 thin slices ham
6 thin slices gruyère
   cheese
flour seasoned with
   salt and pepper

1 egg
fine dry breadcrumbs
2 oz. (¼ cup) butter
2 tablespoons oil

Pound escalopes, if necessary, until very thin. Top each with slice of ham and slice of gruyère cheese. Fold in half, secure with small wooden stick. Dip in seasoned flour and beaten egg, then press on fine dry breadcrumbs. Refrigerate 1 hour.

Heat butter and oil in large frying pan. Cook escalopes turning occasionally, until cooked through. Drain well, remove small wooden sticks.

Serves 6.

Gourmet Veal

6 veal escalopes
½ lb. mushrooms
6 to 8 spring onions
   (scallions)
2 oz. (¼ cup) butter

2 tablespoons oil
¼ pint (½ cup) medium
   cream
salt, pepper
parsley

Pound escalopes until very thin, if necessary. Slice mushrooms, chop spring onions (scallions). Heat butter and oil in large frying pan, fry meat quickly. Remove from pan and keep warm.

Add mushrooms to pan and sauté until tender, add the chopped spring onions, cook a few minutes. Add cream and allow to heat through (do not boil). Season to taste. Pour over the cooked veal. Sprinkle with chopped parsley.

Serves 6.

Veal Chops à la Crème

12 shallots
4 oz. (½ cup or 1 stick)
   butter
6 veal cutlets
6 oz. small mushrooms

salt, pepper
¼ pint (½ cup) dry white
   wine
3 to 4 tablespoons
   medium cream
chopped parsley

Peel the shallots keeping them whole; cook in boiling salted water 10 minutes.

Heat butter in pan, add cutlets, and cook until golden brown on one side. Turn and cook on other side. When done, remove and keep warm on serving dish. Add the small whole mushrooms and parboiled onions to pan, season, cook until tender, and golden brown in colour. Stir in white wine, then add cream. Cook a few minutes, stirring frequently (do not allow to boil). Taste, and correct seasonings. Pour sauce over cutlets, sprinkle with parsley.

Serves 3.

Herbed Shoulder of Veal

1 boned shoulder of
   veal
½ pint (1 cup) chicken
   stock

salt, pepper
1 oz. (2 tablespoons)
   butter

Stuffing

1 small onion
1 oz. (2 tablespoons)
   butter
4 oz. (1¼ cups) fresh
   breadcrumbs
2 tablespoons finely
   chopped parsley

finely grated rind 1
   lemon
1 teaspoon mixed herbs
pinch salt
pepper

Fill shoulder with herbed breadcrumb stuffing; tie firmly into shape. Place in baking dish with stock, salt, pepper and butter. Bake in moderate oven, Mark 4, 350°F., basting frequently, allowing 30 minutes per lb.

Serves 6 to 8.

Stuffing Sauté chopped onion in melted butter; mix with breadcrumbs, parsley, grated lemon rind, herbs, salt and pepper. Beat egg, add to the mixture, and stir until it binds together.

Wiener Schnitzel—golden-crumbed veal slices, seasoned lightly with lemon, are served with traditional topping of egg and anchovy.

Pork, Ham and Bacon

For some families, there's nothing nicer than a roasted leg of pork—the crackling crisp and golden; or slices from a pink, juicy, succulent ham. In this section are the cooking methods and recipes which present pork, in its various forms, at its most appetizing best.

Cuts of Pork, Ham and Bacon

Belly   This corresponds to the breast of lamb or veal. It is usually salted and then boiled (salt pork). It can also be cut into thin slices and fried or grilled like streaky bacon. Allow 4 to 6 oz. per portion.

Blade or Shoulder Butt   Cut from the top part of the foreleg, suitable for roasting. Allow ½ to ¾ lb. per portion.

Hand and Spring or Hock and Forefoot   This is the foreleg, suitable for roasting, boiling or stewing. Allow ¾ lb. per portion.

Leg   This is the hind leg. Can be roasted whole or boned and stuffed. Slices from the top end without bone—fillets—are used for frying and grilling.

Loin   This is the best and most expensive cut. Can be roasted in the piece or cut into chops for frying or grilling. These are the chump chops and usually one is quite sufficient per portion.

   Cutlets are cut from the spare rib and two per portion would be needed.

Spare Rib   This is the top piece just behind the head. It is fairly lean and can be roasted, braised or stewed.

Offal

Head—used for brawn.

Liver—has a fairly strong flavour but excellent for making pâté.

Pig's Fry—is the term given to a selection of offal including kidneys and liver. It is generally fried or baked.

Trotters—can be boiled or stewed.

Apple Sauce

Peel, core and slice 3 tart apples. Cook until soft with 1 tablespoon sugar, 2 tablespoons water, pinch salt, squeeze lemon juice and 1 teaspoon of butter. Beat until smooth, serve hot.

Roast Pork

1 small leg of pork or fillet cut from leg (4 to 5 lb.)	salt ground ginger oil

Ask your butcher to score the pork rind well. Place roast in well-oiled baking dish. Rub skin with generous amount of salt and a little ground ginger. (The salt will ensure crisp crackling). Roast in hot oven, Mark 7, 425°F., 20 minutes, then reduce heat to moderate, Mark 4, 350°F.; continue cooking until meat is well browned and tender, allowing 25 to 30 minutes per lb. cooking time. Make a thin gravy from the pan drippings; serve with gravy and baked apples or apple sauce.

Sweet and Sour Pork

3 dessertspoons sugar	3 to 4 spring onions
1 tablespoon soy sauce	(scallions) or chives
½ teaspoon salt	1 red pepper
1 tablespoon dry sherry	4 oz. mushrooms
1 egg-yolk	½ cucumber
2 to 2½ lb. lean pork	cornflour (cornstarch)
15½ oz. can pineapple pieces	3 to 4 tablespoons vinegar
2 onions	1 dessertspoon tomato sauce
	salt, pepper

Mix together sugar, soy sauce, salt, sherry and egg-yolk; stir well. Cut meat into 1 in. cubes, place in soy sauce mixture. Stir until well coated with marinade. Cover, leave 1 hour; stir occasionally.

   Drain pineapple, reserve the liquid. Slice onions, cut spring onions diagonally. Remove seeds from pepper; cut into thin strips. Slice mushrooms and cucumber into chunky strips. Fry onion in a little hot oil until transparent. Add pepper and spring onions, cook further 3 to 4 minutes. Add mushrooms, cook until softened. Stir in pineapple pieces and cucumber. Remove from heat, keep hot.

   Drain meat from marinade, reserve liquid. Toss meat lightly in cornflour (cornstarch). Heat oil, cook meat until golden brown and cooked through; drain well. Add meat to vegetables, keep hot.

   Blend 1 dessertspoon cornflour (cornstarch) with reserved pineapple liquid. Add vinegar and tomato sauce, stir into remaining marinade. Bring to boil, stirring continually; season to taste. Pour sauce over meat and vegetables, stir to coat evenly. Serve with hot boiled rice.

Serves 6.

Ginger Pork Spareribs

4 lb. pork spareribs	juice ½ lemon
4 tablespoons soy sauce	pepper
1½ gills (¾ cup) water	½ teaspoon ground
4 tablespoons orange	ginger
marmalade	1 dessertspoon grated
1 clove garlic	green ginger

Place spareribs, meaty side down, in well-greased, shallow baking dish. Roast in hot oven, Mark 7, 425°F., 30 minutes. Turn spareribs over, lower temperature to moderate, Mark 4, 350°F., continue cooking further 30 minutes. Pour off excess fat from pan.

Combine soy sauce, water, marmalade, crushed garlic, lemon juice, pepper and gingers; blend thoroughly. Pour this sauce over spareribs, cook further ¾ hour, basting frequently with sauce.

Serves 6.

Chinese Barbecued Pork Fillets

4 slices pork fillet	2 tablespoons dry
about 6 oz. each	sherry
1 dessertspoon sugar	1 clove garlic, crushed
1 tablespoon honey	½ teaspoon mixed spice
3 tablespoons soy sauce	1 tablespoon Hoy Sin
1 teaspoon oil	sauce*—optional
	1 teaspoon salt

* Hoy Sin sauce is available at food halls of large department stores, or at Chinese food stores.

Trim pork, removing surplus fat. Combine remaining ingredients in large mixing bowl, mix well. Add pork, allow to marinate a few hours or overnight, turning occasionally. Drain pork, place on wire rack. Stand rack in shallow baking tray. Bake in hot oven, Mark 7, 425°F., approximately 30 minutes, or until meat is tender, basting frequently with remaining marinade. Turn pork once during cooking. (Place a small amount of water in baking tray to prevent juices from burning).

Alternatively, meat can be grilled under hot grill until tender, turning and basting often.

Brawn

½ pig's head	5 peppercorns
1 lb. lean pork	2 cloves
1 lb. veal shoulder	1 small onion, sliced
salt	1 bayleaf
5 whole allspice	1 small carrot

Clean pig's head, soak in cold water 6 to 12 hours; change water once. Place with other meat in large saucepan, cover with boiling water. Bring to boil again, skim well; add remaining ingredients. Reduce heat; simmer covered, 1½ to 2 hours or until meat is very tender. Remove meat from bones, cut into small pieces. Measure liquid, return liquid to saucepan, continue boiling until liquid is reduced to half quantity; strain. Replace strained liquid and meat in saucepan, bring to boil, season to taste.

Pour into lightly oiled 9 × 5 in. loaf tin; cool, then refrigerate until set.

Serves 4 to 6.

Pork and Cider Casserole

2 lb. boned blade of	2 sticks celery
pork	2 cloves garlic
2 oz. (½ cup) flour	1 pint (2 cups) cider
salt, pepper	¼ pint (½ cup) yoghurt
1 oz. (2 tablespoons)	
fat	
2 onions	

Cut the meat into 1½ in. cubes and coat with seasoned flour. Heat the fat in a pan, add the meat, finely chopped onions, finely chopped celery and crushed garlic and fry altogether until lightly browned. Remove from the heat, gradually stir in cider, return to the heat and bring to the boil, stirring all the time. Add seasoning, cover and simmer slowly for 1½ hours or until meat is tender.

Blend the yoghurt with a little of the hot liquid then stir it into the stew. Correct the seasoning and serve with boiled noodles or spaghetti.

Serves 5 to 6.

Hawaiian Ham

4 gammon rashers cut	2 tablespoons light
¼ to ½ in. thick or	brown sugar
lean thickly sliced	¼ pint (½ cup) pine-
bacon	apple juice
4 oz. (½ cup or 1 stick)	
butter	

Marinate rashers in combined pineapple juice and brown sugar for 3 hours. Drain well.

Heat butter, fry gammon until golden brown on both sides; turn constantly during cooking. Canned pineapple rings, sautéed in hot butter, can be served as an accompaniment.

Serves 4.

Ham-Asparagus Rolls

canned asparagus spears	½ pint (1 cup) mornay sauce
6 slices cooked ham	(see page 105)

Drain asparagus spears well. Take 4 or 5 spears and roll these inside a slice of ham. Arrange neatly in a fireproof dish. Pour sauce over ham-asparagus rolls. Heat through in a moderate oven, Mark 4, 350°F., or under the grill.

Serves 4 to 6.

Boiled Ham

Soak ham for several hours in cold water, then drain and dry. Place in large vessel with enough tepid water to cover. Add a little parsley and thyme and 4 peppercorns. Bring slowly to boil, taking at least 1½ hours. Simmer gently (never boil) for time required, according to size.

To test whether ham is cooked, pull the small bone at the shank end that lies alongside the large one; when it is loose and slips out easily, then ham is done.

Allow to cool in liquid, then peel off skin, and glaze as desired. If boiled ham is to be eaten cold, remove skin, then return to water in which it was cooked and leave until quite cold. This helps to keep it juicy.

Cooking Time per Pound
Up to 12 lb.—20 minutes
12 lb. and over—15 minutes

To Glaze the Ham

If baking a ham that has been already cooked (by boiling), simply peel off skin; score fat into squares or diamonds with sharp knife. Place ham in large baking dish, glaze with any of the following suggested glazes; bake in moderate oven, Mark 4, 350°F., 45 minutes.

Spread orange marmalade over scored ham. Bake, baste with pan drippings.

Arrange pineapple rings and glacé cherries on ham, secure with whole cloves or cocktail sticks. Sprinkle with brown sugar; bake.

Blend together 6 oz. (1 cup) brown sugar, 1 tablespoon dry mustard; mix to a thick paste with dry sherry. Spread over scored ham; bake.

Pork Loins with Prunes

4 lb. loin pork, boned	1 large cooking apple
salt, pepper	lemon juice
4 oz. (⅔ cup) prunes	2 oz. (¼ cup) butter

Make a pocket in the loin by cutting, with a sharp knife, to within ½ in. of both ends; sprinkle with salt and pepper. Pit prunes; peel and dice apple, sprinkle with lemon juice. Stuff pocket with prunes and apple. Roll meat firmly around filling, secure with string. Rub scored crackling around loin lightly with salt.

Melt butter in baking dish; add pork. Cook in moderate oven, Mark 4, 350°F., approximately 1½ to 2 hours. Make thin gravy from pan juices. Red cabbage makes a good accompaniment.

Serves 6.

Boiled Bacon

Whilst in America it is not customary for the housewife to boil bacon, in England this is a popular dish.

The most usual cut for boiling is the gammon which comes from the hind leg of a bacon pig. It can be corner, middle, hock or slipper. The collar is also suitable and generally less expensive. The approximate weights of the joints naturally varies with the size of the pig but a corner of gammon is generally about 4 lb., middle gammon about 5 lb., hock about 4½ lb., and the slipper is a smaller joint about 1½ to 2 lb.

Perhaps 'simmering' would be a better word than boiling for this cooking process, because rapid boiling, over a period, will cause shrinkage and will affect the meat texture and the fat structure. Slow, careful cooking is necessary for best results.

Put bacon into saucepan, cover with cold water and let stand 24 hours; drain. Cover with fresh cold water, bring slowly to boil, then reduce heat until water is just simmering. Cover, cook until bacon is tender. Allow 20 to 25 minutes per lb.

When the bacon has been cooked it can be glazed and baked as a ham. Remove rind while hot, spread with some melted red currant jelly or honey, or spread with a paste of brown sugar, mustard and sherry. The fat can be cut in criss-cross squares and each square studded with a clove. Bake in moderate oven, 350°F., 20 minutes to melt glaze. Apple sauce (see page 72), spiced lightly with cinnamon, is a nice accompaniment.

Chinese Sweet and Sour Pork combines—deliciously!—tender pieces of pork with pineapple and a rich sauce.

The Variety Meats

Simple recipes suit the variety meats best, so that their full, delicate flavour is retained. They are easily prepared and some can be cooked in minutes. Serve them often; in addition to their good taste, they are a rich source of nourishment at a low price.

Pig's Trotters (feet)

4 trotters (feet)	1 chicken stock cube
2 onions	salt, pepper
pinch ground mace	$\frac{1}{2}$ oz. (1 tablespoon)
strip lemon peel	flour
	parsley

Ask the butcher to split the trotters in half lengthwise. Wash them and put into a pan with the sliced onions, mace, lemon peel, stock cube, 1 pint (2 cups) water, and a little salt and pepper. Bring to boiling point, stirring occasionally, cover and simmer for about 2 hours. Remove the trotters and thicken the liquid with the flour blended smoothly with a little cold water. Boil 2 to 3 minutes. Pour over the trotters and serve hot sprinkled with chopped parsley.

Serves 2 to 4 according to the size of the trotters.

Brains

To prepare   Soak brains in cold water several hours. Then place in saucepan with 1 dessertspoon vinegar, a little salt, 1 small sliced onion, 1 small bayleaf and water to cover. Bring slowly just to boiling point. Poach gently for 10 minutes, without allowing water to boil. Drain, cover with cold water to firm; remove membranes.

Brains in Cream Sauce

4 sets brains	1 chicken stock cube
2 oz. ($\frac{1}{4}$ cup) butter	2 egg-yolks
1 small onion	$\frac{1}{2}$ green pepper
1 tablespoon flour	1 teaspoon lemon juice
$\frac{3}{4}$ pint ($1\frac{1}{2}$ cups) boiling water	1 medium tomato
	salt, pepper

Cut prepared brains into slices or cubes. Melt butter in saucepan, add finely chopped onion, cook 1 minute. Stir in flour, cook further 1 minute. Remove from heat, gradually stir in boiling water, in which chicken stock cube has been dissolved. Return to heat, bring to boil, stirring; reduce heat, simmer until thickened, stirring constantly.

Stir 2 tablespoons of this mixture into beaten egg-yolks, gradually add to remaining sauce, stirring constantly. Simmer 5 minutes without boiling. Add brains, chopped pepper, lemon juice, peeled and chopped tomato, salt and pepper. Place in top of double saucepan over hot water, simmer 15 minutes.

Serves 4.

Brains in Black Butter

4 sets brains	juice 1 lemon
seasoned flour	1 teaspoon capers
butter for frying	chopped parsley
4 oz. ($\frac{1}{2}$ cup or 1 stick) butter, extra	

Toss prepared brains in seasoned flour. Sauté in heated butter until golden brown, remove to hot serving dish. Add extra butter to pan, cook until it turns brown. Remove from heat, add lemon juice and capers. Pour the sizzling butter over brains, sprinkle with chopped parsley.

Serves 3 to 4.

Sweetbreads

To prepare   Wash sweetbreads well, soak in cold water 3 to 4 hours, changing water several times. Drain, place in saucepan with sufficient cold water to cover. Bring water slowly to boil, simmer 3 to 5 minutes, according to size. Drain, plunge at once into cold water. Remove as much skin and membrane as possible; dry well.

If desired, they can be spread out on a plate and weighed down by pressing another plate on top of them. In this way, they flatten as they cool. The sweetbreads are now ready to cook in a variety of ways. They can be crumbed and fried, or served in a cream sauce.

Sweetbreads à la King

1 lb. sweetbreads	$\frac{1}{4}$ pint ($\frac{1}{2}$ cup) thin cream
3 oz. ($\frac{3}{8}$ cup) butter	
4 oz. mushrooms	1 tablespoon flour
1 green pepper	$\frac{1}{2}$ pint (1 cup) milk
1 red pepper	salt, pepper
3 to 4 tablespoons dry sherry	4 slices of toast or pastry-cases

Cut prepared sweetbreads into cubes. Melt half the butter in saucepan, add sliced mushrooms and diced peppers; cook gently 2 minutes, then add half the sherry and cream. Simmer sauce until reduced by half, then add sweetbreads.

Melt remaining butter in separate saucepan, stir in flour, cook 1 minute. Remove from heat, gradually add milk. Return to heat, bring to boil, stirring; reduce heat, simmer until thick and smooth, stirring constantly. Add sweetbread mixture, season to taste with salt and pepper. Stir in remaining sherry and cream, reheat without boiling. Spoon mixture into heated pastry cases or serve on slices of hot toast.

Serves 4.

Tripe

To prepare Tripe should be absolutely fresh; if possible, cook and serve it on the day it is bought. Although tripe, when bought, has already been parboiled in processing, a preliminary blanching before cooking is necessary.

Place tripe in large saucepan with sufficient cold water to cover; add squeeze of lemon juice. Bring slowly to the boil, simmer 5 minutes. Drain well, then prepare as desired.

Tripe in Parsley Sauce

1½ lb tripe	1 oz. (2 tablespoons)
water	flour
2 oz. (¼ cup) butter	½ pint (1 cup) milk
2 onions	2 tablespoons chopped
	parsley
	salt, pepper

Cut blanched tripe into strips. Place in saucepan with sufficient cold water to cover. Bring to boil, cover, simmer approximately 2 hours or until tender; drain, reserving ½ pint (1 cup) stock.

Melt butter in saucepan, add chopped onions, cook until transparent. Stir in flour, cook 1 minute. Remove from heat, gradually add reserved stock and milk. Return to heat, bring to boil stirring; reduce heat, simmer until thickened, stirring constantly. Add tripe and chopped parsley; heat through. Season to taste with salt and pepper.

Serves 4.

Tripe Bordelaise

1½ lb. tripe	¾ pint (1½ cups) boiling
2 onions	water
1 oz. (2 tablespoons)	1 chicken stock cube
butter	salt, pepper
1 clove garlic	bouquet garni
3 medium tomatoes	chopped parsley
1 tablespoon tomato	
paste	

Cut blanched tripe into strips. Sauté chopped onions in butter until golden. Add crushed garlic, peeled and chopped tomatoes, tomato paste, boiling water (in which chicken stock cube has been dissolved), seasoning and bouquet garni. Bring to boil, add tripe, reduce heat; cover and simmer slowly until tripe is tender, approximately 2 to 2½ hours. Remove bouquet garni. Correct seasonings. Transfer to serving dish, sprinkle with chopped parsley.

Serves 4.

Ox Tongue

To prepare Wash the tongue. If it is highly salted, it should be soaked in water for approximately 24 hours. (If fresh, unsalted tongue is used, add some salt to water when cooking.) Place tongue in large saucepan with sufficient cold water to cover. Add a few peppercorns, 1 bayleaf, 1 sliced onion and 1 small carrot. Bring to boil, cover, reduce heat and simmer approximately 3 hours depending on size of tongue, allowing 45 to 60 minutes cooking time per lb. Remove skin from tongue while still hot.

Allow pickled tongue, which is served cold, to cool in the cooking liquid.

Glazed Ox Tongue

1 cooked ox tongue	3 cloves
½ oz. (2 tablespoons or	3 thin strips lemon rind
2 envelopes) gelatine	1 dessertspoon lemon
¾ pint (1½ cups) cold	juice
water	2 thin slices onion
¼ pint (½ cup) hot water	2 sprigs parsley
1 tablespoon white	1 teaspoon salt
vinegar	

Pack cooked tongue into tongue presser or basin. Pour in just enough aspic to cover tongue. Place saucer or plate and a weight on top. Leave to cool, then refrigerate overnight.

Aspic Jelly Soak gelatine in hot water. Place all other ingredients into saucepan, stir lightly with fork until boiling, add soaked gelatine. Cool and strain through fine strainer lined with clean cloth. Pour over tongue (you may not need all the aspic).

Kidneys

To prepare Wash kidneys, remove skin. Cut lamb's kidneys in half. Remove hard core and any fat or gristle. When frying halved kidneys, place them cut side down in pan and press lightly. This will seal the cut edge, thus retaining all juices.

Ox kidney should not be fried: it needs long, gentle simmering to soften it, as in the filling for Steak and Kidney Pie.

Kidneys Chasseur

8 lamb's kidneys
salt, pepper
4 oz. (½ cup or 1 stick) butter
1 tablespoon finely chopped shallots
1 dessertspoon plain flour
¼ pint (½ cup) madeira or port wine
¼ pint (½ cup) dry white wine
4 oz. mushrooms
triangles of fried bread
parsley

Soak kidneys in salted water for 15 minutes. Remove outer skin and fat from kidneys, cut into slices. Sprinkle with salt and pepper. Melt half the butter in frying pan, add kidneys, cook quickly until just beginning to brown; remove from pan.

Add shallots and flour to pan drippings, cook 2 minutes. Add madeira and white wine; return kidneys. Bring just to boil, simmer 5 minutes. In separate pan, sauté sliced mushrooms a few minutes in remaining butter. Spoon kidney mixture on serving dish, top with mushrooms. Serve with triangles of fried bread. Garnish with parsley.

Serves 4.

Devilled Kidneys

8 lamb's kidneys
3 oz. (⅜ cup) butter
1 clove garlic
1 small onion
salt, pepper
1 tablespoon Worcestershire sauce
1 tablespoon dry sherry
2 to 3 tablespoons finely chopped parsley

Wash kidneys, remove skin, fat and hard core; slice kidneys. Melt butter in pan, add crushed garlic, finely chopped onion, salt and pepper, cook a few minutes. Add kidneys, cook quickly on both sides. Add Worcestershire sauce, sherry and parsley to pan, blend well. Spoon on to slices of hot buttered toast—delicious as a supper dish; or serve with hot rice, into which some finely chopped parsley has been tossed.

Serves 4.

Oxtail Casserole

2 large onions
2 large carrots
4 oxtails
1 oz. (2 tablespoons) butter
1 dessertspoon dark brown sugar
4 tablespoons flour
6 tomatoes
3 cloves garlic, crushed
few sprigs parsley
1 bayleaf
½ teaspoon thyme
3 pints (6 cups) beef stock
1 pint (2 cups) red wine
salt, pepper
1 15½ oz. can cream of tomato soup
4 oz. (¼ cup) haricot beans*

Slice onions, dice carrots, cut oxtails into 2 in. sections. Heat butter, gradually add onions, carrots and oxtail pieces, sauté, stirring constantly until well browned. Drain off any surplus fat during cooking.

Place browned meat and vegetables into a large casserole dish, sprinkle with brown sugar and flour. Peel tomatoes and chop finely, add with remaining ingredients (except haricot beans) to casserole, cover, bake in slow oven, Mark 1, 275°F., 4 hours. Cool, refrigerate overnight.

Cover haricot beans well with water, stand overnight. Next day, drain, place beans in salted water, boil 1 hour, or until tender.

Remove fat from top of casserole, remove bayleaf. Reheat casserole in slow oven, Mark 2, 300°F., for approximately 1 hour; stir in beans during last 15 minutes. Adjust seasoning, serve sprinkled with parsley.

Serves 6 to 8.

* Green beans can be substituted for haricot, but do not need soaking overnight.

A wonderful meal for men—subtle blending of hearty flavours makes this Oxtail Casserole the perfect dish for cold-weather entertaining.

Poultry

Chicken, so easily available at an economical price, has become almost a standard feature on weekly menus, either for family meals or for entertaining. Turkey, too, now available in small sizes, gives lots of good eating when you have a number of people to entertain.

In this section are all the basic ways of cooking the various birds, plus a wide selection of the world's most popular ways with poultry, plus stuffings and accompaniments.

To Choose a Chicken

The skin should be white and free from wrinkles, the breast plump and the breast bone pliable. A boiling fowl may have a slightly yellow tinge to the skin.

Young birds weigh from 2½ to 3 lb. and are suitable for roasting, grilling or frying or sautéing. Older birds weigh from 3½ to 5 lb. and are boiled or used for fricassées, casseroles or similar dishes.

A capon is a male bird that has been specially treated and reared to make it particularly 'meaty' and may weigh up to 8 lb.

Poussins are baby chickens 4 to 8 weeks old weighing 1 to 2 lb. and may be roasted, sautéed or grilled. According to their size, they are either cooked whole or cut in half. Spring chickens are generally 8 weeks to 4 months old.

A 2½ to 3 lb. bird is sufficient for 4 to 5 people. A larger one will serve 6 to 8 people. If the chicken is stuffed and roasted it should be weighed after stuffing in order to calculate the time for cooking. Allow 25 minutes to the lb.

Chicken joints, fresh or frozen are convenient for small families and for special occasions.

How to Joint a Chicken

Many chicken recipes call for the chicken to be jointed, or cut into sections. Here's how to do it. You'll need a good sharp knife and a pair of poultry shears or a strong pair of kitchen scissors.

A chicken will joint into 8 sections: 2 legs, 2 wings, 2 breast portions, and the backbone, which is split into 2 pieces.

To remove legs Cut through skin connecting leg to body; bend leg out, away from body, find the joint where leg hinges, cut through this (there is no need to cut any bone).

To remove wings Cut a slice of breast meat with the wing to make a better serving portion, then bend wing away from body to find where wing joins body; cut through this. Fold wing into a neat shape with breast meat tucked under.

To remove breast Separate breast and back by cutting through rib-bones along each side of body. Cut down centre of breastbone to divide breast in 2; trim away excess skin and fat. (These breast portions, when removed from the bone, are called the supremes).

The backbone Break back in 2 where ribs end. These back portions are generally not considered as individual serving portions, but can be served to accompany another portion such as a wing, or they can be used to make soup, etc.

For many recipes—particularly those to be served with a white or cream sauce—some cooks prefer to remove the skin of the chicken before cooking. However, for those recipes where the chicken pieces are browned before cooking, the skin browns more easily and gives protection to the juicy meat beneath.

Roast Chicken

For roasting, a chicken is generally stuffed (see page 89) and can be cooked in an uncovered dish, wrapped in foil or in a covered roaster. (Spring chickens and poussins are not stuffed.)

The stuffing is put in at the neck end and should not be packed too firmly.

Rub the breast and legs with butter or bacon fat and cook in a moderately hot oven, Mark 6, 400°F., for the calculated time. If the chicken is in a covered roaster or has been wrapped in foil, allow an extra 10 to 15 minutes cooking time and remove the lid or foil 15 minutes before the end of the cooking to allow the skin to brown and crisp.

Accompaniments to Roast Chicken

Bread Sauce Peel an onion and stud with 2 or 3 cloves. Put into saucepan with ½ bayleaf, 2 or 3 peppercorns, a small blade of mace and ½ pint (1 cup) milk. Bring slowly to boil, cover, simmer 5 minutes; strain, retaining liquid and discarding onion. Return liquid to rinsed-out saucepan, add 2 oz. (¾ cup) fresh breadcrumbs, season to taste. Simmer, stirring, 2 or 3 minutes. Stir in a little butter or cream before serving.

Giblet Gravy Melt 1 tablespoon butter in small saucepan, stir in 1½ dessertspoons flour; cook, stirring, few minutes. Gradually stir in ½ pint (1 cup) hot giblet stock (made by cooking giblets in water with a little onion and celery) season to taste. A few of the finely chopped giblets can also be added.

Or stir some flour into pan drippings, pour in the strained giblet stock; cook, stirring, until sauce boils and thickens slightly; season.

French Roast Chicken

1 chicken (2½ to 3 lb.)	giblets
prepared stuffing	½ pint (1 cup) stock or
4 oz. (½ cup or 1 stick)	water
softened butter	salt, pepper

Fill chicken with prepared stuffing, spread legs and breast with softened butter. Place in baking dish with giblets and stock or water. Roast in moderately hot oven, Mark 6, 400°F., until chicken is well browned and tender, basting and turning frequently, and adding extra water or stock if this reduces too much.

Transfer cooked bird to hot serving platter. Strain pan juices into saucepan, skim well, bring to the boil, cook 1 or 2 minutes, season to taste, strain; serve with chicken.

Serves 4.

Chicken in a Basket

This is one of the most popular chicken dishes, particularly for a small, informal party.

Allow one small chicken (about 1½ lb.) for each person; roast in usual way. Serve in small basket, lined with paper napkin. Packaged potato crisps (heat them in oven first) and fried onion rings are the correct accompaniments.

Chicken in the Basket is finger food, so serve finger bowls filled with warm water, with a slice of lemon floating in the water. As the water cools, the lemon can be used to remove any grease from fingers.

There's a correct way to eat this dish: Break off one leg first. Eat this before breaking off any further pieces. In this way the chicken retains its heat.

One hand only should be used to convey the food to the mouth. Rinse fingers often in the finger bowl. Make sure the dinner napkins are a good big size.

Chicken in Aspic

3 lb. chicken	piece of lemon rind
1 carrot	salt, pepper
1 stick celery	½ oz. (2 tablespoons or
1 medium onion	2 envelopes) gelatine
1 clove garlic	2 tablespoons chopped
1 bayleaf	parsley

Place chicken in a pan with sliced carrot, sliced celery, sliced onion, crushed garlic, bayleaf, lemon rind and a sprinkling of salt and pepper. Cover with water and bring to the boil; reduce heat and simmer until chicken is cooked.

Lift out chicken, remove meat from bone, return bones and skin to pan and allow to boil a further 10 minutes. Cut meat into small pieces, soften gelatine in a little water.

Strain bones and vegetables from stock, then strain again through muslin.

Take 1 pint (2 cups) of this stock and add the gelatine, add salt to taste. Mix together chicken, parsley and stock, pour into oiled mould. Refrigerate until set, stirring occasionally to distribute meat evenly.

Serves 4 to 5.

Coq au Vin

2 2½ lb. chickens	3 to 4 tablespoons
2 oz. (¼ cup) butter	brandy
¼ lb. lean salt pork	¾ pint (1½ cups) dry red
12 tiny onions	wine
salt, pepper	¼ pint (½ cup) stock
½ lb. mushrooms	bouquet garni
1 to 2 cloves garlic	1 oz. (2 tablespoons)
	butter, extra
	2 tablespoons flour

Joint the chickens. Heat butter in heavy saucepan, add diced pork and peeled, blanched and drained onions. Cook a few minutes, then add chicken joints; brown well, season. Add sliced mushrooms and crushed garlic, cook 5 minutes. Strain off all excess fat, add brandy. Add red wine, stock and bouquet garni.

Transfer to casserole, cover; cook in moderate oven, Mark 4, 350°F., 40 minutes or until chicken is tender. (Or cook in saucepan on top of stove.) Mix extra butter with flour and add gradually to sauce to thicken it. Stir over heat a few minutes. Check seasoning. Serve with hot garlic bread (see page 137) and a tossed green salad.

Serves 6.

Chicken Tetrazzini

3 lb. chicken	2 oz. (¼ cup) butter
½ pint (1 cup) water or chicken stock	3 tablespoons flour
½ pint (1 cup) dry white wine	¾ lb. (2 cups) spaghetti
1 onion	½ lb. mushrooms
1 bayleaf	2 oz. (¼ cup) butter, extra
pinch thyme	¼ pint (½ cup) heavy cream
a few bacon rinds	1 tablespoon sherry
salt, pepper	

Gently poach chicken in combined wine and water, with chopped onion, bayleaf, thyme, bacon rinds, salt and pepper. When tender, cool, drain, strain the stock and reserve.

Remove the flesh from the chicken bones and cut into thin pieces. Melt the butter, stir in the flour, and cook over gentle heat 2 minutes. Gradually add ½ to ¾ pint (1 to 1¼ cups) of the reserved stock, stirring continually until mixture boils and thickens. Cook a few minutes, then set aside.

Cook spaghetti in plenty of boiling salted water until tender; drain thoroughly, place in deep, hot serving bowl. Finely slice the mushrooms, melt extra butter in frying pan and sauté the mushrooms gently until tender. Drain the mushrooms and add to the sauce with the sliced chicken and seasoning to taste. Reheat until nearly boiling.

Stir in the cream and sherry and stir over heat until heated thoroughly. Pour over spaghetti.

Serves 4 to 6.

Chicken Chow Mein

3 lb. chicken	½ cabbage
½ lb. lean pork	3 shallots
salt, pepper	2 to 3 sticks celery
1½ teaspoons soy sauce	1 green pepper
1 teaspoon brandy or dry sherry	1 clove garlic
1 dessertspoon cornflour	1 pint or 1 packet frozen prawns (shrimp)
4 tablespoons oil	2 tablespoons water

Remove meat from uncooked chicken. Cut chicken meat and pork into fine shreds, place in bowl, sprinkle with salt. Add soy sauce, brandy, ½ teaspoon of the cornflour, and 1 teaspoon of oil; mix well.

Prepare vegetables, cut into thin strips. Heat remaining oil in pan, add crushed garlic and chicken and pork mixture. Cook quickly 3 minutes, stirring constantly, sprinkle with pepper. Add prepared vegetables, fry until vegetables are tender, but still slightly crisp. Add shelled prawns. Mix remaining cornflour with water, add to pan,

bring to boil, stirring gently. Serve on top of crisp fried noodles.

Serves 4 to 6.

Crisp Fried Noodles

Drop ½ lb. (2 cups) fine dried egg noodles into large saucepan of rapidly boiling salted water; stir with fork to separate, cook 3 to 4 minutes; drain well. Arrange on a clean teatowel over wire cake cooler, spread noodles over this to drain. Leave at least 6 hours.

When ready to serve, drop noodles, a few at a time, into shallow hot oil. (To ensure thorough cooking, it is best to fry the noodles in 3 or 4 lots). They cook in seconds; turn once during cooking.

Chicken Paprika

lard or oil for frying	2 tomatoes
2 onions	¾ pint (1½ cups) stock
4 chicken joints	salt, pepper
1 tablespoon paprika	¼ pint (½ cup) sour cream

Heat lard or oil in large frying pan, add chopped onions, sauté until tender. Add chicken pieces to pan, cook until brown. Add paprika, then peeled, chopped tomatoes, stock, salt and pepper. Cover, simmer over gentle heat 1 hour or until chicken is tender.

Remove chicken from sauce, stir in sour cream, return chicken; stir over low heat until well blended and hot.

Serves 4.

Paella

4 small joints frying chicken	1 chicken stock cube
1 onion	pinch saffron
1 clove garlic	2 scallops
2 tablespoons oil	8 large prawns (shrimps)
2 pints (4 cups) water	6 to 8 mussels
2 tomatoes	8 oz. (2 cups) cooked peas
4 oz. (⅔ cup) rice	1 red pepper

Cut up the chicken, slice onion, crush garlic and fry in the oil until golden brown. Add half the water and simmer 15 minutes. Add peeled and sliced tomatoes, rice, stock cube and remaining water. Simmer for 5 minutes then add saffron. Mix in well then add all other ingredients. Continue cooking until rice is tender and most of the liquid has been absorbed.

Chicken in a Basket—a good dish for an informal luncheon or dinner. Serve the small, golden chickens with fried onion rings, potato chips.

Chicken Casserole

1 onion
4 chicken breasts
1 teaspoon salt
4 oz. (½ cup or 1 stick) butter
2 teaspoons paprika
3 tablespoons flour

¼ pint (½ cup) water
1 chicken stock cube
¼ pint (½ cup) sour cream
½ pint (1 cup) white wine
14 oz. can artichoke hearts

Chop onion finely, sprinkle chicken breasts with salt. Heat butter in frying pan, add chicken breasts, fry until golden brown; drain on absorbent paper. Add onion and paprika to remaining melted butter, sauté until onion is soft. Remove pan from heat, stir in flour, return to heat, cook 1 minute. Gradually add water in which stock cube has been dissolved; stir until mixture boils and thickens. Add cream and wine, stir well, heat gently; do not boil.

Place chicken and drained artichoke hearts in ovenproof dish, top with sauce. Cover, bake in moderate oven, Mark 4, 350°F., 1 hour. If desired, before serving, garnish with crisp fried bacon and toasted slivered almonds.

Serves 4.

Burmese Chicken Curry

½ coconut grated*
1 pint (2 cups) chicken stock
3 lb. chicken
2 medium onions
4 tablespoons oil
3 cloves garlic
1 teaspoon ground ginger
1 dessertspoon curry powder

¼ pint (½ cup) boiling water
1 teaspoon salt
2 tablespoons cornflour (cornstarch)
3 tablespoons cold water
1 lb. broad noodles, cooked
1 red chilli
2 hard-boiled eggs
3 chives

* If fresh coconut is not available use 4 oz. (⅔ cup) desiccated coconut.

Combine coconut and chicken stock in saucepan; bring to the boil stirring constantly; remove from heat, let stand 15 minutes, stirring occasionally.

Strain mixture, pressing coconut well with wooden spoon, to extract as much flavour as possible. Reserve liquid, discard coconut.

Remove meat from chicken, cut into bite-sized pieces, chop onions.

Heat oil in large saucepan, add onions, crushed garlic, and ginger, sauté 10 minutes; add curry powder, sauté further 2 minutes. Add chicken, cover, simmer 15 minutes. Stir in ½ pint of the coconut liquid, boiling water and salt; simmer, uncovered, 30 minutes.

Blend cornflour (cornstarch) with cold water,

add to chicken mixture, stir until mixture boils and thickens, add further ½ pint coconut liquid, bring back to boil, remove from heat. Arrange hot noodles on serving plate, sprinkle with finely chopped chilli, chopped eggs and sliced chives, top with chicken mixture.

Serves 4 to 5.

Chicken à la King

3 to 4 lb. chicken
1 small green pepper
1 oz. (2 tablespoons) butter
¼ lb. sliced mushrooms
1 dessertspoon grated onion
1 tablespoon flour
salt

½ pint (1 cup) milk or light cream
½ pint (1 cup) chicken stock
3 egg-yolks
1 dessertspoon lemon juice
½ teaspoon paprika
½ teaspoon celery salt
2 tablespoons dry sherry

Steam chicken until tender; remove meat from bones and cut into large dice or pieces.

Remove pith and seeds from green pepper; blanch in boiling water 5 minutes. Drain and chop finely.

Heat butter in saucepan, add green pepper, mushrooms and grated onion; sauté a few minutes. Sprinkle in flour and salt, cook, stirring, 2 minutes. Gradually blend in milk or cream and stock; add chicken. Stir over gentle heat until sauce thickens, simmer 3 minutes.

Stir a little of sauce into beaten egg-yolks, return to saucepan. Add lemon juice, paprika and celery salt. Reheat very gently, stirring, but do not allow to boil. Just before serving, stir in sherry.

Serves 4 to 6.

Chicken Maryland

1 egg
1 tablespoon milk
3 lb. chicken
2 oz. (½ cup) seasoned flour

dry breadcrumbs
2 oz. (¼ cup) butter
4 tablespoons oil

Beat egg and milk together. Cut chicken into joints, roll in seasoned flour, dip in the beaten egg, then coat with crumbs. Heat butter and oil in heatproof casserole, add chicken pieces, sauté until golden on all sides. Drain off excess oil, cover casserole, cook in moderate oven, Mark 4, 350°F., until tender (about 30 to 45 minutes).

Serve with fried bananas, corn fritters, bacon rolls and grilled tomato halves.

Serves 4.

Corn Fritters Sift 4 oz. (1 cup) plain flour with 1 teaspoon baking powder and ¾ teaspoon salt. Beat

the yolk of 1 egg and 4 tablespoons of milk; mix with 1 11 oz. can whole kernel corn, add to dry ingredients; mix thoroughly. Beat egg-whites until stiff, fold in. Deep-fry dessertspoons of mixture in hot oil until golden. Drain well.
Fried Bananas Peel bananas, cut in halves cross-wise, dip in beaten egg, then breadcrumbs. Fry in butter until golden. Drain well.

Chicken Fricassée

3 lb. chicken
salt, pepper
2 oz. (¼ cup) butter
1 clove garlic
1½ gills (⅔ cup) dry white wine
¾ pint (1½ cups) chicken stock
3 shallots
1 oz. (2 tablespoons) butter, extra
4 oz. mushrooms
2 tablespoons flour
¼ pint (½ cup) milk
2 tablespoons light cream

Cut chicken into serving pieces, season with salt and pepper. Melt butter in large pan, add chicken joints, and cook until a light brown on all sides. Add crushed garlic, wine, chicken stock, chopped shallots, salt and pepper, cover and cook gently until chicken is tender.

Melt extra butter in separate pan and sauté sliced mushrooms for 5 minutes, drain.

When chicken is tender, remove joints from pan, blend flour with the milk, add gradually to pan, stir over gentle heat until sauce thickens. Return chicken pieces to pan, add mushrooms, reheat and adjust seasoning, if necessary. Just before serving, add cream, keep hot but do not boil.

Serves 4 to 5.

Chicken Croquettes

½ pint (1 cup) milk
few peppercorns
1 onion, sliced
1 carrot, sliced
1½ oz. (3 tablespoons) butter
2 oz. (½ cup) plain flour
1 lb. chopped cooked chicken
2 egg-yolks
½ lb. mushrooms
salt, pepper
1 egg
dry breadcrumbs
oil for frying

Combine milk, peppercorns, onion and carrot in saucepan. Bring to boil, simmer 5 minutes; strain.

Melt butter in separate saucepan. Stir in flour, cook 1 minute. Remove from heat. Gradually stir in hot milk, blend well. Return to heat. Bring to boil, then reduce heat and simmer until thickened, stirring constantly. Remove from heat.

Add finely chopped chicken, egg-yolks, and finely chopped mushrooms which have been sautéed in a little butter. Season to taste with salt and pepper. Blend well together.

Spread mixture on greased tray, cover with greased paper. Refrigerate until cold and set. Divide mixture into 16 pieces and mould each into croquette shape approximately 2½ in. long. Dip in lightly beaten egg, then in breadcrumbs. Refrigerate 1 hour. Fry in hot oil until brown.

Makes 16 croquettes.

Chicken Chasseur

3 lb. chicken
3 shallots
1 lb. mushrooms
2 large tomatoes
flour
salt, pepper
1 oz. (2 tablespoons) butter
¼ pint (½ cup) dry white wine
½ pint (1 cup) chicken stock

Joint the chicken, chop the shallots, slice the mushrooms, peel and chop the tomatoes. Dredge the chicken pieces in flour seasoned with salt and pepper. Heat butter in frying pan, sauté chicken pieces gently, browning lightly on all sides.

Remove chicken pieces from pan. Add shallots and mushrooms, cook a few minutes, then add tomatoes, wine and stock. Return chicken to the pan, bring to boil, then reduce heat, cover pan, and simmer until chicken is tender. Taste and adjust seasoning.

Serves 4 to 5.

Chicken Marengo

3 lb. chicken
2 tablespoons oil
2 cloves garlic
2 tablespoons flour
½ pint (1 cup) dry white wine
½ pint (1 cup) chicken stock
salt, pepper
pinch mixed herbs
½ lb. sliced mushrooms
1 small onion
3 tomatoes

Cut chicken into serving pieces. Heat oil in pan, add crushed garlic and chicken pieces, brown chicken on all sides; remove from pan.

Stir flour into oil, cook a few minutes, then add wine and stock gradually, stirring, until mixture boils and thickens. Season with pepper, salt and mixed herbs, add sliced mushrooms, chopped onion and peeled, chopped tomatoes. Cook about 5 minutes, then return chicken to the pan, cover and simmer 45 minutes or until chicken is tender.

Serves 4 to 5.

Chicken Cacciatore

3 lb. chicken	1 lb. tomatoes
2 tablespoons oil	salt, pepper
2 cloves garlic	½ teaspoon oregano
2 large onions	¼ pint (½ cup) red wine
½ lb. mushrooms	

Cut the chicken into serving pieces. Heat the oil in a pan and add the crushed garlic, sliced onions, and mushrooms; brown lightly. Remove and reserve.

Add the chicken pieces and brown on all sides. Return the onions and mushrooms to the pan. Peel and chop the tomatoes and add with the salt, pepper and oregano. Pour in the red wine, bring to boil; reduce heat, cover and simmer for ½ hour. Uncover and simmer for 15 to 20 minutes longer or until sauce is reduced and chicken very tender. Sprinkle with chopped parsley, if desired.

Serve with noodles or hot fluffy rice.
Serves 4 to 5.

Assamee Chicken Curry

3 lb. chicken	¾ teaspoon ground ginger
2 oz. (¼ cup) butter	
salt	2 1 in. pieces cinnamon
1 teaspoon ground black pepper	3 to 4 cloves crushed garlic
2 to 3 bayleaves	1 in. piece green ginger
1 tablespoon turmeric	2 onions
pinch chilli powder	½ pint (1 cup) chicken stock
½ teaspoon cloves	
¾ teaspoon cardamom	2 tablespoons cornflour (cornstarch)
½ teaspoon cumin	
½ teaspoon coriander	water

Joint chicken. Heat butter in saucepan, add all ingredients except chicken, chopped onions, cornflour (cornstarch) and stock; fry 5 minutes. Add chicken joints, brown well on all sides. Add chopped onions and cook gently, stirring occasionally, 25 to 30 minutes. Gradually add stock, simmer 1 hour, or until chicken is tender.

Blend cornflour (cornstarch) with a little water, add to pan, simmer further 3 minutes. Allow to cool, refrigerate overnight. Remove any excess fat, reheat gently.
Serves 4 to 5.

Chicken Liver Risotto

4 oz. (½ cup or 1 stick) butter	½ lb. (1⅓ cups) long grain rice
2 onions	1½ pints chicken stock
3 sticks celery	2 oz. (½ cup) grated Parmesan cheese
1 lb. chicken livers	
	salt, pepper

Heat half the butter in large saucepan. Add finely chopped onions and sliced celery, sauté 10 minutes, stirring occasionally.

Cut cleaned chicken livers into quarters. Add to pan, cook further 5 minutes. Stir in well-rinsed rice and remaining butter, and cook further 5 minutes. Add stock, bring to the boil; reduce heat and simmer, covered, until rice is tender and liquid absorbed (about 20 to 25 minutes). Stir in cheese, adjust seasoning.

Serves 4.

Chicken Chop Suey

3 lb. chicken	oil
½ small firm cabbage	salt
3 to 4 sticks celery	chicken stock
¼ lb. carrots	16 oz. can bean sprouts
¼ lb. green beans	1 dessertspoon corn-
1 onion	flour (cornstarch)

Steam chicken until tender, cool; remove meat from bones, cut into large dice.

Shred cabbage, slice celery, carrots, beans diagonally, chop onion. Heat oil in large pan, add vegetables, sauté until just tender but still crisp, season with salt. Add chicken pieces and chicken stock to cover, add drained bean sprouts. Reheat gently, then thicken with cornflour (cornstarch) which has been blended with a little water; stir until thickened.

Serves 4 to 5.

Honeyed Chicken

3 oz. (⅜ cup) butter	3 lb. chicken

Sauce

4 spring onions (scallions)	1 tablespoon honey
	1 tablespoon soy sauce
1 teaspoon finely chopped green ginger	½ teaspoon salt
	¼ pint (½ cup) sherry

Melt butter in baking dish, add chicken, brush well with butter, bake in moderately hot oven, Mark 4, 350°F., 45 minutes; baste frequently with the butter. Pour sauce over chicken, continue cooking for further 30 minutes, or until tender and golden brown. Baste chicken frequently with sauce during last 30 minutes.
Sauce Chop spring onions (scallions) finely, combine with remaining ingredients.
Serves 4 to 5.

Chicken Casserole combines tender chickens with artichoke hearts, wine, paprika; a perfect dish for a small dinner party.

Roast Duck

1 duckling, 4 to 5 lb.   1 tablespoon flour
prepared stuffing   ½ pint (1 cup) chicken
melted butter   stock
                            salt, pepper

Fill duck with prepared stuffing (see page 89); place in baking dish, brush well with melted butter. Roast in hot oven, Mark 7, 425°F., 15 minutes, then reduce heat to moderate, Mark 5, 375°F., and cook until tender. During cooking, baste and turn bird occasionally. Allow 15 to 20 minutes per lb. Remove duck to a warm serving dish, keep hot.

Pour excess fat from baking dish, sprinkle in flour, stir over gentle heat until brown. Stir in stock, simmer, stirring, 3 or 4 minutes. Strain.
Serves 4.

NOTE: If desired, towards end of cooking time duck can be brushed with a little honey; this helps to crisp the skin. Don't use too much or skin will become too brown. For a Chinese flavour, a little crushed green ginger can be mixed into the honey.

Orange Roast Duckling

3 oranges   1 dessertspoon lemon
2 small ducklings   juice
1 stick celery   3 teaspoons arrowroot
1 carrot   ¼ pint (½ cup) sweet
1 small onion   sherry
2 oz. (¼ cup) butter   salt, pepper
1 tablespoon sugar   2 to 3 tablespoons
1 dessertspoon vinegar   Grand Marnier or
1 pint (2 cups) chicken   other orange liqueur
   stock

Remove rind from 2 oranges, cut into thin strips; squeeze juice from the 3 oranges. Set aside for sauce.

Cut ducklings in half lengthwise. Place chopped celery, carrot and onion into baking dish, add butter; place ducklings on top. Roast in hot oven, Mark 7, 425°F., 15 minutes reduce heat to moderate, Mark 4, 350°F., continue cooking until ducklings are tender, allowing approximately 20 minutes per lb.; baste occasionally with pan juices. Remove from pan, keep warm.

Orange Sauce Skim off fat from pan, strain pan juices. Add sugar and vinegar to pan, cook over gentle heat until sugar caramelises slightly. Add strained pan juices, stock, orange juice and rind and lemon juice. Cook rapidly until sauce is reduced in quantity by half. Blend arrowroot and sherry, stir gradually into sauce; cook, stirring, 6 to 8 minutes over gentle heat; season to taste.

just before serving, stir in orange liqueur.

Spoon the hot Orange Sauce over each serving of duckling, or pass sauce separately.
Serves 4.

Chinese Braised Duck

1 plump young duck   pepper
   (3½ to 4 lb.)   1 teaspoon soy sauce,
6 dried mushrooms   extra
1 dessertspoon soy   1 tablespoon oil
   sauce   ½ teaspoon salt
1 tablespoon dry sherry   2 cloves garlic
1 teaspoon very finely   1 small can bamboo
   chopped green   shoots
   ginger   1 small can water
water   chestnuts
1½ dessertspoons corn-   1 pint (2 cups) stock or
   flour (cornstarch)   water
½ teaspoon sugar

Wash duck, cut into joints. Wash mushrooms, soak in hot water 20 minutes. Rinse, squeeze dry, cut in halves.

Combine dessertspoon of soy sauce, the sherry and ginger; add 1 dessertspoon water. Mix together the cornflour (cornstarch), sugar, pepper and extra soy sauce; stir in ¼ pint (½ cup) water.

Heat oil with salt and crushed garlic, add duck pieces, and fry, stirring until well browned. Add mushrooms, sliced bamboo shoots, and sliced water chestnuts; cook further 2 minutes. Stir in soy sauce mixture; cook 2 minutes, stirring. Add stock, cover, bring to boil. Reduce heat, simmer until duck is tender. Stir in cornflour (cornstarch) mixture and cook, stirring, until sauce thickens. Transfer duck to serving dish, spoon sauce over.

Serve with hot, fluffy rice.
Serves 4.

To Choose a Turkey

Turkeys should be plump with white flesh. Short spurs and smooth black legs are indications that the bird is young. Much has been done over the past years to breed small plump breasted birds. They are frequently marketed frozen and sold by dressed weight i.e. drawn with feet and legs removed and ready for the oven. They should be left in the polythene bag and allowed to thaw out slowly at room temperature which may take about 2 days.

A turkey can weigh as much as 20 lb. but for family use a medium sized bird 10 to 12 lb. is usually most popular. For roasting, the turkey is stuffed to keep it moist and add flavour. It can be roasted in the same way as chicken—see page 80—or slow roasted. The French method ensures that the flesh remains succulent and tender. See page 81.

Roast Turkey

Stuff the turkey and truss it making it as plump and even in shape as possible. Then weigh the bird and calculate the time for cooking. Allow 15 minutes per lb. and 15 minutes over for a bird up to 12 lb. Over 12 lb. allow 10 minutes per lb. and 10 minutes over.

Heat some dripping or bacon fat in the roasting tin—enough to cover the tin to a depth of 1 in. Put in the turkey, baste with the hot fat then cover with greaseproof paper and cook in a hot oven, Mark 6, 425°F., for 45 minutes then reduce the heat to moderate, Mark 4, 350°F., for the required time, basting frequently during cooking. If the turkey is cooked in foil it is not necessary to baste.

Slow roasting

Rub the turkey all over with butter or bacon fat and wrap in foil. Cook at Mark 3, 325°F., allowing 20 minutes per lb. and 30 minutes over for a bird up to 14 lb.

Unwrap about 30 minutes before the end of the cooking to allow the turkey to brown.

Accompaniments for Roast Turkey

Bread sauce or cranberry sauce, bacon rolls, chipolata sausages and watercress to garnish.

Roast Goose

1 goose (9 to 10 lb.)   flour
prepared stuffing   melted butter
1 cooking apple

Stuff goose with prepared stuffing. Place in baking dish with quartered apple, brush with little melted butter. Put little extra melted butter in base of baking dish. Roast in hot oven, Mark 7, 425°F., 15 to 20 minutes, reduce to moderate, Mark 4, 350°F., and allow 20 to 25 minutes per lb. If bird appears to be browning too rapidly, cover with piece of well-greased paper.

When almost cooked, prick skin of bird lightly with fine-pronged fork or skewer; this will allow excess fat to run off. Do not prick flesh of bird, or juices will run out. Dredge breast lightly with flour, baste with hot fat, and continue cooking until tender.

Transfer cooked goose to serving dish, serve with well-seasoned gravy made from pan drippings.

Stuffings for Poultry

Chestnut Stuffing (for Turkey)

15 oz. can unsweetened chestnut purée
½ lb. (3 cups) fresh breadcrumbs
1 finely chopped onion
1 tablespoon chopped parsley
1½ oz. (3 tablespoons) melted butter
salt, pepper
beaten egg to bind

Sieve chestnut purée into bowl. Blend with remaining ingredients.

Sage and Onion Stuffing (for Duck and Goose)

2 onions chopped
¼ lb. (1½ cups) fresh breadcrumbs
1½ teaspoons dried sage
1 oz. (2 tablespoons) melted butter
salt, pepper
pinch nutmeg
½ teaspoon sugar

Place onions in saucepan. Add cold water to cover, and salt. Bring to boil; reduce heat and simmer until almost tender. Combine drained onion with remaining ingredients. Add sufficient onion water to bind, about 1 tablespoon.

Simple Herb Stuffing (for Chicken)

¼ lb. (1½ cups) fresh breadcrumbs
1 oz. (2 tablespoons) softened butter
2 tablespoons chopped parsley
1 teaspoon grated lemon rind
1 teaspoon mixed dried herbs
1 small onion chopped
salt, pepper
beaten egg to bind

Mix together all ingredients, except egg. Add sufficient beaten egg to bind.

Forcemeat (for Turkey)

1 small onion
2 oz. ham or bacon
1 oz. (2 tablespoons) butter
½ lb. lean minced (ground) veal or sausage meat
6 oz. (1⅓ cups) fresh breadcrumbs
pinch grated lemon rind
1 dessertspoon chopped parsley
½ teaspoon mixed herbs
pinch nutmeg
salt, pepper
1 egg
milk

Chop onion and bacon finely, sauté in heated butter until onion is transparent. Add minced meat, breadcrumbs and seasonings; bind with beaten egg; add a little milk if mixture seems too dry.

Fondues

Cheese fondue is a different and delightful dish for entertaining. And the other fondues—tomato (a variation of the cheese fondue) beef, fish, and even a dessert fondue—are equally popular.

For cheese fondue, a thick earthenware pot called a 'caquelon' is used; this gives the gentle heat necessary for cheese cookery. If cooked too quickly, or overheated, cheese would become stringy. For Beef Fondue (or Fondue Bourguignonne, as it is sometimes called) a cast-iron (as shown in the picture), copper, or enamel fondue pot is used. Any small heatproof bowl or casserole can be used for the dessert fondue. For all fondues, a spirit lamp with an adjustable flame is necessary. Special fondue forks, with long handles and prongs, are available.

Cheese Fondue

crusty French bread
1 clove garlic
¾ pint (1½ cups) white burgundy
¾ lb. Gruyère cheese

¾ lb. Cheddar cheese
3 tablespoons kirsch
2 tablespoons cornflour (cornstarch)

Cut bread into cubes; each cube should have some crust on it. Push the fondue fork through the crust; this will hold the bread firmly on the fork and help prevent it dropping into the fondue.

To prepare the fondue Rub round inside of fondue dish with cut garlic clove. Add wine, heat to boiling point. Add the grated cheeses gradually, stirring continually, until cheese melts and mixes with wine. Add the kirsch, blended with cornflour (cornstarch). Continue to cook until mixture thickens (about 3 to 4 minutes) stirring all the time in the form of a figure eight.

Some like to add a light sprinkling of nutmeg or paprika, or both, to the fondue; add these with the cheese.

One after another, the guests take up a piece of bread on the prong of the fork and dip it in the thick, creamy fondue.

There's no need for hurry with fondue, but it must be stirred so it remains evenly thick. The swirling of the bread in the fondue is generally sufficient for this.

Slowly, the 'Grillon', or rich brown crust, forms at the bottom of the fondue dish. Some consider this the best part of fondue; everybody should share in this delicacy.

A crisp green salad is a good accompaniment to cheese fondue. And don't forget to have the pepper mill on the table.

If serving wine, it should be the same as used in the fondue.

NOTE: If kirsch is not available, brandy or gin can be substituted. The fondue will not have the traditional taste, but it will be very good.

There's a traditional forfeit paid by those who drop their bread in the fondue—a kiss, if it's a lady; a bottle of wine, if it's a man.

Tomato Fondue

1 clove garlic
¾ pint (1½ cups) white burgundy
1½ lb. Cheddar cheese
¼ pint (½ cup) tomato purée

2 tablespoons cornflour (cornstarch)
salt, pepper
paprika

Rub round inside of fondue dish with cut garlic clove. Add wine, heat to boiling point. Add grated cheese gradually, stirring constantly until cheese melts and mixes with wine. Add tomato purée blended with cornflour (cornstarch). Continue cooking until mixture thickens, approximately 3 to 4 minutes, stirring constantly. Season to taste with salt, pepper and paprika.

Beef Fondue (or Fondue Bourguignonne), wonderful for a party, is served with a variety of sauces and accompaniments. In smaller pictures, popular Cheese Fondue and Chocolate Dessert Fondue.

Beef Fondue

Allow about ¾ lb. steak per person. Any tender steak can be used. Remove all fat, cut steak into 1 in. cubes. Add equal quantities of oil and butter to fondue pot. The melted butter, combined with the oil, should fill fondue pot about three-quarters full. A clove of garlic can be added to the oil for flavour.

To save time, the oil and butter mixture can be heated on the stove and transferred to the fondue pot, then placed over spirit lamp.

Each guest spears a morsel of beef on a fondue fork and cooks it in the hot oil and butter, then slides it on to the plate with another fork. (The fork which has been in the fondue pot would be too hot to use for eating.) Another piece of beef can be cooking while the first is being eaten.

Have a selection of sauces and condiments. Offer at least two of the following: Bearnaise sauce, chilli sauce, mustard, bottled horseradish sauce, caper sauce, any savoury steak butter. Accompaniments can be simple—a good green salad, asparagus spears, onion rings, a baked potato or heated potato crisps, etc. Serve with hot crusty bread and a good red wine or beer.

Steaks to use　Any tender steak can be used; rump will have best flavour, but there will be less wastage with fillet because of its lack of fat.

Round steak can be used, but will need to be marinated first to make it tender.

Marinade　Combine 4 tablespoons salad oil, ¼ pint (½ cup) red wine, 1 dessertspoon chopped onion. Let meat pieces marinate in this several hours, turning occasionally. Drain well, pat dry.

Here are two variations of the classic beef fondue.

Add other meats—kidney, veal, chicken—to the beef. Put first on the fork or skewer the meat that needs least cooking; put on last the meat that needs the most cooking. If using foregoing combination, you would put the square of kidney on first, then veal, then chicken and finally the cube of beef, which will be immersed in the hot oil.

Use boiling beef bouillon in place of oil in fondue dish. Cut the steak into wafer-thin strips, wrap round the prongs of fondue forks. The steak cooks very quickly in the hot bouillon. And, when the meal is finished, don't discard the bouillon; enriched by the steak cooked in it, it makes an excellent soup for the following day.

Fish Fondue

A fish fondue can be prepared in two ways: with an oil and butter mixture (as for Beef Fondue), for shellfish, or with fish stock to cook fish fillets.

For Shellfish　Prepare oil and butter mixture as for Beef Fondue. Prawn (Shrimp) Fondue makes an excellent supper dish, but prawns (shrimps) must be uncooked; cooked prawns fried in this way would be very hard and tough.

For Chinese style Prawns (Shrimps)　Shell prawns (shrimps), cut deep slit down back of each, taking care not to cut through completely. Coat prawns (shrimps) in cornflour, shaking off excess. Dip in eggs which have been beaten lightly with soy sauce (you will need 2 eggs and 1 teaspoon soy sauce for 2 lb. or 2 pints prawns (shrimps)). Coat prawns well in breadcrumbs, pressing down with palm of hand to flatten.

Prawns (shrimps) can be prepared in this way several hours in advance, and refrigerated until guests arrive. Guests spear a prawn (shrimp) on fondue fork, lower in to the hot oil and butter for few minutes; prawns (shrimps) cook quickly. Serve with Hoi Sin Sauce (obtainable from Chinese food stores) or with Chinese Plum Sauce (see page 149) for dipping.

For Fish Fillets　Make a good fish broth. Place fish trimming and bones into saucepan (fish with firm flesh, halibut, turbot, etc. is best), add 1 chopped onion, 1 or 2 chopped sticks celery, 1 chopped carrot, a bayleaf and few parsley sprigs. Add water to cover; about 2 pints (4 cups) water should be sufficient. Bring to boil, skim well, reduce heat, simmer 20 minutes; strain. Add salt and pepper to taste.

Pour this liquid into fondue pot, add ½ pint (1 cup) dry white wine and, if desired, three slices fresh green ginger and 1 or 2 teaspoons soy sauce. Bring to boil.

Have fish cut into 1 or 1½ in. squares. Spear fish on fondue fork, dip into broth; it will cook very quickly. Serve with small dishes of soy sauce and chopped cucumber.

Fish fillets can also be cooked in the butter and oil mixture. Cut fillets into 1½ in. pieces, put piece on fondue fork, and dip into hot oil; it cooks quickly. Serve with mustard or tartare sauce (see page 148, 149).

Chocolate Dessert Fondue

2 large cans evaporated milk	8 oz. (8 squares) plain chocolate
1½ oz. (scant ¼ cup) sugar	2 teaspoons instant coffee powder
	1 dessertspoon rum

Place milk, sugar, grated chocolate and coffee powder in fondue dish. Heat to boiling point, stirring, then lower heat and simmer gently 5 minutes, stirring constantly. Stir in rum. A small fondue dish is used for this rich dessert sauce. Pineapple, pears, bananas—in fair-sized pieces—go well with the chocolate flavour. Or any other fresh or canned fruits can be used.

Rice

Rice is one of the most versatile of all grains; it can be used for sweet and savoury dishes with equal success.

In this section we give the various methods of cooking rice; all work well, it's just a matter of choosing the method which suits you best.

Hints for Cooking Rice

Add a good squeeze of lemon juice to the rice when cooking; this will whiten and flavour the grains. Some cooks also like to throw in the $\frac{1}{2}$ or $\frac{1}{4}$ of lemon from which the juice was squeezed. For additional flavour, 1 or 2 small stock cubes can be crumbled into the water.

Boiled or steamed rice can have many flavourful additions lightly forked through, such as finely chopped chives, parsley, or mint; grated carrot with finely chopped shallots; raisins, toasted halved or slivered almonds; diced, cooked vegetables; chopped hard boiled eggs. The choice is as wide as the imaginative cook cares to make it.

Rice almost triples in bulk during cooking. Allow approximately 2 oz. ($\frac{2}{3}$ cup) cooked rice for each main dish serving. In other words, 1 lb. of rice, when cooked will give 8 to 10 servings.

Fluffy and Boiled Rice

Put $3\frac{1}{2}$ pints (7 cups) water into large saucepan, bring water to rapid boil, add 1 dessertspoon salt. Then, gradually letting it dribble through your fingers so the water does not go off the boil, add 8 oz. ($1\frac{1}{3}$ cups) rice. Boil rapidly, uncovered, 12 to 15 minutes. Cooking time depends on the type of rice used and also on the way you like your rice—tender, or still with a slight firmness left in the grain. Start testing at the end of 12 minutes. Lift a few grains from the pan with a fork and bite into the grain. When cooked to your liking, drain at once in a colander.

Steamed 'Pearly' Rice

Put rice into saucepan, add water to come 1 in. above level of rice. Add salt to taste. Bring water rapidly to boil, then cover tightly, reduce heat to the lowest simmer and cook further 20 minutes. For a firmer grain, many cooks prefer to simmer the rice 15 minutes only; then remove from heat, let stand—still tightly covered—for 5 to 10 minutes.

Oven-Steamed Rice

Place $\frac{1}{2}$ lb. ($1\frac{1}{3}$ cups) rice into casserole dish, sprinkle lightly with salt. Pour over $1\frac{3}{4}$ pints ($3\frac{1}{2}$ cups) boiling water, cover tightly. Cook in moderately hot oven, Mark 4, 350°F., 20 to 25 minutes.

Reheating Rice

Rice which you have cooked in advance and stored in the refrigerator can be reheated in any of the following ways:

To reheat with steam Place cooked rice in colander, stand over saucepan of simmering water. Cover colander with lid, steam until rice is heated through. Another method of steaming cooked rice is to pour just enough water into saucepan to cover the base of pan. When boiling, add rice, cover, steam 5 minutes or until water is absorbed and rice is hot. The size of saucepan will depend on the amount of rice to be reheated; use a large saucepan for a large amount of rice so the steam can penetrate the grains.

To reheat in oven Spread rice in greased, shallow ovenproof dish, sprinkle with little water or milk, dot with butter. Cover dish with lid or aluminium foil. Place in moderate oven, Mark 4, 350°F., until heated through.

To reheat in frypan Melt a little butter in frypan, add rice; stir with fork until heated through.

Pilaf

1 tablespoon butter or oil	1 tablespoon melted butter, extra
1 small onion	3 oz. ($\frac{1}{2}$ cup) raisins
12 oz. (2 cups) long grain rice	2 oz. ($\frac{1}{4}$ cup) blanched slivered toasted almonds
2 pints (4 cups) chicken stock	

Heat butter or oil in pan that can be covered tightly. Add finely chopped onion, cook gently until it is soft but not brown. Add rice, stir well over gentle heat a few minutes; add boiling chicken stock.

Cover tightly, cook in moderately hot oven, Mark 4, 350°F., 25 to 30 minutes, or until liquid is absorbed and rice is tender. Turn rice on to heated serving dish, separate grains with fork, stir in melted butter, raisins and almonds.

Serves 6 to 8.

Nasi Goreng

½ lb. (1¼ cups) long grain rice	2 medium onions
boiling salted water	4 spring onions (scallions) or chives
½ lb. or ½ pint prawns (shrimps)	cucumber
3 oz. (⅜ cup) butter	2 cloves garlic, crushed
1 lb. fillet steak or pork	salt, pepper
3 cabbage leaves	2 tablespoons soy sauce
2 red peppers	1 small can bean sprouts
thin omelets (see below)	

Add rice gradually to large quantity of boiling salted water, boil rapidly for approximately 15 minutes, or until tender; drain, keep hot. Shell prawns (shrimps), sauté in 1 oz. (2 tablespoons) of the butter, set aside.

Thinly slice steak or pork, cabbage, red peppers and omelets. Chop onions, cut spring onions (scallions) into 1 in. pieces. Peel and thinly slice cucumber.

Heat remaining butter in a large pan, add onion and garlic, sauté 1 minute or until onion is transparent. Add steak or pork, sauté until tender, season with salt and pepper. Add cabbage, peppers, spring onions or chives and hot rice, toss with a fork to mix well; add half the omelet strips, sautéed prawns, soy sauce and bean sprouts. Heat thoroughly, stirring continually.

Add a little more butter if mixture appears too dry; season to taste. Serve on hot platter, garnish with remaining omelet strips and sliced cucumber.

Serves 4 to 6.

Thin Omelets

5 eggs	salt, pepper
3 tablespoons milk	butter

Beat eggs lightly with milk, season to taste with salt and pepper. Grease pan with butter, when hot, pour in enough of the egg mixture to make 1 very thin omelet. When cooked, roll, slice into thin strips. Repeat with remaining egg mixture.

Risotto

1 oz. (2 tablespoons) butter	1 dessertspoon melted butter, extra
1 onion	1 tablespoon grated Parmesan cheese
12 oz. (2 cups) long grain rice	
2½ pints (5 cups) chicken stock	

Melt butter in large saucepan, sauté finely chopped onion until it starts to turn golden. Add rice, mix well. Gradually add boiling stock, about ½ pint (1 cup) at a time; wait until liquid has been absorbed before adding next quantity. Stir at each addition.

Cover pan and cook for remainder of cooking time. The rice should cook about 20 minutes from time first ½ pint (1 cup) of stock is added. The rice should be very tender, liquid all absorbed and mixture creamy at the end of this time.

Add melted butter and Parmesan cheese, mix in carefully with fork. Serve immediately, topped, if desired, with extra Parmesan cheese.

Chinese Fried Rice

Among English speaking people, this is one of the most popular of Chinese dishes. Boil or steam rice the day before you want to fry it; it then has time to dry out completely so that it will fry with every grain separate.

Rice is fried in a small quantity of hot oil, and a variety of good tasting, colourful ingredients are added.

1 tablespoon oil	1 egg
¼ lb. cooked pork	1 teaspoon soy sauce
½ lb. (1⅓ cups) long grain rice, cooked	1 teaspoon water
salt	2 spring onions (scallions) or chives
¼ to ½ pint prawns (shrimps)	2 oz. ham

Heat oil in frying pan, add chopped pork. Fry 1 or 2 minutes, then add rice and salt. Cook 10 minutes, stirring to prevent rice sticking. Add shelled prawns (shrimps), mix well, then clear small space in rice and drop in egg, breaking yolk. When nearly cooked, stir and mix through rice.

Add soy sauce mixed with the water, and finely chopped spring onions (scallions) or chives. Mix well, sprinkle with finely chopped ham.

Fried Rice, traditional accompaniment to many Chinese dishes, is also a colourful, good-tasting dish for a buffet party.

Pastas

Finding your way among the different macaroni foods—or pastas, as they are called—can be a little puzzling at first because of the varying names. But it is a treasure hunt that will reward you with good food for all the family.

Many nations have claimed to have invented macaroni (the generic term which is applied to all shapes and flavours of pasta), but it is in Italy that pasta-making was perfected. As a result, most of the macaronis bear Italian names. When these names are translated, they describe the shape or type of pasta.

Spaghetti, the long, tube-like strands, means 'little string', lasagne means 'broad-leafed', farfalle is 'butterfly', and so on.

Macaroni products can be divided into four basic groups—cords, tubes, ribbons and special shapes such as shells, crests, etc. There is a wide range of sizes and shapes within each of these groups.

Different shapes have evolved for different dishes. Generally, very small shapes—such as alphabet or animal noodles (these are really just for fun, and children love them!) or tubettini—are cooked in clear broths. Cut macaroni or shells are used in heartier soups or in salads. Wide ribbon shapes are for casserole use layered with sauces.

Spaghetti is available in two forms; thin spaghetti and thicker, or 'tubular' spaghetti. Cooking time is approximately the same for both.

Some of the macaronis—spaghetti, shells, elbows, noodles, crests, gnocchi, spirali, alphabets, animals, etc.—are sold in packages and are easily available. For the more unusual types you might need to shop at an Italian or Continental food store.

Green noodles—coloured with spinach juice—can also be purchased.

Oriental noodles, from China or Japan, are much finer than Italian pasta, and they are in plainer form—cords or ribbons of varying degrees of fineness. They are used in three ways: in soup, cooked noodles, drained and mixed with seasonings, or they can be fried.

How to Cook Pasta

Cook all forms of pasta in plenty of boiling water; a gallon of water to 1 lb. of pasta is not too much. Use large saucepan and bring water to a fast, rolling boil; add sprinkling of salt.

Add pasta gradually so water does not go off the boil.

When cooking spaghetti, vermicelli, or any of the 'long goods', as they are called, hold long strands at one end and place other ends into the boiling water. The pasta will begin to soften in the hot water and it is then simple to lower strands into saucepan, coiling them neatly inside pan.

Approximate Cooking Time

Spaghetti, 12 to 20 minutes; vermicelli (resembles very fine spaghetti), 6 to 10 minutes; macaroni, 12 to 20 minutes; noodles, 10 to 20 minutes, depending on width.

Cooking time of pasta varies according to individual manufacturers; freshness of the product, too, will affect cooking time. Pasta should not be overcooked; it should be tender but firm.

Start testing at the minimum cooking time given above and, when the pasta is cooked just to your liking, add a cup of cold water to the pan to stop the cooking instantly. Pour pasta into colander, drain well. If you wish, mix a knob of butter or a little oil through the pasta to prevent it sticking together.

Provided sufficient water has been used in cooking, there will be no starch adhering to the pasta, so do not rinse it under cold water; this will only cause the tender pasta to become hardened.

Spaghetti and macaroni almost double in volume during cooking; noodles remain the same in volume.

1. *Gemelli*	6. *Spirali*	11. *Large Shells*	16. *Tubettini*
2. *Spinach Noodles*	7. *Farfalle*	12. *Small Shells*	17. *Elbows*
3. *Fine Noodles*	8. *Gnocchi*	13. *Alphabets*	18. *Macaroni*
4. *Medium Noodles*	9. *Animals*	14. *Spaghetti*	19. *Lasagne*
5. *Wide Noodles*	10. *Rigatoni*	15. *Crests*	

Meatballs in Tomato Sauce

1 medium onion	1 tablespoon chopped
1 lb. minced beef	parsley
1 egg	salt, pepper
1 oz. ($\frac{1}{4}$ cup) dry	oil for frying
breadcrumbs	
1$\frac{1}{2}$ tablespoons grated	
Parmesan cheese	

Tomato Sauce

1 small onion	1 pint (2 cups) water
1$\frac{1}{2}$ tablespoons oil	salt, pepper
5 oz. can tomato paste	

Finely chop onion, combine with remaining ingredients, mix well. Shape mixture into balls approximately the size of an egg. Fry in hot oil until evenly browned.

Remove from pan, drain well, place in prepared sauce, bring to boil; reduce heat, simmer, uncovered, for approximately 1 hour or until tender. Spoon meatballs and sauce over hot spaghetti. Serves 4.

Tomato Sauce Finely chop onion, sauté in heated oil until soft, add remaining ingredients, stir well to combine. Bring to boil, stirring constantly.

Meatballs in Tomato Sauce have the good, rich flavour of Italian-style cooking. Spoon them over piping hot spaghetti.

Spaghetti Marinara

2 oz. ($\frac{1}{4}$ cup) butter	1 lb. or 1 pint prawns
1 clove garlic	(shrimps)
2 tablespoons finely	4 to 6 scallops
chopped parsley	salt, pepper
6 large tomatoes	1 lb. spaghetti
1 8 oz. can oysters	

Melt butter in saucepan, add crushed garlic, parsley and peeled, chopped tomatoes. Simmer until mixture is well blended and soft; mix in oysters, shelled prawns (shrimps), and scallops cut in halves or quarters, cook gently 5 to 7 minutes. Season to taste.

Drain hot cooked spaghetti. Return to saucepan, stir the sauce through. Or, alternatively, spoon sauce over individual servings of spaghetti. Serves 6.

Spaghetti Bolognese

1 large onion	salt, pepper
2 tablespoons oil	$\frac{1}{4}$ teaspoon oregano
1 lb. minced (ground)	$\frac{1}{4}$ teaspoon thyme
steak	$\frac{3}{4}$ lb. spaghetti
1 pint (2 cups) water	grated Parmesan
8 oz. can tomato paste	cheese
2 beef stock cubes	

Sauté the finely chopped onion in the heated oil until golden, add minced steak; cook very well, stirring with fork all the time, until steak browns well. Pour off any surplus fat. Add water, tomato paste, crumbled stock cubes, salt and pepper to taste, and herbs.

When sauce comes to the boil, reduce heat, cook gently 1 to 1$\frac{1}{2}$ hours, uncovered, adding a little more water if sauce becomes thick too quickly. The longer this sauce is cooked the better it is.

Cook spaghetti, drain well and arrange in individual bowls, making a slight well in the centre. Spoon in the sauce. Top with grated Parmesan cheese.

Serves 4 to 6.

Spaghetti alla Carbonara

1 lb. spaghetti	2 oz. ($\frac{1}{2}$ cup) grated
boiling salted water	Parmesan cheese
$\frac{3}{4}$ lb. bacon	freshly ground pepper
$\frac{1}{4}$ pint ($\frac{1}{2}$ cup) white	chopped parsley
wine	extra grated Parmesan
2 eggs	cheese

Cook spaghetti in large saucepan of salted boiling water 10 to 12 minutes or until tender but still firm. While spaghetti is cooking, remove rind from bacon, cut into $\frac{1}{2}$ in. squares. Sauté in pan until cooked through but not crisp.

Add wine, simmer gently 3 minutes. Drain spaghetti well, return to saucepan. Immediately add bacon and wine. Blend together, then add well-beaten eggs and cheese. Toss together over low heat. Add a little freshly ground pepper. Make sure spaghetti is well coated with egg-and-cheese mixture. Serve in individual dishes sprinkled with parsley and extra grated cheese.

Serves 6.

NOTE: If completed spaghetti is a little dry, add a little extra white wine to moisten.

Meatballs in Tomato Sauce have the good, rich flavour of Italian-style cooking. Spoon them over piping hot spaghetti.

Baked Rigatoni

½ lb. rigatoni noodles   grated Parmesan
                                          cheese

Filling

1 tablespoon oil   3 oz. (1 cup) fresh
2 onions, chopped   breadcrumbs
1 clove garlic, crushed   1 egg
1½ lb. minced (ground)   1½ teaspoons salt
    steak   pepper

Sauce

oil for frying   ½ pint (1 cup) juice from
1 onion, chopped   can (made up to ½
1 clove garlic, crushed   pint (1 cup) with
14 oz. can drained,   water if necessary)
    peeled tomatoes   1 bayleaf
                               salt, pepper

Cook rigatoni in boiling salted water until just softened (about 5 minutes); drain and, for this dish, rinse under cold water because they must be cool enough to handle immediately.

Filling Heat oil, brown onions and garlic lightly. Combine with all remaining ingredients.

Using small teaspoon, stuff rigatoni with filling mixture. Arrange stuffed rigatoni in casserole, spoon sauce over. Top with sprinkling of grated Parmesan cheese. Bake in moderate oven, Mark 4, 350°F., 30 minutes.

Sauce Heat a little oil in saucepan, add onion and garlic; sauté until onion is transparent. Add all remaining ingredients (crush tomatoes well), simmer uncovered until sauce has thickened.

Serves 4 to 6.

Macaroni Cheese

6 oz. macaroni   10 oz. can tomato soup
3 oz. (⅜ cup) butter   ¼ lb. bacon
1 oz. (2 tablespoons)   1 onion
    flour   1 small green pepper
salt, pepper   1 teaspoon
1 teaspoon dry mustard   Worcestershire sauce
¼ teaspoon paprika   extra grated cheese
½ pint (1 cup) milk
6 oz. (1½ cups) grated
    firm cheese

Cook macaroni in boiling salted water 12 to 15 minutes or until tender; drain.

Melt butter in saucepan, remove from heat, stir in flour and seasonings. Return to heat and cook 1 minute. Add milk gradually, stirring until sauce boils and thickens, remove from heat. Add grated cheese and tomato soup, mix well. Gently heat sauce, do not boil.

Fry lightly, chopped bacon, chopped onion and chopped pepper, add to sauce. Add macaroni and Worcestershire sauce, mix thoroughly. Place mixture into casserole dish, sprinkle with extra grated cheese. Bake in moderate oven, Mark 4, 350°F., 25 to 30 minutes.

Serves 4 to 6.

Lasagne

¼ lb. lasagne noodles

Meat Sauce

1½ lb. tomatoes   ½ clove crushed garlic
1 tablespoon oil   1 teaspoon oregano
1 lb. minced (ground)   ¼ teaspoon basil
    steak   ¼ teaspoon rosemary
small can tomato juice   1 teaspoon salt
1 tablespoon finely   ½ teaspoon sugar
    chopped onion
small can or 2 oz.
    button mushrooms

Cheese Sauce

2 oz. (¼ cup) butter   4 oz. (1 cup) grated
3 tablespoons flour   processed cheese
1 pint (2 cups) milk   salt, pepper

Topping

2 oz. (½ cup) grated   3 to 4 tablespoons
    Parmesan cheese   cream

Cook lasagne noodles in boiling, salted water until tender, 15 to 20 minutes. Drain well. Peel and chop tomatoes. Heat oil, add steak, cook, stirring, until browned. Add all other ingredients, cook until meat is tender. Place half the noodles in ovenproof dish, spread with half the meat sauce, then half the cheese sauce. Repeat layers.

Sprinkle top with grated Parmesan cheese. Cook in moderate oven, Mark 4, 350°F., 15 minutes. Five minutes before end of cooking time, pour cream over top of cheese.

Cheese Sauce Melt butter in saucepan, stir in flour, cook gently for 2 minutes. Gradually add milk, stir over low heat until boiling. Stir in grated cheese and seasoning, stir until cheese has melted.

Serves 4 to 6.

Vegetables

Vegetables are an important part of our daily diet. We use them in salads, as colourful, good tasting accompaniments to main meals, or they can be a complete meal in themselves.

To cover or not to cover vegetables when cooking them on top of the stove is a question often debated; as with most forms of cookery, everybody has a favourite method. But experts agree on this—vegetables should be cooked as quickly as possible, so they are crisp, full of flavour, and retain as much of their vitamin contents as possible.

Artichoke

There are two types of artichoke—the Jerusalem and the globe. Many people consider the globe artichoke to be the most delicately flavoured and refined of all vegetables.

Globe Artichokes Wash artichokes, then cut off stem at base. Remove any old outside leaves, shorten the tips with scissors. Plunge into large saucepan of boiling salted water; add juice of ½ lemon, cover and cook 30 to 40 minutes, according to size. Artichokes are cooked when leaves come away easily when pulled gently. Drain well, place on individual serving dishes. Serve with bowl of melted butter, with juice of lemon and salt and pepper added.

Each diner pulls off the leaves, dips them in melted butter and eats fleshy end. Remove central hairy 'choke', when reached, and eat base.

Artichokes cooked in this way can also be served cold, with a vinaigrette sauce.

Jerusalem Artichokes Not really an artichoke but a member of sunflower family. Does not look or taste like the globe artichoke, but resembles a knotty potato. Has a sweet nutty flavour.

The tubers are small and irregular in size and shape. Scrub them well, soak in slightly salted cold water 30 minutes, then drain and rinse well. Cover with cold salted water, cook 20 to 30 minutes until tender, depending on size.

Some cooks prefer to peel the artichokes before cooking; small, sharp-pointed knife should be used for this.

However, it is much easier to peel the skins off after cooking. They are now ready to be used in a variety of ways, or they can be served topped with butter.

Asparagus

Cut off tough ends of asparagus, scrape spears a few inches up from end, tie in a bunch. Stand in deep, tall saucepan (top of double boiler is also suitable), and add boiling salted water to come half way up spears. Cover tightly, bring to boil, reduce heat and simmer until asparagus is tender (about 20 minutes, although very young, tender asparagus will take only 10 to 15 minutes). Drain asparagus well. Serve with melted butter.

Aubergine

See Eggplant.

Beans

Broad Beans Seasonal: April to July. Very young broad beans (fresh from the garden) can be cooked whole. But usually they should be shelled, as for peas, and the pods discarded. Cook beans in boiling salted water until tender (15 to 20 minutes). Top with butter and sprinkling of finely chopped parsley.

French or Runner Beans, (Green or Shap Beans) Wash beans, then top and tail, remove strings. Young beans can be left whole for cooking, but older beans should be sliced. Cook in small amount of boiling salted water until tender (10 to 15 minutes). Drain well, season with salt and pepper, top with pat of butter. Serve at once.

Artichoke

Runner Beans

Spanish Beans

1 large onion	1 dessertspoon
1 tomato	flour
1 chilli	1 to 1½ pints (2 to
1 red or green	3 cups) stock
pepper	1 lb. runner
1 oz. (2 table-	(green) beans
spoons) butter	1 teaspoon salt

Slice the vegetables thinly. Cook the onion, tomato, chilli and pepper in the butter until soft and golden brown. Add the flour, stir until brown then add the boiling stock. Bring again to boiling point, add the sliced beans and salt and cook about ½ hour. Serve as an accompaniment to meat or as a savoury.
Serves 3 to 4.

Runner (Green) Beans with Carrots

½ lb. young	salt, pepper
carrots	2 tablespoons oil
1 lb. runner	
(green) beans	

Scrape the carrots and cut into very thin rounds. String and slice the beans thinly. Put 1 in. water into a strong saucepan, add the carrots, salt and pepper, cover and cook for 10 minutes. Add the beans and oil and continue cooking further 20 minutes or until tender. Correct the seasoning as necessary.
Serves 4.

French Beans Almondine

1 lb. French	1 oz. (3 to 4 table-
(green) beans	spoons)
2 oz. (¼ cup)	slivered
butter	almonds
pinch salt	1 dessertspoon
	lemon rind

Top and tail beans. Cook whole, or sliced, in little boiling salted water until tender; drain. Melt butter over low heat, add almonds, sauté a few minutes. Stir in salt and lemon juice. Pour over hot beans.
Serves 4.

Beetroot

Wash well. Leave on 1 in. or more of stems and root end. If cut too near stem the bright colour will leak into water, leaving cooked beetroot a pale pink instead of its bright natural colour. Cook, covered, in boiling salted water to cover until tender when tested with fork. Small young beetroot will take 30 to 40 minutes, older beetroot up to 1½ hours. When tender, drain and slip off skins, root and stems.

Broccoli

Wash broccoli, trim off ends of stalks and coarse leaves. Cut deep cross in base of extra thick stalks to facilitate cooking. Place in saucepan with small amount of boiling salted water; boil until tender (10 to 15 minutes). Drain, add salt, pepper, pat of butter and squeeze of lemon juice. Serve at once.

For additional flavour, add ½ clove garlic to cooking water. Remove garlic before serving.

Broccoli with Lemon-Cream Sauce

1½ oz. (3 table-	1 lb. cooked
spoons butter	broccoli spears
1 dessertspoon	(or use quick-
flour	frozen broccoli)
salt, pepper	1 oz. (3 to 4
large can	tablespoons
evaporated	blanched,
milk or cream	slivered
2 egg-yolks	almonds
1½ tablespoons	
lemon juice	

Melt ½ oz. (1 tablespoon) butter in a saucepan, add flour and seasonings, stir until smooth. Cook 1 minute. Gradually add the evaporated milk. Bring to the boil, stirring constantly. Remove from heat. Beat egg-yolks, slowly beat a little hot sauce into the eggs, return to sauce in the pan, stir in remaining butter and lemon juice carefully.

Place the cooked broccoli spears in a shallow dish, pour over the hot sauce and garnish with almonds.
Serves 4.

Brussels Sprouts

Remove any wilted outer leaves from sprouts, remove hard end of stem; cut a cross in base of stems to ensure even cooking. Wash thoroughly. Cook in little boiling salted water until tender (10 to 15 minutes depending on size). Drain well, dot with butter, sprinkle with salt and pepper. Serve at once.

At top, from left, Zucchini, Eggplant. Below, Beans.

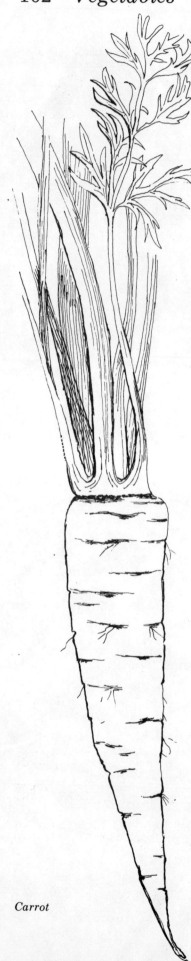

Carrot

Cabbage

Remove coarse outer leaves from cabbage, cut out hard core. Wash thoroughly, cut into fine shreds. Place in saucepan, add little salt, lump of butter and squeeze of lemon juice. Add minimum amount of boiling water, let water come again to boil, then stir cabbage well. Boil rapidly, covered, until tender.

Alternatively, put cabbage into saucepan with salt, add boiling water to cover: bring water rapidly again to boil, boil 3 minutes, then drain. Season with freshly ground pepper, top with knob of butter. This gives a very crisp vegetable, in the Chinese style.

Half a cup of chopped celery added to cabbage when cooking gives a new and delightfully fresh flavour.

Cabbage American

1 medium sized cabbage	½ teaspoon curry powder
3 oz. (⅜ cup) butter	grated rind and juice of 1 lemon
1 teaspoon chutney	

Shred the cabbage and cook for 4 minutes in 1 quart (4 cups) boiling salted water. Drain well. Brown the butter in a small pan, add curry, chutney, orange rind and juice. Pour over the cabbage and leave in a warm place for 10 minutes before serving.
Serves 4.

Dolmas

12 cabbage leaves	¼ teaspoon Tabasco
1 lb. lean pork	½ teaspoon marjoram
1 onion	½ pint (1 cup) cider
¼ teaspoon garlic salt	sliced cooked carrots for garnish
¼ teaspoon black pepper	

Wash the cabbage leaves and cook for 5 minutes in boiling salted water until just soft and pliable, drain well.

Mince or grind the pork and onion, add seasoning, Tabasco and marjoram. Spread over the cabbage leaves, roll firmly and put into a casserole. Add the cider, cover and cook in a very moderate oven, Mark 3, 325°F. for 1 hour. Arrange in a hot dish and garnish with carrots.
Makes 12 dolmas.
If liked the remaining cider can be thickened with a little cornflour and served with the dolmas. When thickened add seasoning and a little tomato purée.

Red Cabbage

This, unlike green cabbage, is never boiled in water. It should be finely shredded or grated and then cooked slowly, covered, with butter or lard and vinegar; water may then be added. This initial cooking with butter and vinegar ensures a rich purple colour to the cabbage; if cooked with water, the cabbage will 'bleed' and become pale pink.

½ red cabbage	1 apple
1 oz. (2 table-spoons) lard	¼ pint (½ cup) water
2 oz. bacon	6 peppercorns
1 medium onion	1 bayleaf
3 tablespoons sugar	4 whole cloves
¼ pint (½ cup) white vinegar	1 teaspoon salt

Finely shred cabbage, discarding any coarse leaves. Melt lard in large saucepan, add chopped bacon and onion, sauté until onion is golden. Add sugar, cook over medium heat 1 minute. Add shredded cabbage, vinegar, peeled and chopped apple; cover, simmer gently 10 minutes, turning occasionally. Stir in water and seasonings, cover; simmer gently further 1½ hours. Serve as accompaniment to any meats.
Serves 4.

Capsicums

See Peppers

Carrots

One of the most popular root vegetables. Their bright colour adds appetite appeal to many dishes, especially when served raw in salads; their sweet fresh taste teams well with many foods. Carrots are rich in vitamins.

Carrots Vichy

1 lb. young carrots	2 oz. (¼ cup) butter
1 teaspoon sugar	water
salt, pepper	chopped parsley

Scrape carrots and cut into slices about ½ in. thick. Put in pan with the sugar, seasoning and butter, barely cover with water. Cook quickly, turning occasionally, until all the water has evaporated and the carrots are tender, and lightly coated in butter. Sprinkle with parsley.

Serves 4.

Cauliflower

Trim cauliflower, removing outer green leaves and part of core. Make several deep cuts in core to facilitate cooking. Place in saucepan, add boiling water almost to cover cauliflower. Add salt to flavour, and a teaspoon of lemon juice or little milk; this will help keep cauliflower white. Cook gently 20 to 30 minutes or until tender (do not overcook); drain.

Alternatively, the cauliflower can be broken into flowerets and cooked for a shorter time.

Cauliflower au Gratin

1 cauliflower	fresh bread-
Mornay sauce	crumbs
(see below)	melted butter
grated Parmesan	
or Cheddar	
cheese	

Cook cauliflower until tender, drain well. Spread about ¼ pint (½ cup) Mornay Sauce in ovenproof dish, place drained cauliflower on top of this. Spoon over ½ pint (1 cup) of Mornay Sauce, or more, if necessary, to cover. Sprinkle with grated cheese and fine, fresh breadcrumbs. Spoon over little melted butter. Cook in hot oven, Mark 7, 425°F., or place under hot grill until top is lightly brown.

Mornay Sauce

2 egg-yolks	1 dessertspoon
1 tablespoon	butter
cream	2 tablespoons
1 pint (2 cups)	finely grated
hot white	Parmesan or
sauce (see	Cheddar
page 146)	cheese

Mix egg yolks and cream into hot white sauce. Cook, stirring constantly, until mixture just reaches boiling point; remove from heat. Stir in butter and grated cheese.

Celery

Trim heads thoroughly—for best results for cooked celery, only the tender inner stalks should be used. Scrub these, plunge into boiling water; cook 10 minutes. Then drain, dry and tie tops of heads together; cook as desired.

The simplest way to cook celery is to blanch it as above, then continue cooking in boiling salted water until tender (about 20 minutes). Drain, serve with a well-seasoned white sauce.

Don't throw away the discarded leaves and outer stalks—these are a wonderful addition to the stock or soup pot, and young, fresh celery is delicious, of course, to eat fresh or use as a salad ingredient.

Celery Victor

1 head celery	tomato wedges
stock	few strips
well-seasoned	anchovy
French	shredded lettuce
dressing	ripe olives
freshly ground	
black pepper	

Clean celery, cut head in halves lengthwise. Trim off top and if head is large, cut in half again crosswise. Place in saucepan with hot stock to cover, cook until tender. Drain well, place in shallow dish to cool. Pour over sufficient French dressing to moisten well. Refrigerate, turning pieces occasionally. At serving time, arrange on platter on bed of shredded lettuce. Sprinkle with pepper, lay few strips of anchovy over each piece. Decorate with tomato wedges, black olives.

Serves 4 to 6.

Braised Celery

2 small heads	1 small onion
celery	1 tablespoon
½ pint (1 cup)	flour
chicken stock	paprika
1 tablespoon	salt, pepper
butter	

Trim and blanch celery as directed, drain and tie up. Place in saucepan with chicken stock, cover, bring to boil; simmer until tender. Drain, remove string, keep warm; reserve cooking liquid. Heat butter in saucepan, add finely chopped onion, sauté until golden. Blend in flour, gradually add cooking liquid. Cook, stirring, until mixture boils and thickens, adding little extra stock if sauce seems too thick. Season to taste. Spoon sauce over celery, sprinkle with paprika.

Celery

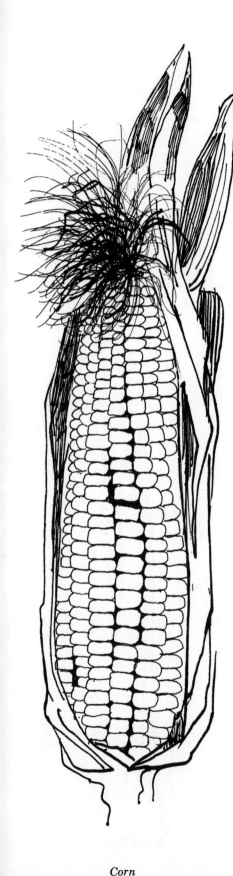

Corn

Celery au Gratin

1 head celery	2 oz. (½ cup)
1 oz. (2 table-	grated
spoons) butter	Parmesan or
1 oz. (2 table-	Cheddar
spoons) flour	cheese
¼ pint (½ cup)	salt, cayenne
celery water	pepper
¼ pint (½ cup)	browned bread-
milk	crumbs

Prepare the celery and cut into dice. Cook in a little boiling salted water until tender, drain well. Make a white sauce with the butter, flour, celery stock and milk. Add half the cheese and season carefully. Fill a greased fireproof dish with alternate layers of sauce and celery. Sprinkle the rest of the cheese and a few breadcrumbs on top. Reheat in the oven or under the grill.

Serves 3 to 4.

Celery and Fruit Jelly

1 pkt. lemon jelly	1 teaspoon salt
1 pkt. lime jelly	1 pint (2 cups)
1 pint (2 cups)	cold water
hot water	3 oz. (½ cup)
4 tablespoons	diced celery
lemon juice	1 apple
2 small bananas	

Dissolve lemon and lime jellies in the hot water. Add lemon juice, salt and cold water. Chill in the refrigerator until slightly thickened. Fold in celery, diced bananas and diced unpeeled apple. Pour into 1 large or 8 individual moulds and refrigerate until set. Serve on lettuce with mayonnaise (see page 121).

Serves 8.

Chicory (Endive)

Generally imported. In France this vegetable is called Endive Belge. It is generally eaten raw in salads or can be braised.

Chicory (Endive) Soufflé

6 to 8 heads of	3 eggs
chicory	salt, pepper
(endive)	nutmeg
½ pint (1 cup)	grated firm
bechamel	cheese
sauce (see	
page 146)	

Wash the chicory (endive), removing the outside leaves and cook in boiling salted water for 20 minutes. Drain and chop finely. Add to the sauce with beaten egg-yolks, salt, pepper and nutmeg to taste.

Fold in the stiffly beaten egg whites, turn into a buttered soufflé dish and bake in a moderately hot oven, Mark 5, 375°F., for 20 minutes. Serve with a sprinkling of grated cheese.

Serves 4.

Chilli

See Peppers

Corn

Corn deteriorates more rapidly after picking than any other vegetable. The sugar in the corn rapidly converts to starch. Freshly picked young corn is sweet to taste; corn which has been picked for some time develops a floury taste. Ideally, corn should be cooked as soon as possible after picking. Look for corn with dark green, fresh husks, with plump, well-filled kernels. Fresh corn looks moist and juicy; if you scratched a grain with your fingertips it would be soft. Old corn looks hard and dull. Do not buy corn that has had the husks removed.

Do not remove husks until ready to cook the corn. Have ready a deep saucepan filled with boiling water; water should be deep enough to cover cobs when they are in saucepan. Salt can be added to the water, but some cooks believe this tends to toughen the kernels; instead, they add a little sugar. Remove green leaves and the silky 'hair' from cobs, drop cobs into the boiling water, let water return to the boil, then cook for 20 minutes. Overcooking will toughen the kernels; the corn becomes harder, not softer, through longer boiling.

Lift cobs from water with tongs. Serve with butter and pepper.

Corn is also good for a barbecue. Remove husk and silk from corn. Spread cobs generously with softened butter, season well with salt and pepper. Wrap each cob in a double thickness of aluminium foil, twisting or folding ends to make a seal. Place on grill of barbecue over hot coals. Cook, turning often, 15 to 20 minutes, depending on heat of fire.

Or cobs can be boiled for 10

Mild, sweet peppers (or capiscums) come in a variety of colours. Yellow-green Banana Chillies (mild as peppers) and small, hot red chilli are also shown.

Leek

minutes, removed from the water, and brushed generously with melted butter; then barbecued on grill over hot coals for 10 minutes, and brushed occasionally with melted butter.

Cucumbers

Although generally used as a salad vegetable, cucumbers are excellent when cooked and served hot.

Buttered Cucumbers

2 to 3 cucumbers
boiling salted
  water
2 tablespoons
  melted butter

salt, pepper
lemon juice
2 tablespoons
  chopped
  parsley

Peel cucumbers, score them with fork. Cut into quarters, lengthwise, or into ½ in. slices. Drop into boiling salted water, simmer 2 minutes, drain.

Melt butter in frying pan, add well-drained cucumber, sprinkle with salt and pepper. Cook, turning once, until cucumbers are lightly golden; do not overcook. Add a good squeeze of lemon juice, stir this lightly through cucumbers. Sprinkle with parsley.

This is a delicious accompaniment to fish.

Serves 4.

Cucumbers in Sour Cream

2 medium
  cucumbers
1 tablespoon salt
1 tablespoon
  vinegar
¼ pint (½ cup)
  sour cream

2 tablespoons
  chopped chives
salt, pepper to
  taste
pinch cayenne

Peel cucumbers and slice thinly. Sprinkle slices with salt and vinegar, let stand 30 minutes. Drain off liquid, and mix cucumber with sour cream, chives and seasonings to taste. Serve well chilled. Excellent as a curry accompaniment.

Serves 4 to 6.

Eggplant or Aubergine

To prepare for cooking, simply wipe with damp cloth and remove stem and calyx. Can be peeled or left unpeeled. Eggplant is a watery vegetable; if cut into thick slices, salted and covered with plate with weight on top, some of the excess moisture will drain away.

When frying eggplant, do not cover pan—the slices should be crisp.

Cut unpeeled eggplant crosswise in thin slices. Coat lightly with seasoned flour, fry in hot butter until pale golden brown. Serve piping hot as vegetable accompaniment with meat, fish, etc.

Aubergines à la Boston

4 aubergines
salt, pepper
flour
oil for frying
2 onions
½ oz. (1 table-
  spoon) butter
1 egg

2 oz. (½ cup)
  grated
  Parmesan
  cheese
¼ pint (½ cup)
  thin white
  sauce (see
  page 146)

Cut unpeeled aubergines in half lengthways. Run the point of a knife round the inside of the skin to a depth of 1 in. and make several cuts across the fleshy part.

Sprinkle with salt and leave to stand for ½ hour. Drain, dry with a cloth and sprinkle with flour. Fry for about 8 to 10 minutes on the cut side only. Remove from the pan and leave to cool. Then, with a metal spoon, scoop out the flesh and chop up. Soften the peeled and chopped onions in the butter, add to the aubergine flesh with beaten egg, cheese and seasoning. Fill the aubergine cases with this mixture, place in a fire-proof dish and cook for 10 minutes in a hot oven, Mark 7, 425°F. Pour over the sauce and serve in the same dish.

Mild, sweet peppers (or capsicums) come in a variety of plain and variegated colours—red, green, yellow; shown, also, is the rarer creamy-white pepper. Yellow-green Banana Chillies (mild as peppers) and the small, hot red chilli are also shown.

Kale

This is a vegetable of the cabbage family. The leaves are closely curled, prettily variegated in colours of green, white and mauve.

Cut leaves from heavy stems, wash well. Cook as for spinach over gentle heat, but allow slightly longer cooking time. Drain, season with a little grated nutmeg, top with butter.

Kale can also be substituted in any recipe that calls for spinach.

Kohlrabi

Looks like a turnip and has similar taste, but more delicate grain. Actually, is a member of the cabbage family. Select leaves that are pale green and crisp, roots about the size of medium-sized onion. Trim off leaves, peel roots, slice. Cook in boiling salted water to cover until tender, about 25 minutes. Drain, season with salt, pepper, melted butter, or serve with a medium white sauce.

Leeks

Cut off roots, trim green tops, leaving about 3 in. of green part. Peel off outside layer, then make 2 cuts, about 2 in. long, first one way and then the other, on top of green parts of leek. This makes it easy to ruffle back the tops when washing. (This is essential because all particles of grit lying between leaves must be removed.) Then place leeks in saucepan with little boiling salted water. Cover, bring to boil, simmer until tender (about 30 minutes). Drain well, season with salt and pepper, pour over little melted butter.
Leeks Vinaigrette Cook leeks as directed, drain and cool. Serve with vinaigrette sauce (three parts oil mixed with one part vinegar, with salt and pepper to taste), sprinkle with chopped parsley or chives.

Braised Leeks

8 small leeks	½ pint (1 cup)
1 tablespoon	chicken stock
butter	salt, pepper
1 small onion	slices of buttered
	toast

Wash leeks thoroughly and trim. Melt butter in wide shallow saucepan, add chopped onion, sauté until soft and golden. Add leeks, pour in stock; add salt and pepper. Cover, simmer until leeks are just tender. Serve on slices of buttered toast.
Serves 4.

Lettuce

Widely used as a salad vegetable, lettuce can also be cooked to serve as a green vegetable. Remove wilted leaves, wash lettuce under running water. Cut heads into quarters. Put into saucepan with a little chicken stock (about 2 tablespoons for each medium-size lettuce). Cover, cook until tender, about 5 to 10 minutes. Drain, season with salt and pepper, pour over a little melted butter.

Marrow (Squash)

When small known as Courgettes or Zucchini (see picture on page 102 and page 115). Seasonal April to August, sometimes imported.

Peel marrow, cut into neat pieces, cook in boiling salted water until just tender, or steam over boiling water. Serve topped with butter or parsley sauce. Marrows can also be filled with a savoury stuffing and baked in the oven.

Stuffed Vegetable Marrow (Acorn or Hubbard Squash)

1 medium vegetable marrow (squash)	salt, pepper
	1 dessertspoon chopped parsley
½ lb. (1½ cups) cold cooked meat	2 oz. (½ cup) grated Cheddar cheese
3 oz. (1 cup) diced cooked vegetables	1 oz. (scant ½ cup) soft breadcrumbs
1 tomato	
about ¼ pint (½ cup) white sauce (see page 146)	1 dessertspoon butter

Cut marrow in half lengthwise, do not peel, remove seeds. Mince or dice meat finely, skin and chop tomato. Combine meat, vegetables, tomato, white sauce, salt, pepper and parsley; fill into each half of marrow. Sprinkle tops with combined cheese and breadcrumbs, dot with butter. Place marrow (squash) in baking dish with small quantity of water in bottom of dish, bake in moderate over, Mark 4, 350°F., for approximately 45 minutes or until tender.
Serves 4.

Mushrooms

Classified as a fungus rather than a vegetable, but used as a vegetable they are delicious! Two kinds of mushrooms are generally available —the cultivated mushrooms, pink-brown underneath with creamy-white top; and the darker, generally larger and more open-capped field mushroom, which grows wild.

Mushrooms should be used when they are fresh. From the time they

Mushrooms

are picked, they gradually lose weight by dehydration; they contain 75 per cent of water.

To help cut down evaporation, if they are to be kept, store in plastic bag, or well wrapped in plastic food wrap or waxed paper, in refrigerator. Don't try to keep them too long—a week is maximum, if they are to have any flavour.

Before cooking, wash mushrooms lightly. Don't let them soak in water, because this dilutes their flavour. For cultivated mushrooms, a wiping with clean, damp cloth is generally sufficient.

To prepare, slice off dry end of stem. It is not necessary to peel the cultivated mushrooms, but you might like to remove darker skin of field mushrooms before cooking. They can be sliced, if large, or left whole.

Here is a simple way of cooking mushrooms.

Prepare as directed above. Sauté in heated butter until barely tender (about 5 minutes). Add squeeze of lemon juice to pan, with a small clove of crushed garlic, some chopped parsley, salt and pepper. Cook a further moment or two. Nice with grills.

Stuffed Mushrooms

½ lb. small mushrooms	1 dessertspoon chopped parsley
2 oz. (¼ cup) butter	1 small shallot
1 small clove garlic	2 tablespoons soft bread-crumbs, approx.
salt, pepper	oil

Wash and stem mushrooms; chop stems finely. Melt butter in frying pan, add stems and crushed garlic, sauté 2 minutes. Add salt and pepper to taste, parsley and very finely chopped shallot, cook gently 1 minute. Remove from heat and add enough breadcrumbs to mix to a light stuffing.

Fill mushroom caps with this mixture, spreading evenly. Place in shallow, well-greased ovenproof dish, pour 1 teaspoon oil over each mushroom. Bake in moderate oven, Mark 4, 350°F., 10 to 15 minutes. The mushrooms should not be over-cooked.

Serve as a first course or as an accompaniment to meat.

Sautéed Mushrooms

3 tablespoons butter	⅛ teaspoon ground nutmeg and clove mixed
1 teaspoon flour	
1½ lb. mushrooms	salt
	4 tablespoons sherry

Melt butter in a shallow pan over low heat. Add flour, then gradually add mushrooms turning each over to absorb some of the butter. Just cover with water, add salt, cover and cook slowly for 10 minutes. Uncover, increase heat a little and cook until liquid has been well reduced. Add sherry and spice, bring to the boil and serve at once.

Serves 4.

Onions

A versatile vegetable, they adapt themselves well to almost all ways of cooking. Can be sliced and fried to top a succulent grill; baked whole with the joint; boiled and served with parsley sauce; or can be chopped, boiled, and added to a savoury white sauce to top corned beef.

Fried Onion Rings

4 onions	¼ teaspoon salt
½ pint (1 cup) milk	4 oz. (1 cup) plain flour
1 egg	oil for frying

Skin onions, slice thinly, separate into rings. Put into bowl, add the milk, let stand 1 hour. Drain, reserve milk. Beat egg well, beat in reserved milk, salt and sifted flour. Dip each onion ring into batter, drop into hot oil a few rings at a time so heat of oil does not decrease. Fry until golden brown. Drain well, sprinkle with salt.

Stuffed Onions

4 large onions	2 tablespoons grated Parmesan cheese
1 clove garlic	
1 stick celery	
1½ teaspoons oil	salt, pepper
1 teaspoon thyme	
2 oz. (¼ cup) dried bread-crumbs	2 tablespoons melted butter

Peel onions, cut off top ¾ of the way up onion. Cut out enough of the inside to leave a shell about ¾ in.

Onion

thick. Salt the cavities well and let the onions stand while making the stuffing. Chop onion pulp finely with crushed garlic and celery. Fry slowly in oil for 5 minutes, then add thyme, breadcrumbs, cheese, salt and pepper to taste. Mix thoroughly, fill the onions; stand them flat in an oven-proof dish in which there is the melted butter and a little salt and pepper. Cover and bake in a moderately hot oven, Mark 5, 375°F., for 1 hour, or until onions are tender.

Spoon over the juices in base of the casserole.

Parsnips

Wash, trim and peel. Slice, if desired, or leave whole. Cook in small amount of boiling water until tender (about 25 to 30 minutes for whole parsnips—sliced parsnips will not take as long). Drain, season with salt and pepper, pour over little melted butter.

Parsnips are also delicious if baked around a roast. Peel parsnips and cut in halves, lengthwise. Place in baking dish with meat, spooning little of hot fat from pan over each. Bake about 45 minutes or until tender and browned.

Parsnip Croquettes

2 rashers bacon	1 small egg
1 lb. parsnips	2 tablespoons
1½ gills (⅔ cup) milk	plain flour
	salt, pepper
1 oz. (2 tablespoons) butter	seasoned flour
	egg glazing
2 to 3 tablespoons finely chopped chives	dried bread-crumbs
	oil for frying

Remove rind from bacon, cut bacon into small pieces. Fry until crisp, drain, set aside. Peel parsnips, cut into small pieces; put into saucepan with milk. Simmer, covered, until parsnips are tender and liquid is almost absorbed; mash. Add butter, chopped chives, egg, plain flour, and bacon. Season with salt and pepper, mix well. Drop tablespoons of mixture into seasoned flour, shape into croquettes; roll in flour, dip in beaten egg, toss in dry breadcrumbs. Press crumbs firmly on to croquettes. Refrigerate 1 hour. Deep fry in hot oil until golden brown.

Makes approx. 1½ dozen small croquettes.

Peas

Shell peas just before cooking, place in saucepan with small amount of boiling salted water. Add salt, little sugar and sprig of mint; cook until peas are tender. Cooking time will depend on age of peas, but is usually from 10 to 15 minutes. Drain, season with salt and pepper; add nut of butter; serve at once.

Peas Bonne Femme

1 heart of lettuce	1 dessertspoon flour
1½ to 2 lb. peas	
1½ oz. (3 tablespoons) butter	½ pint (1 cup) chicken or vegetable stock
6 chives or spring onions (scallions)	bouquet garni
2 rashers bacon	salt, pepper

Shred lettuce finely, shell peas. Melt butter in saucepan, add sliced chives and chopped bacon, shake over heat for a few minutes. Stir in flour, cook 2 to 3 minutes, then add lettuce. Pour on stock, bring mixture to boil, add peas, bouquet garni, salt and pepper. Cover, cook gently 20 to 30 minutes, stirring frequently. Remove bouquet garni.

Serves 6 to 8.

Peppers

Size of pepper usually indicates how to use it in cooking. Small pointed varieties (chillies) are very hot. Like garlic, a small amount goes a long way in seasoning casseroles, pickles, relishes, etc. Banana chillies are long, pale greenish-yellow in colour, are mild in flavour, like the big red and green peppers (or capsicums). Peppers can be used in many dishes; they add flavour to casseroles, and are a popular, colourful addition to salads.

To prepare peppers for cooking, remove slice from stalk end, scoop out seeds and membranes. Young, tender peppers can be used fresh, but older peppers should be blanched in hot water for 2 to 3 minutes to soften.

Perhaps the most popular way of using peppers is to stuff them with a savoury mixture and bake them; they make an easy, economical dish.

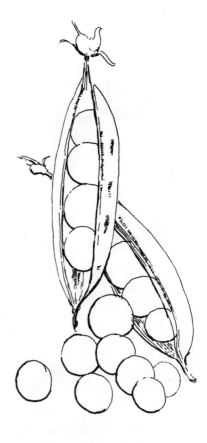

Peas

Peppers

Stuffed Peppers

4 green peppers	2 to 3 sticks
1 tablespoon oil	chopped celery
salt, pepper	½ lb. minced (1
2 oz. (¼ cup)	cup ground)
butter	raw meat
1 small onion	2 oz. (⅔ cup)
	cooked rice

Cut tops from peppers, or cut peppers in half lengthwise; remove seeds and membranes. Place peppers in boiling water with oil, boil 5 minutes; drain well. Season inside of peppers with salt and pepper. Heat butter, add finely chopped onion and celery, sauté until tender; add meat and rice, season with salt and pepper. Cook, stirring constantly, until meat changes colour.

Place meat mixture into pepper halves, place in shallow baking dish, cover. Bake in moderate oven, Mark 4, 350°F., 30 to 40 minutes, serve at once.

Serves 4.

Stuffed Peppers with Frankfurters

4 peppers	2 oz. butter

Filling

1 onion	3 dessert apples
1 can frank-	1½ oz. (3 table-
furters	spoons) butter
(medium size)	seasoning

Sauce

½ oz. (1 table-	1 cooked cabbage
spoon) butter	2 tablespoons
½ oz. (1 table-	water
spoon) flour	2 tablespoons
¼ pint (½ cup)	tomato purée
liquid from	seasoning
frankfurters	

Cut the tops off the peppers, remove core and seeds. Cook in hot butter for about 7 minutes, drain and keep hot. Peel and chop onion, chop frankfurters, chop unpeeled apple. Add remaining butter to that left in the pan, add onion, frankfurters and apple and fry until tender. Season. Fill the peppers and keep hot.

For the sauce—melt the butter, stir in the flour and cook for a few minutes. Add the liquid from the can of frankfurters gradually, stir until boiling. Add the tomato purée and cook until thickened. Season well. Arrange the cooked cabbage round the peppers and pour the sauce over.

Potatoes

They are eaten boiled, baked, roasted and fried—there are a hundred different methods of cooking them.

New Potatoes Scrub well before cooking. Cook in boiling salted water to which a sprig of mint or chopped parsley has been added until tender, 15 minutes or a little longer, depending on size. (Don't add too much mint, this darkens the potatoes). Drain, peel potatoes, return to pan, toss in butter, sprinkle with a little finely chopped mint. Or, as the skins on new potatoes are very thin, some cooks prefer to serve them unpeeled; just cut them in half for serving, top with a little butter and mint.

Baked Potatoes Choose potatoes of uniform size so they will finish cooking at the same time; scrub skins well, prick several times with a fine-tined fork. Rub over well with oil (this will ensure a crisp skin), sprinkle with salt. Bake in moderately hot oven, Mark 5, 375°F., 1¼ to 1½ hours, depending on size of potatoes; the skins should be crisply brown.

Remove from oven, make 2 cuts in top of each potato, forming a cross. Press sides of each potato so it opens out. Top each with knob of butter and sprinkling of salt and freshly ground pepper.

If desired, add sprinkling of chopped chives, parsley or crumbled bacon, spoonful of thick sour cream or sprinkling of grated Parmesan cheese.

Alternatively (and this is a delicious course at a dinner party) scoop out inside of cooked potato carefully, mash well, mix with some cooked cod's roe and enough sour cream to give a firm but rather creamy consistency. Spoon back into potato jacket.

Pommes Dauphinoise

2 lb. potatoes	1 cut clove garlic
salt, pepper	1 egg
nutmeg	4 tablespoons
½ pint (1 cup)	grated Gruyère
milk	cheese
few onion slices	butter

Peel potatoes, slice thinly. Arrange in ovenproof casserole, sprinkle with salt, pepper, grated nutmeg. Heat milk with onion slices and garlic, strain, combine with beaten egg; pour over potatoes. Sprinkle with

cheese, dot with butter. Bake in moderate oven, Mark 4, 350°F., 45 to 50 minutes, or until potatoes are soft when tested with skewer.
Serves 4 to 6.

Paprika Potatoes

2 lb. potatoes	¼ pint (½ cup)
3 oz. (⅜ cup) lard or butter	sour cream
	2 tablespoons
3 chives	milk
salt, pepper	1½ teaspoons paprika

Peel and wash potatoes, cut into 1 in. cubes. Heat lard in large frying pan, add potatoes; cover and cook over low heat, stirring occasionally, until potatoes are tender and lightly golden brown. Add chopped chives, cook few minutes longer; season with salt and pepper. Mix together sour cream, milk and paprika, add to potatoes. Heat slowly over low heat (do not boil). Serve immediately.
Serves 4.

Potato Scallops

1 lb. potatoes	1 egg
boiling water	1 tablespoon oil
½ lb. (2 cups) plain flour	about ½ pint (1 cup) hot water
¼ teaspoon salt	

Peel potatoes, wash well. Cut into slices ¼ in. thick. Place in heatproof basin, cover with boiling water, let stand 1 hour.
Meanwhile, prepare batter. Sift flour and salt into basin. Make a well in centre, add beaten egg and oil; beat in enough hot water to make a fairly thick coating batter. Beat until smooth.
Drain potatoes, pat dry. Coat each slice well with batter, deep-fry in hot oil, a few at a time, until batter is golden brown and crisp. Drain on kitchen paper, sprinkle with salt.

Potatoes Anna

2 lb. potatoes	salt, pepper
water	parsley
approx. 4 oz. (½ cup or 1 stick) butter	

Peel potatoes, slice as thinly as possible. Drop them into iced water, let them stand 30 minutes. Drain, dry well. Take round mould or small baking dish, butter generously. Place layer of potatoes in base, spread over some softened butter. Repeat layers of potatoes and butter, ending with butter; sprinkle each layer with salt and pepper. Bake in hot oven, Mark 7, 425°F., 45 to 55 minutes, or until potatoes are soft when tested with thin skewer. To serve, invert on to serving dish. Garnish with parsley.
Serves 4.

Duchesse Potatoes

3 lb. potatoes	2 oz. (¼ cup)
salt, pepper, nutmeg	butter
	melted butter
4 egg-yolks	

Peel potatoes, boil in salted water until tender, then drain well, mash or push through strainer. Place in bowl, season with salt, pepper and nutmeg; add yolks and softened butter, work to smooth paste. Place in piping bag with star tube, pipe small pyramids on greased baking sheets. Brush with little melted butter. Bake in hot oven, Mark 7, 425°F., until tipped with brown.

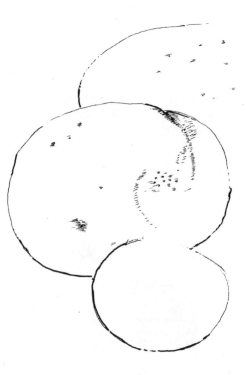

Potatoes

Pumpkin and Squash

Of the same family and sometimes classed as fruit. Both are popular in America and Australia and are becoming popular in Britain. Pumpkin is good made into soup and for the American favourite—pumpkin pie. As a vegetable, it can be cooked and mashed like turnips. See Marrow (page 109).

Spinach

Should be thoroughly washed before cooking and every speck of dirt removed. Can be cooked in either of the following ways:
Wash spinach thoroughly. One popular variety of spinach has rather coarse white stems; these should be cut out before cooking. Place spinach in saucepan with only the water clinging to leaves. Cover tightly, cook until tender. Drain, pressing out all moisture, return to pan with salt, pepper and squeeze of lemon juice. Shake over heat 2 or 3 minutes before serving.

Spinach and Mushroom Cream

2 lb. spinach	nutmeg
¼ lb. mushrooms	salt, pepper
1 oz. (2 table-spoons) butter	1 hard boiled egg
¼ pint (½ cup) white sauce (see page 146)	

Prepare and cook spinach as usual. Drain well, chop finely and keep hot.

Sauté the chopped mushrooms in butter, add them to the white sauce together with grated nutmeg and seasoning.

Reserve the yolk of the hard boiled egg for garnish, chop the white and add to the sauce. Arrange the spinach in a border on a hot dish. Reheat the sauce and pour in the centre. Garnish with sieved egg yolk.

Serves 4.

Spinach à la Creme

2½ lb. spinach	lemon juice
2 oz. butter	freshly ground pepper
2 tablespoons flour	fried croutons (see page 14)
1½ gills milk	1 to 2 table-spoons hot medium cream
salt, pepper	
sugar, nutmeg	

Cook the spinach and drain well. Put into a pan over gentle heat to dry off, add half the butter and stir in the flour. Cook for a few minutes then add the milk, salt, pepper and a pinch of sugar. Bring to boiling point, cover and simmer over low heat for about 15 minutes. Add a pinch of nutmeg and adjust the seasoning. Just before serving add the remaining butter in small pieces, a squeeze of lemon juice and a dash of pepper. Serve with croutons and if liked, add 1 to 2 spoonfuls of hot cream.

Serves 4.

Sweet Potato

This is an edible tuber resembling an ordinary potato in appearance but with a sweetish flavour. Sweet potatoes are also known as yams. They can be boiled or baked, and are delicious if simply scrubbed and baked in their jackets; this will take 1 to 1½ hours, depending on size. When cooked, serve them split open and topped with a pat of butter.

They can also be peeled, quartered, or halved and cooked with roast meat in the same way as ordinary potatoes.

Peel them just before cooking; if left to stand after peeling, their colour rapidly darkens.

Tomatoes

Should be washed thoroughly before use. Some recipes require peeled tomatoes. This is quite simple; place tomatoes in bowl, pour over sufficient boiling water to cover. Leave a moment, then drain and plunge into cold water. Skins will slip off easily.

Other recipes require juices and seeds to be discarded and only firm flesh of tomato used. To remove juices and seeds, halve tomatoes, squeeze out seeds and juice into basin. Strain juice, if desired, and use in place of some of liquid in recipe.

Baked Tomatoes

6 large tomatoes	2 to 3 table-spoons chopped parsley
salt, pepper	
1 teaspoon sugar	
1 onion	soft white breadcrumbs
	1 oz. (2 table-spoons) butter

Peel tomatoes, cut into firm slices. Arrange layer of tomatoes in greased ovenproof dish. Sprinkle with salt, pepper, sugar, finely chopped or grated onion and parsley. Top with another layer of tomatoes, sprinkle over any remaining onion, parsley, etc. Top with layer of breadcrumbs, dot with butter. Bake in moderately hot oven, Mark 5, 375°F., about 20 minutes. Delicious with roast meats.

Serves 4 to 6.

Tomato Concassé

1 lb. tomatoes	butter
2 shallots or 1 small onion	1 clove garlic crushed
	salt, pepper

Plunge tomatoes into boiling water, then into cold water. Skin, seed and chop. Chop shallots or onion finely. Sauté shallots in little hot butter until softened, but not browned. Add tomatoes, garlic, salt and pepper to taste. Simmer gently, pressing mixture with fork occasionally.

Serve over chops, steaks or sausages; delicious as filling for omelets.

Turnips

Young, small turnips can be washed, peeled and cooked whole in boiling salted water to cover until soft (about 30 minutes). Bigger turnips can be cut into large dice or halved. Drain them well, toss in a little butter and serve sprinkled with chopped parsley.
Swede Turnips Peel, dice or cut into quarters and cook as above. They are best served mashed with salt, pepper and a little butter.

Stuffed Turnips

4 medium sized turnips	salt, pepper
1 tablespoon chopped parsley	½ lb. (2 cups) cooked peas
	2 oz. (¼ cup) butter

Peel the turnips and cook whole in boiling water until tender. Drain and scoop out the centres, leaving the cases about ½ in. thick. Heat the parsley, seasoning, peas and butter and fill the turnip cases.
Serves 4.

Zucchini or Courgettes

Small Italian marrows; French name is courgettes. Delicately and delightfully flavoured. To prepare, trim stems. Young, small zucchini can be cooked whole and unpeeled in boiling salted water until just tender. Serve with butter. Or, when cooked, slice and mix with some finely chopped mushrooms which have been sautéed until tender in a little butter.

Zucchini with Mushrooms

1 lb. zucchini	2 oz. (¼ cup) butter
1 clove garlic	salt, pepper
4 oz. mushrooms	2 tablespoons chopped parsley
1 large onion	

Cut zucchini diagonally into 1 in. slices, crush garlic, slice mushrooms, chop onion. Melt butter in large frying pan, add vegetables, sauté until golden brown and tender. Season with salt and pepper. Sprinkle with chopped parsley and serve.

Herbs and Flavourings for Vegetables

Aubergine	Basil, dill, garlic, marjoram, oregano, rosemary.
Beetroot	Celery or caraway seeds, dill, mustard, tarragon, thyme.
Broccoli	Basil, garlic, lemon, mustard, nutmeg, onion, oregano.
Brussels Sprouts	Basil, celery seed, curry powder, lemon, mustard, oregano.
Cabbage	Dill, onion, nutmeg, chives, parsley, tarragon.
Carrots	Bayleaf, basil, curry powder, garlic, ginger, mint, nutmeg, onion, parsley, rosemary, thyme.
Cauliflower	Basil, caraway seed, chives, mace, lemon, oregano, parsley, rosemary.
Celery	Basil, onion, parsley, tarragon.
Green Beans	Basil, chilli powder, garlic, nutmeg, onion, tarragon, thyme.
Mushrooms	Basil, chives, garlic, parsley.
Peas	Chives, mint, garlic, onion.
Peppers	Basil, garlic, onion, oregano.
Spinach	Basil, garlic, lemon, nutmeg, onion, rosemary.
Tomatoes	Celery salt, chives, garlic, onion, oregano, parsley, tarragon, basil.

Salads

Salads can be a light, colourful accompaniment to a main meal, or substantial enough to be a main meal in themselves. All types of salad recipes are given here—old favourites, such as coleslaw, rice, potato— as well as wonderful new salads. And we've given a selection of good-tasting salad dressings.

Classic Green Salad

1 lettuce
salt, pepper

French dressing (see page 121)

Wash lettuce, dry thoroughly; place in plastic bag in refrigerator to crisp. At serving time, tear into small pieces; place in salad bowl. Sprinkle with salt and pepper; pour over sufficient dressing to moisten, then toss lightly.

There should be just enough dressing to lightly coat each leaf.

The classic green salad uses lettuce only; however, other greens—endive, young spinach, etc.— can be added for contrasting colours of green.

Prawn and Rice Salad

2 medium onions
3 oz. ($\frac{3}{8}$ cup) butter
4 oz. mushrooms
$\frac{1}{2}$ lb. ($2\frac{2}{3}$ cups) cooked long grain rice
3 oz. ($\frac{3}{4}$ cup) cooked peas
1 green pepper

2 tablespoons chopped parsley
4 oz. ham
1 lb. or 1 pint prawns (shrimps)
French dressing (see page 121)
shredded lettuce
sliced tomatoes and cucumber

Sauté finely chopped onions in 1 oz. (2 tablespoons) heated butter until lightly browned; remove from pan. Add remaining butter to pan. Fry sliced mushrooms in this until tender (about 3 minutes). Spoon onion and mushroom mixture into rice, adding pan juices as well. Mix in peas, chopped green pepper, parsley, chopped ham and shelled prawns (shrimps) (reserving about 1 dozen with tails still on for garnishing).

Mix together lightly, pour over enough French dressing to moisten; mix lightly. Arrange rice in ring on large platter. Surround with shredded lettuce and alternate slices of tomato and cucumber. Fill centre of ring with shredded lettuce, arrange reserved prawns in crown shape on top of rice ring.

Serves 4 to 6.

Creamy Potato Salad

2 lb. potatoes
$\frac{1}{4}$ pint ($\frac{1}{2}$ cup) French dressing (see page 121)
3 to 4 sticks sliced celery
few chopped spring onions

$\frac{1}{4}$ pint ($\frac{1}{2}$ cup) mayonnaise (see page 121)
4 tablespoons sour cream
1$\frac{1}{2}$ teaspoons prepared mustard
salt
$\frac{1}{4}$ small cucumber, diced

If using old potatoes, peel and cook until tender but still firm; if new potatoes, cook in their jackets and peel when cooked. Slice potatoes or cut into large dice while still warm. Put into bowl, pour over the French dressing, toss gently to coat potato pieces. Let stand 1 hour. Add celery and spring onions. Combine mayonnaise, sour cream and mustard, blend well; mix into potato, together with salt to taste; refrigerate. Just before serving mix in the cucumber.

Serves 4 to 6.

Indian Curry Salad

$\frac{1}{4}$ pint ($\frac{1}{2}$ cup) French dressing (see page 121)
$\frac{1}{2}$ teaspoon Worcestershire sauce
salt, pepper
1$\frac{1}{2}$ teaspoons curry powder

$\frac{1}{2}$ small cauliflower
$\frac{1}{4}$ lb. ($\frac{2}{3}$ cup) long grain rice, cooked
2 lb. or 2 pints prawns (shrimps)
1 green pepper
$\frac{1}{2}$ head celery, sliced
2 small onions, finely sliced

In basin combine French dressing, Worcestershire sauce, salt, pepper and curry powder. Cut cauliflower into small flowerets, mix with cooked, drained rice; pour the combined dressing over and marinate 1$\frac{1}{2}$ hours, stirring occasionally. Shell prawns, cut into $\frac{1}{2}$ in. pieces. Cut green pepper into thin 2 in. strips. Stir remaining vegetables and prawns into rice. Refrigerate until required.

Serves 6 to 8.

Delicious Garden Salad

½ small cauliflower
1 large onion
1 small cucumber
1 large green pepper
1 large red pepper
½ lb. young spinach

1 teaspoon paprika
2 teaspoons sugar
1 teaspoon thyme
¼ pint (½ cup) French
    dressing (see
    page 121)
salt, pepper

Soak cauliflower in salted water 30 minutes, wash and drain, trim off leaves and stems leaving small flowerets. Dice onion and unpeeled cucumber; cut green and red peppers into thin strips. Wash and dry spinach, remove stalks, roughly chop leaves. Combine prepared vegetables with remaining ingredients, toss lightly with fork. Refrigerate well before serving.
Serves 6 to 8.

Haricot Bean Salad

1 lb. haricot beans
boiling salted water
2 oz. (⅓ cup) green
    olives
1 clove garlic,
    crushed

¼ pint (½ cup) French
    dressing (see
    page 121)
1 oz. (½ cup) chopped
    parsley
salt, pepper
2 oz. (⅓ cup) black
    olives

Cover beans well with water, allow to stand overnight. Drain, add to boiling salted water, boil 1 to 1½ hours or until tender, drain well; allow to become cold. Pit and slice green olives, add to beans with garlic, dressing and parsley. Season with salt and pepper, toss lightly to combine. Garnish with black olives. Refrigerate before serving.
Serves 6.

Chicken Salad with Lychees

4 lb. cooked chicken
4 to 5 sticks chopped
    celery
1 small green pepper,
    chopped

¼ pint (½ cup) French
    dressing (see
    page 121)
salt, pepper
large can lychee nuts
salad greens

Mayonnaise Dressing

6 tablespoons mayon-
    naise (see page 121)
2 tablespoons sour
    cream
2 teaspoons curry
    powder

2 tablespoons grated
    onion
2 tablespoons chopped
    parsley

Remove meat from chicken, chop into cubes. Add celery and green pepper, season with salt and pepper. Add French dressing, toss until all ingredients are lightly coated. Refrigerate ½ hour, tossing occasionally.

Heap chicken salad on to serving platter. Drain lychees, arrange on top of salad. If desired, some canned mandarin segments can be used for garnish; slip one segment into each lychee nut. Serve with salad greens. Serve the mayonnaise dressing separately to spoon over individual servings.
Mayonnaise Dressing Blend together all ingredients. Refrigerate until well chilled.
Serves 6.

Home-Style Potato Salad

2 lb. potatoes
2 medium carrots
1 dessertspoon finely
    chopped onion
1 teaspoon finely
    chopped mint

pinch cayenne pepper
4 tablespoons mayon-
    naise (see page 121)
2 oz. (½ cup) cooked
    peas

Peel and dice potatoes and carrots. Cook in boiling salted water until tender; drain and allow to cool. In a basin combine onion, mint, cayenne and mayonnaise, mix well; fold in potatoes, carrots and cooked peas. Refrigerate before serving. Spoon servings into crisp lettuce leaves.
Serves 6.

Party Chicken Salad

¼ lb. mushrooms
¼ pint (½ cup) French
    dressing (see
    page 121)
2 small lettuce
1 cooked chicken
    (3½ lb.)

1 small can artichoke
    hearts
1 small red pepper
½ lb. (2 cups) sliced
    cooked green beans
salt, pepper
2 oz. (¼ cup) slivered
    almonds

Slice mushrooms thinly, place in shallow dish. Pour French dressing over, stand 1 hour, stirring occasionally. Wash and drain whole lettuce, discarding outer leaves. Cut each lettuce crossways into 6 wedges, arrange in base of large deep salad bowl. Discard bones and skin of chicken, chop meat roughly. Drain and lightly wash artichoke hearts, slice pepper into thin strips.

In separate basin, combine chicken meat, artichoke hearts, cooked beans, strips of pepper, mushrooms and dressing. Toss lightly, adding salt and pepper to taste. Refrigerate until ready to serve. Toast almond slivers under grill until lightly brown, remove from heat. To serve, spoon chicken mixture over lettuce in large salad bowl, toss lightly. Sprinkle over toasted almonds.
Serves 6.

Waldorf Salad

3 red skinned eating
    apples
juice of 2 lemons
6 sticks celery

2 oz. (½ cup) chopped
    walnuts
lettuce leaves
mayonnaise (see page
    121)

Core and dice unpeeled apples, sprinkle with lemon juice. Add sliced celery and walnuts. Toss together with enough mayonnaise to moisten thoroughly. Pile into salad bowl lined with lettuce leaves.
    Serves 4 to 6.

Caesar Salad

2 small lettuce
    (Romaine)
2 slices bread
1 clove garlic, crushed
1 oz. (2 tablespoons)
    butter

2 rashers bacon
chopped parsley
grated Parmesan
    cheese

Dressing

¼ pint (½ cup) French
    dressing (see
    page 121)
1 teaspoon salt

1 coddled egg
1 teaspoon prepared
    mustard

Wash lettuce well, discard tough outer leaves. Tear leaves into pieces, mix with dressing. Cut bread into ½ in. cubes. Brown cubes with garlic in hot butter. Cook chopped bacon separately until crisp. Drain on absorbent paper.
    Scatter bread croutons over salad with bacon pieces, chopped parsley and grated cheese.
Dressing To coddle egg, gently lower egg into boiling water, boil 1 minute. Remove egg from shell; combine with remaining ingredients. Blend well.
    Serves 4 to 6.

Oregano-Tomato Salad

1 lb. firm tomatoes
2 small white onions
1 teaspoon ground
    oregano
1 teaspoon sugar
1 teaspoon salt

freshly ground pepper
2 tablespoons dry white
    wine
2 tablespoons oil
chopped parsley

Wash, dry and slice tomatoes; peel and thinly slice onions. Layer tomatoes and onions in bowl. In another bowl mix together seasonings, add oil and wine; stir until well mixed. Pour over tomatoes and onions, refrigerate several hours. Serve sprinkled with chopped parsley. Garnish, if desired, with black olives.
    Serves 6.

Prawn (Shrimp) and Green Bean Salad

1 lb. green beans
salted water
2 tablespoons French
    dressing (see
    page 121)

½ lb. or ½ pint shelled
    prawns (shrimps)
little extra French
    dressing
2 hard-boiled eggs

Top, tail and string beans, cook in boiling salted water until tender. Drain, pour the 2 tablespoons French dressing over. Toss lightly, arrange on platter.
    Top with shelled prawns and sprinkle these with a little additional French dressing. Garnish with the eggs cut into quarters.
    Serves 6.

Ratatouille

3 to 4 tablespoons oil
2 large onions
2 cloves garlic
2 small eggplants
    (aubergines)
4 zucchini (courgettes)

2 green peppers
1 small head celery
1 lb. ripe tomatoes
1 teaspoon dried basil
1½ teaspoons salt
pepper

Heat oil in shallow pan, add sliced onions and crushed garlic; cook slowly until soft. Add the eggplant, cut into cubes, sliced zucchini, peppers cut into strips and sliced celery. Mix well, cook quickly 5 minutes. Add peeled, chopped tomatoes and seasonings, cover and simmer about 1 hour, stirring occasionally. Then remove cover and allow mixture to cook down until most of liquid has evaporated and mixture is thick. Serve cold.
    Serves 4 to 6.

Asparagus Rice Salad

½ lb. (1⅓ cups) long
    grain rice
boiling salted water
1 large onion
1 oz. (2 tablespoons)
    butter
7 oz. can asparagus tips

2 tablespoons chopped
    parsley
2 tablespoons French
    dressing (see
    page 121)
salt, pepper

Add rice gradually to large quantity of boiling salted water, boil rapidly 10 minutes or until tender. Drain, allow to cool. Dice onion, sauté in butter 2 to 3 minutes until tender (do not brown). Drain asparagus well, discard liquid.
    Add onion mixture, asparagus, parsley and French dressing to rice, season with salt and pepper, toss lightly.
    Serves 6.

Chicken Salad with Lychees—perfect for a summer luncheon, as shown with Oregano Tomato Salad and classic Green Salad. Flamed Caramel Pineapple—delightfully informal dessert; guests cook their own. It's a perfect dessert for a summer barbecue.

Almond Coleslaw

½ medium cabbage	¼ pint (½ cup) mayon-
2 sticks celery	naise (see page 121)
½ cucumber	1 tablespoon vinegar
½ green pepper	salt, pepper
1 large onion	1 oz. (¼ cup) toasted
	flaked almonds

Wash cabbage; discard outer leaves and hard central stalk. Shred finely. Chop celery, slice cucumber; thinly slice pepper, finely chop onion. Combine prepared vegetables in bowl.

Mix together mayonnaise and vinegar; season to taste with salt and pepper. Add mayonnaise mixture to vegetables, and mix with two forks until evenly coated. Top salad with almonds.

Serves 4 to 6

Coleslaw

½ medium cabbage	4 sticks celery
2 carrots	1 red skinned apple
3 to 4 spring onions	

Dressing

1 tablespoon lemon	good pinch cayenne
juice	½ tablespoon salt
¼ pint (½ cup) mayon-	freshly ground black
naise (see page 121)	pepper
½ teaspoon dry mustard	3 tablespoons cream

Remove stalk and shred cabbage very finely; grate carrots. Cut celery and spring onions, including green parts, into diagonal pieces. Wash, but do not peel apple, core and cut into dice. Mix together all prepared vegetables and apple and add enough dressing to give even coating. Mix well.
Dressing Place all dressing ingredients in small basin, mix well.

Serves 4 to 6.

Rice Coleslaw

½ medium cabbage	1 medium sized onion
shredded finely	10 oz. can whole kernel
6 oz. (1 cup) long grain	corn
rice	¼ pint (½ cup) French
½ small red and ½ small	dressing (see
green pepper,	page 121)
chopped	½ teaspoon dry mustard
6 to 8 sliced radishes	pinch pepper
1 teaspoon salt	1 dessertspoon sugar
	1 clove garlic, crushed

Cook rice in usual way, drain well. Place cabbage into large bowl. Add rice, red and green peppers, radishes, grated onion and drained corn. Place

remaining ingredients into screwtop jar, shake well. Pour over rice and vegetables, toss thoroughly.

Serves 6.

Smoked Oyster Salad

½ lb. (1⅓ cups) long	1 teaspoon curry
grain rice	powder
¼ pint (½ cup) French	6 chives or spring
dressing (see	onions (scallions)
page 121)	1 red or green pepper
	2 cans smoked oysters

Cook rice in usual way, drain well. Combine French dressing and curry powder in small jar, shake well.

Arrange rice in serving dish, pour dressing over; fork dressing lightly through rice. Cool.

Chop celery, chives and pepper. Add to rice with the drained smoked oysters, toss lightly.

Serves 4 to 6.

Mushroom Salad

1 lb. very fresh	chopped parsley
mushrooms	juice of ½ lemon
salt	freshly ground pepper
garlic	lettuce leaves
oil	

Wipe mushrooms, slice finely. Place little salt in bowl, rub bowl with garlic. Add mushrooms, pour over sufficient oil to moisten. Mix lightly, set aside until mushrooms have absorbed most of oil (about 5 minutes).

Sprinkle with lots of chopped parsley, add lemon juice and pepper. Taste mixture, add a little more salt, pepper, lemon juice if needed. Serve on lettuce.

Serves 4.

Egg and Bacon Salad

¼ lb. bacon	1 clove garlic, crushed
1 lettuce	3 to 4 tablespoons
2 to 3 chives or spring	French dressing (see
onions (scallions),	page 121)
chopped	2 tomatoes
3 to 4 sticks celery,	4 quartered hard boiled
diced	eggs

Cook bacon until crisp, crumble into pieces. Tear lettuce into bite-sized pieces, place in salad bowl. Add half the crumbled bacon, with chives and celery. Add garlic to French dressing, shake well, pour over salad. Toss. Garnish with tomatoes and eggs cut into wedges. Top with remaining bacon.

Serves 4.

Salad Dressings

A simple salad can become something really special when you add a well-flavoured dressing.

Mayonnaise

2 egg-yolks	1½ teaspoons vinegar
½ teaspoon salt	½ pint (1 cup) olive or
½ teaspoon dry mustard	salad oil
	½ teaspoon lemon juice

Rinse bowl with hot water; dry well. Put in egg-yolks, salt, mustard and 1 teaspoon vinegar. Beat vigorously with beater or at low speed with electric mixer; add oil, drop by drop, until a little more than a quarter of the oil has been added. Add ½ teaspoon vinegar, still beating, then very slowly pour in remainder of oil in thin stream, beating continually. When all oil has been added, add lemon juice.

Cooked mayonnaise

2 tablespoons vinegar	½ teaspoon salt
2 tablespoons water	½ to 1 teaspoon dry
2 tablespoons sugar	mustard
½ oz. (1 tablespoon)	1 beaten egg
butter	

Combine all ingredients in saucepan, stir over low heat until butter melts and mixture thickens slightly. Remove from heat, cool.

French Dressing

3 parts olive or salad	½ teaspoon salt
oil	½ teaspoon freshly
1 part white vinegar	ground pepper

Place all ingredients in screw-top jar, shake thoroughly before pouring over salad.
NOTE: Crushed garlic, dry or prepared mustard or chopped herbs can be added, if desired. The garlic, salt, pepper and mustard are first mixed with the oil, then the vinegar is added. Herbs are added last.

The above are the classic proportions for French dressing. However, equal parts of oil and vinegar can be used, if you like a less oily dressing.

Russian Dressing (1)

½ pint (1 cup) mayon-	1 to 2 teaspoons
naise	chopped chives
1½ tablespoons chilli	
sauce	

Blend chilli sauce and chives into mayonnaise; a little chopped red pepper or canned pimento can also be added. Use with egg or vegetable salads or with fish.
NOTE: Strength of chilli sauce varies greatly. With a mild, American chilli sauce, the above quantity is correct. If using a hot chilli sauce, add only ½ teaspoon at first; then taste, and add a little more if desired.

Russian Dressing (2)

½ pint (1 cup) mayon-	1 to 2 teaspoons bottled
naise	horseradish sauce
3 to 4 tablespoons	
finely chopped	
cooked beetroot	

Combine mayonnaise and beetroot, blend in bottled horseradish sauce or relish.

Thousand Island Dressing

½ pint (1 cup) mayon-	1 tablespoon finely
naise	chopped green olives
1 tablespoon chilli	1 dessertspoon finely
sauce	chopped chives

Combine all ingredients, mix well. Good with meat or fish salads. See Russian Dressing for note on chilli sauce.

Aioli

2 egg-yolks	3 teaspoons lemon juice
2 cloves garlic	salt, pepper
½ pint (1 cup) oil	

Beat egg-yolks in bowl with crushed garlic. Add oil, drop by drop. When half the oil has been used, add half the lemon juice, then beat in remaining oil, drop by drop. Season with salt and pepper and add remaining lemon juice.

Green Goddess Dressing

1 clove garlic	2 tablespoons cream
1 oz. (½ cup) parsley	3 dessertspoons tar-
2 tablespoons chopped	ragon vinegar
chives	1 dessertspoon anchovy
½ pint (1 cup) mayon-	paste
naise	

Crush garlic; finely chop parsley. Combine all ingredients and stir until dressing is smooth. Serve with seafood salads.

International cookery

Every year more and more people spend their holidays travelling abroad and eating unfamiliar dishes. Once back home, they like to re-capture some of the enjoyment and try out for themselves some of the interesting food of other countries.

Many people too, enjoy dining in Chinese and Indian restaurants, and in this chapter—apart from popular Continental dishes we give you some very good recipes for dishes from the South Pacific, China and India.

Unusual ingredients are explained or alternatives given. Green ginger is used in some dishes and this is quite often available, but if ground ginger is substituted, use only ¼ of the amount specified.

The food of each country can be presented as a complete menu. Quantities given will serve 4 to 6. The Hawaiian menu is suggested as an outdoor party, a wider choice of dishes is given and quantities will serve 8.

Germany

German cooking varies from district to district and, as with Switzerland, the cooking in the various sections is influenced by the other countries on the borders. Recipes given here are representative of Bavaria, Southern Germany.

German food is hearty, and not highly spiced. Black and rye breads are popular; potato and cabbage are part of everyday meals. Beer, wine and Schnapps are the popular drinks. Kirsch and Kummel are famous German liqueurs.

Sauerkraut

2 15 oz. cans sauerkraut	½ teaspoon whole peppercorns
2 tablespoons oil	1 dessertspoon flour
6 oz. fat pork in one piece	1 pint (2 cups) water
1 medium onion	1 large potato

Drain sauerkraut, wash lightly under cold running water. Heat oil in large saucepan, add pork, cook few minutes on both sides. Add chopped onion; cook, covered, over low heat until soft but not brown. Lightly mix in sauerkraut, peppercorns and flour; add 1 pint (2 cups) water. Bring to boil; cover, cook for 30 minutes, stirring occasionally. Peel potato, grate finely, stir into mixture. Continue cooking, stirring occasionally, further 30 minutes, adding little more water if necessary. Remove pork; discard.

Serve sauerkraut hot or cold.

NOTE: To keep sauerkraut a good colour, place a sheet of plain white paper on top of mixture, under lid, during boiling.

Roast Pork

1 leg or loin of pork	1 large carrot
salt, pepper	approx. 1 pint (2 cups) boiling water
1 large onion	

Wipe meat with clean cloth, score skin into small squares with sharp knife (or have butcher do this for you). Sprinkle over plenty of salt and pepper. Place meat skin-side down in large, greased baking dish. Add peeled and sliced onion and carrot, carefully pour over boiling water. Bake in hot oven until meat is tender (allow approximately 30 to 35 minutes per lb.). You may need to add more boiling water during cooking. Halfway through cooking time turn meat so that skin is uppermost.

Serve with potato balls and sauerkraut.

Flamed Caramel Pineapple—delightfully informal dessert; guests cook their own. It's a perfect dessert for a summer barbecue.

Potato Balls

1 lb. potatoes	1 teaspoon salt
½ lb. (2 cups) plain flour	1 large or two small eggs

Steam potatoes in their jackets over boiling water until cooked. Cool, refrigerate overnight. Next day, peel and mash well.

Sift together flour and salt, add alternately to potato with lightly beaten egg. Knead well. Mixture should not be sticky. Roll mixture into small balls, and drop gently into large saucepan of boiling water. Boil steadily, uncovered, 15 minutes. Drain, serve immediately.

Apple Strudel

Pastry

½ lb. (2 cups) plain flour	approx. ¼ pint (½ cup) warm water
½ teaspoon salt	
2 oz. (¼ cup) butter	

Sift flour and salt into bowl, rub in softened butter. Add a little warm water gradually, kneading to soft dough. Turn out on lightly floured surface, continue kneading and adding water until mixture is smooth and shiny. This should take about 15 minutes. Hit dough a few times with heavy wooden spoon during kneading. Form dough into a ball, place in warmed bowl or saucepan. Cover and stand in warm place 1 hour.

Filling

4 or 5 cooking apples	extra sugar
4 tablespoons sugar	extra cinnamon
finely grated rind 1 small lemon	½ pint (1 cup) sour cream
2 teaspoons cinnamon	melted butter
2 oz. (⅓ cup) sultanas	icing sugar

Filling Peel, core and slice apples very thinly, stir in sugar, lemon rind and cinnamon, mix well. Place sultanas in small bowl, add enough hot water to cover, set aside.

Divide pastry into thirds; roll each piece out very thinly on floured surface. Spread ⅓ apple mixture in centre of dough, sprinkle over a little extra sugar and cinnamon. Drain sultanas, pat dry; sprinkle a few over apples. Lightly spread ⅓ of sour cream over mixture. Roll up pastry into a long shape and seal edges.

Prepare remaining two rolls in the same way. Grease a deep 8 in. round tin. Place rolls side by side in tin, curving them carefully to fit. Bake in moderately slow oven, Mark 3 or 325°F., approximately 1¾ hours. Brush a little melted butter over strudel several times during cooking.

When golden brown and crisp, remove from oven, glaze again with melted butter. Leave in tin 15 minutes before turning out on to serving plate. Sift over a little icing sugar. Serve with whipped cream.

Hawaii

Hawaiian food is very similar to that of other islands in the South Pacific. All types of fish are easily available; pork is popular—particularly for a luau, or feast, when it is cooked in a pit, under the ground. Bananas, baked, are eaten as a vegetable, in addition to sweet potatoes or yams.

Tropical Dip

¼ pint (½ cup) mayonnaise (see page 121)	1 teaspoon dry mustard
⅛ pint (2 tablespoons) whipping cream	lemon juice
1 tablespoon bottled horseradish relish	salt, pepper

Combine whipped cream, mayonnaise, horseradish relish and dry mustard; blend well. Season to taste with lemon juice, salt and pepper. Refrigerate. Place into serving bowl. Place all kinds of interesting titbits in sauce, such as shelled prawns, oysters, ripe olives, water chestnuts, raw vegetables, etc. Each guest arms himself with a cocktail stick and 'fishes' in the sauce.

Makes approx. ⅜ pint.

Avocado Chicken Salad

3 avocados	1 teaspoon paprika
3 to 4 lb. steamed chicken	½ teaspoon nutmeg
1 cucumber	1 teaspoon salt
4 sticks celery	½ teaspoon pepper
½ green pepper	¼ pint (½ cup) cream
2 oz. (¼ cup) blanched slivered almonds	2 tablespoons mayonnaise (see page 121)

Peel, stone and slice avocados. Remove chicken meat from bones. Cut meat into 1 in. cubes. Slice cucumber, celery and green pepper and layer in dish or bowl with toasted almonds, chicken and half the avocado slices.

Blend paprika, nutmeg, salt and pepper with

cream, mayonnaise and lemon juice; pour over chicken and vegetables. Decorate with remaining avocado slices, sprinkle with extra paprika.

NOTE: If preparing this dish in advance, dip avocado slices in lemon juice so they will keep their fresh colour.

Baked Honeyed Pork

1 leg pork	2 teaspoons ground
2 tablespoons grated	ginger
green ginger	2 teaspoons salt
2 tablespoons oil	3 to 4 tablespoons
	honey

Get the butcher to score the pork thoroughly. Run knife between the skin and meat to form a pocket. Using long-bladed knife, spread grated green ginger into pocket. In basin mix oil, ground ginger and salt. Place pork in baking dish, brush leg with oil and ginger mixture. Bake in moderate oven, Mark 4, 350°F., allowing 30 minutes per lb.; brush occasionally with remaining oil and ginger mixture. Fifteen minutes before the end of cooking time, brush leg completely with honey. Serve hot or cold.

Hawaiian Chicken

4 tablespoons soy sauce	4 oz. ($\frac{1}{2}$ cup or 1 stick)
$\frac{1}{4}$ pint ($\frac{1}{2}$ cup) white	butter
wine	2 onions
juice 1 lemon	flour seasoned with
1 clove garlic	salt and pepper
$\frac{1}{2}$ teaspoon curry	$\frac{3}{4}$ lb. (2 cups) rice
powder	2 large cans pineapple
$\frac{1}{2}$ teaspoon ground	slices
ginger	1 oz. (2 tablespoons)
$\frac{1}{4}$ teaspoon pepper	butter, extra
4 lb. chicken pieces	2 oz. ($\frac{1}{4}$ cup) toasted
	slivered almonds
	1 red pepper

Mix together soy sauce, half the white wine, lemon juice, crushed garlic, curry powder, ginger and pepper. Pour over chicken, marinate several hours, turning occasionally. Melt butter in frying pan, add sliced onions, cook until golden brown, remove onions. Dry chicken, coat with seasoned flour. Cook in frying pan until brown. Add onions and marinade, cover and simmer gently 45 minutes or until tender, uncovering pan for the last 15 minutes.

Meanwhile, cook and drain rice and keep hot. Cut pineapple slices in half and brown in extra butter, also fry chopped pepper until tender.

To serve, mix rice, toasted almonds and pepper. Heap on large serving platter, arrange chicken pieces and pineapple slices round edge. Add remaining white wine to pan drippings, heat well and pour over.

Flamed Caramel Pineapple

Take a ripe pineapple, cut into 4 pieces, cutting carefully through the green top. With sharp knife, slice off the hard core. Cut pineapple down into wedges, then run a knife along base of wedges, releasing them from the shell.

(If the pineapples are not too large, allow 1 pineapple for 4 persons).

Take another pineapple, cut off top about quarter-way down. Hollow out inside of pineapple to take a small metal bowl. (The hollowed-out pineapple pieces can be reserved and used to replenish the pineapple quarters as they empty.)

Place metal bowl in position. Place hollowed-out pineapple in centre of heat-proof dish (a large wooden plate is good), arrange pineapple quarters decoratively around.

Arrange small bowls of rum or brandy, brown sugar and whipped cream round dish. Have a small fork and plate for each guest.

When ready to serve the dessert, three-quarters fill metal bowl with methylated spirit and set aflame.

Guests use fork to spear a juicy piece of pineapple, dip it in the rum, roll it in brown sugar, then hold it over the flame until the sugar caramelizes —it will take about a second. Then dip in the whipped cream—and eat!

Strawberries are delicious served this way, too, but have more flavour if allowed to stand in rum 10 to 15 minutes. Serve small bowls of rum-soaked strawberries round the pineapple.

NOTE: When lit, methylated spirit will burn for some time. If necessary to use more spirit, put it in another perfectly clean bowl; do not add more spirit to that already burning; do not pour fresh spirit into a hot bowl.

Bananas with Rum

8 bananas	2 oz. ($\frac{1}{3}$ cup) dark
1 oz. (2 tablespoons)	brown sugar
butter	3 tablespoons rum
juice of 1 lemon	cream

Peel and halve the bananas and arrange in a well buttered dish. Mix the lemon juice with 2 tablespoons water and pour over the fruit. Sprinkle with the sugar.

Bake in a moderately hot oven, Mark 5, 375°F. for 20 minutes. Add the rum and cook another 2 minutes.

Serve hot with cream.

Scandinavia

The smorgasbord—or 'cold table'—is part of the hospitality of all Scandinavian countries. Norway, Denmark, Sweden, all have their own individual versions—but, basically, the cold table of each country offers a selection of hot and cold dishes, as set out below.

Scandinavian cooking is simple. Fish of all types is widely used; potatoes, beetroot, cucumber are favourite vegetables; dill is used often for seasoning.

Smorgasbord

The Smorgasbord is said to have originated long ago at Swedish country parties, to which each housewife brought the speciality of her own kitchen. All these dishes were arranged on a long table round which the guests walked, filling their plates several times.

A Smorgasbord can be as comprehensive and varied as desired, with rich and inviting delicacies; or it can be a simple, well-chosen and well-prepared selection, comprising only a few dishes.

There is a definite rule in the procedure of dishes. Fish dishes begin the meal; favourites are pickled herrings, anchovies, herring salad—with them might be served potatoes flavoured with dill. A hot, baked fish dish might also be offered.

Then come the meats; meatballs—very important to a Smorgasbord—smoked sausages, ham, roasted pork with apple sauce and prunes. And so it goes on . . . ending with cheese.

A typical Smorgasbord might comprise a wide variety of fish dishes such as herrings, sardines, anchovies; small meatballs, sliced ham, pâté and other meats; lobster or potato salad, cucumber, radishes, pickled beetroot, mushrooms; egg dishes, tiny omelets with assorted fillings; plain boiled potatoes, cheese and assorted breads with butter.

A simple Smorgasbord can be prepared by choosing a selection from any of these dishes. A whole ham, sliced, or a sliced canned ham; herrings (from the delicatessen) with pickled onion and chopped gherkin; potato salad; smoked oysters; canned salmon with white onion rings, chopped shallots and a light vinegar dressing; smoked tuna; slices of cold roast beef, pork, lamb or seasoned veal; sliced pickled beetroot; salami or other Continental sausage; canned sardines; condiments, such as chutney, etc.; smoked salmon with scrambled eggs; cheese board.

Lamb in Cabbage

3 lb. leg of lamb
½ large cabbage
1 oz. (2 tablespoons) butter
2 oz. (½ cup) flour
salt
2 teaspoons peppercorns
2 medium carrots
1½ pints (3 cups) water or stock
1 tablespoon finely chopped parsley

Trim meat, cut into large cubes; do not remove bones, these add extra flavour to the stock. Remove coarse outer leaves from cabbage. Cut cabbage into thick segments, removing centre core. Melt butter in large saucepan. Place alternate layers of meat and cabbage in pan, starting with meat and finishing with cabbage. Sprinkle flour, salt and peppercorns between each layer. Place peeled, sliced carrots on top. Pour water or stock down side of saucepan. Bring to boil, cover, reduce heat and simmer 1½ to 2 hours or until meat is tender. Shake pan occasionally; do not stir during cooking to avoid disturbing the arranged layers. Season to taste; sprinkle with chopped parsley. Serve with boiled potatoes.

NOTE: Peppercorns can be tied in muslin bag for easy removal after cooking.

Strawberry Mousse

1 lb. strawberries
1 dessertspoon water
½ oz. (2 tablespoons or 2 packets) gelatine
2 egg-whites
3 oz. (⅜ cup) castor (superfine) sugar
½ pint (1 cup) whipping cream
1 tablespoon lemon juice

Wash and hull strawberries, mash well. There should be about ½ pint purée. Add gelatine to water, stand 5 minutes, dissolve over hot water. Beat egg-whites until soft peaks form, gradually add sugar, beating until dissolved. Whip cream until soft peaks form; fold into egg-white mixture. Add strawberries, lemon juice and gelatine, fold in lightly. Pour into wetted mould, or into individual serving dishes. Refrigerate until set.

Cheeseboard has pride of place on a Smorgasbord. Offer a variety of cheeses. Shown here are, from back, Cheddar, Danish Tilsit, Edam, Blue Cheese.

China

The Oriental, it is said, 'eats with his tongue'—flavour is all-important. And Chinese food, with its subtle, well-balanced blending of flavours, has become very popular.

There are five main schools of Chinese cooking, named after the areas in which they originated. They are:

Canton Has succulent pork, chicken and duck dishes, delicious soups. Quick-frying is the favourite method of cooking; fried rice and crisp noodles are popular. Cantonese dishes, served with a variety of sauces, are delicately flavoured, not highly seasoned. Because the majority of Chinese restaurants outside China are owned or operated by Southern Chinese, Cantonese food has become better known throughout the world than the other styles of Chinese cooking.

Fukien Sucking pig is a favourite dish; soups of many varieties are served between courses. Popular Spring Roll is from this school.

Szechuen Also famous for soups. Foods, generally, are hot and highly spiced.

Shanghai Concentrates on steamed, rather than fried foods. More highly spiced than Cantonese, but less than Szechuenese.

Peking Peking-Duck is a world-renowned dish; so is Bird's-Nest Soup. Food is well spiced, of great variety.

Crab and Sweet Corn Soup

1 dessertspoon oil
¼ clove garlic
1 thin slice green ginger
6½ oz. can crab meat
1 dessertspoon dry sherry
1 small can cream-style sweet corn
1¼ pints (2½ cups) chicken stock
1 egg-white
1 tablespoon cornflour (cornstarch)
salt, pepper

Heat oil in large heavy saucepan, add crushed garlic, finely chopped ginger and crab meat which has been drained and shredded. Fry quickly 1 minute, stirring constantly. Add sherry, corn and stock. Bring to boil, reduce heat and simmer 5 minutes. Whisk egg-white lightly, stir into soup with fork. Mix cornflour (cornstarch) with a little cold water; add to soup, stirring constantly until mixture thickens. Add salt and pepper to taste. Mix well, serve immediately.

Prawn (Shrimp) Omelet

2 oz. mushrooms
oil
3 to 4 chives
2 sticks celery
1 lb. or 1 pint prawns (shrimps)
8 eggs
10 oz. can bean sprouts
salt, pepper

Sauce

1 dessertspoon cornflour (cornstarch)
2 tablespoons cold water
½ pint (1 cup) chicken stock
1 teaspoon sugar
1 tablespoon soy sauce
salt

Chop mushrooms, cook in a little hot oil until tender; drain, set aside. Chop chives and celery finely; chop shelled prawns, if large. Beat eggs lightly, as for omelet. Add prawns, chives, celery, mushrooms and drained bean sprouts. Add seasonings and mix lightly. Heat a little oil in fry-pan, pour in enough omelet mixture to make small omelets about 5 in. in diameter. (Several can cook at the same time.) When firm on one side, turn, cook other side. Stack on warm plate while cooking remainder of omelets; keep warm. To serve, stack 3 omelets on top of each other; for each serving spoon sauce over.
Sauce Blend cornflour (cornstarch) with cold water. Place remaining ingredients in small saucepan, bring to boil. Stir in blended cornflour. Cook, stirring, until sauce boils and thickens.

Chicken and Almonds

4 chicken breasts
1½ teaspoons salt
1 tablespoon cornflour (cornstarch)
1 egg-white
1½ tablespoons sherry
oil
4 oz. green beans
2 sticks celery
½ red pepper
4 oz. mushrooms
½ 10 oz. can water chestnuts
2 tablespoons chopped chives
1 oz. (2 to 3 tablespoons) toasted almonds

Sauce

½ pint (1 cup) water
1 chicken stock cube
1 tablespoon soy sauce
1 tablespoon cornflour

Bone chicken breasts, cut meat into ½ in. cubes. Combine chicken pieces, salt, cornflour, egg-white and sherry in bowl. Heat oil in fry-pan. Deep-fry chicken until just changing colour;

drain. String beans (or use quick-frozen beans). Cut beans, celery and pepper into 1 in. strips; parboil 5 minutes. Slice mushrooms. Drain water chestnuts, cut in half. Pour off excess liquid from pan and leave enough to sauté all vegetables together. Add prepared vegetables and return chicken to pan. Season to taste, heat through thoroughly. Pour sauce over chicken mixture. Arrange on warm serving dish, sprinkle with toasted almonds.

Serves 4 to 6.

Sauce Combine water, crumbled chicken stock cube, soy sauce and cornflour (cornstarch) in saucepan; blend well. Stir over low heat until sauce boils and thickens, simmer 2 minutes.

Almond Junket

1½ dessertspoons gelatine	3 oz. (⅜ cup) sugar
¼ pint (½ cup) cold water	¼ pint (½ cup) boiling water
¾ pint (1½ cups) evaporated milk	few drops almond essence

Soften gelatine in cold water, add sugar. Pour boiling water over and stir until sugar and gelatine have dissolved. Add milk and almond essence, stir well. Pour mixture into four individual serving dishes, set aside until cool, then refrigerate until firm. Top with sliced preserved ginger, with a little of the ginger syrup poured over.

Italy

Like most European countries, Italy draws heavily on the natural products of her provinces—the luscious fruits and olives, the wonderful seafood which abounds in the waters bordering her shores.

Antipasto—the equivalent of the French hors d'oeuvre—is a pleasant start to any meal and, with a bowl of soup to follow, can be a complete meal in itself. Pasta is used in many forms.

Italian wines are very cheap in their own country, and very pleasant; the Chianti is world-famous. Wine is drunk with all main meals, and the meals are usually preceded by a glass of sweet or dry vermouth or Campari, the latter, a deep red and tangy bitters, and one of the most famous Italian aperitifs.

Antipasto

8 oz. can tuna	thinly sliced ham
mayonnaise (see page 121)	black and green olives
	anchovy fillets
1 tablespoon capers	quarters of hard boiled eggs
thinly sliced celery	
sliced peeled tomatoes	canned artichoke hearts
sliced salami	

Arrange drained tuna (in one piece) in centre of large, round platter. Coat with mayonnaise, sprinkle with capers. Arrange remaining ingredients in decorative pattern round tuna.

Cannelloni

Batter

4 oz. (1 cup) plain flour	1 egg
pinch salt	½ pint (1 cup) milk

Filling

oil for frying	pinch mixed herbs
1 onion	salt, pepper
1 clove garlic	1 dessertspoon tomato paste
1 lb. minced (ground) steak	
	1 teaspoon paprika
1 tablespoon flour	
¼ pint (½ cup) red wine	

Bechamel Sauce

1 bayleaf	½ pint (1 cup) milk
parsley stalks	½ oz. (1 tablespoon) butter
1 slice onion	
4 peppercorns	1 tablespoon flour
sprig of thyme or parsley	salt, pepper

Tomato Sauce

1 dessertspoon oil	2 tablespoons tomato paste
1 onion	
1 clove garlic	salt, pepper
2 large ripe tomatoes	bayleaf

Batter Sift flour and salt into bowl. Make well in centre, add egg. Mix with wooden spoon, blending in a little of the flour from the side. When mixture begins to thicken, gradually begin to add the milk, blending thoroughly. Heat a little oil in small frying pan. Pour in enough batter to cover base. Tilt pan until batter spreads. Keep pancake as thin as possible. When cooked on one side, turn and cook the other side. Remove from pan, cook the next pancake, stacking them as you cook.

Filling Put a little oil in saucepan; when hot gently sauté chopped onion and crushed garlic. When tender add the meat, cook until brown, stirring occasionally with fork. Add the flour blended with the wine, stir well. Add remaining ingredients, simmer gently ½ to ¾ hour until liquid is absorbed.

Divide mixture between pancakes, roll up. Arrange in casserole.

Bechamel Sauce Place bayleaf, parsley stalks, onion slice, peppercorns and thyme in saucepan, add milk. Bring slowly to boiling point, remove from heat, stand 5 minutes. Melt butter in saucepan, remove from heat, add flour, stir until smooth, gradually add strained milk, stirring constantly. Return to heat, stir until sauce boils and thickens. Season to taste with salt and pepper. Pour over pancakes.

Tomato Sauce Heat oil, fry chopped onion and crushed garlic until tender but not brown. Add skinned, chopped tomatoes, tomato paste, salt, pepper and bayleaf. Simmer gently 20 minutes.

Spoon carefully over the white sauce.

If desired, sprinkle with a little grated cheese. Bake pancakes in hot oven, Mark 7, 425°F., 10 to 15 minutes.

Zabaglione

5 egg-yolks	¼ pint (½ cup) marsala
1½ oz. (3 tablespoons) sugar	

Beat egg-yolks and sugar in top of double boiler. Add the marsala, and cook, beating constantly, until thick and foamy, approximately 10 minutes. Serve warm. Sponge fingers are a good accompaniment.

India

Through the centuries, Arabia, Persia, Central Asia and Mongolia have all contributed towards the unique cuisine of India. The success of Indian cookery rests on the subtle use of a variety of spices. The art of curry-making lies not in hot spicing but in the delicacy of flavour blending.

In such a vast country, with varying climatic and agricultural conditions, it is natural to expect a great variation in curries, also. In the north, curries are mild—like those of Pakistan. The farther south you travel, the hotter the curries become. In Madras, chillies grow abundantly and are used generously; Madras curries, therefore, are much hotter than those of the north.

Rice is the traditional accompaniment to curry. A choice of side dishes or sambals can also be served; choose from coconut, plumped raisins, crumbled bacon, chopped hard-boiled eggs, cucumber in yoghurt, wedges of lemon, bananas dipped in lemon juice, chopped dried apricots, peanuts.

Beef Vindaloo

2 large onions	salt
3 cloves garlic	2 lb. topside or round of beef
2 red chillies or ¼ teaspoon cayenne pepper	1 dessertspoon butter
1 teaspoon ground ginger	1 teaspoon turmeric
2 tablespoons curry powder	¼ teaspoon dry mustard
1 tablespoon vinegar	3 cardamom seeds (crushed)
	1 teaspoon chopped mint

Place 1 chopped onion, 1 crushed clove garlic, 1 finely chopped chilli, ginger, 1 tablespoon curry powder, vinegar and salt into a bowl. Mix well together. Cut beef into 1 in. cubes, add to mixture in bowl. Mix thoroughly and allow to stand at least 3 hours.

Melt butter in frying pan and fry the remaining chopped onion, crushed garlic and chopped chilli until light brown. Add turmeric, remaining curry powder, mustard, cardamom and meat mixture. Cook 5 minutes, reduce heat to simmer, add sufficient hot water just to cover the meat; add salt to taste. Cook gently, covered, until meat is tender,

approximately 1 hour 20 minutes; add a little extra water, if necessary, during cooking time. Lastly add mint. Serve with hot rice.

Chicken Tandoori

1 chicken	2 oz. (¼ cup) butter

Marinade

1 clove garlic	1 teaspoon garam masala (see page 145)
½ pint (1 cup) yoghurt	
1 teaspoon ground ginger	1 teaspoon salt

Crush garlic and mix into the yoghurt with spices and salt. Joint chicken and marinate in yoghurt mixture for 6 hours or overnight. Melt butter in baking dish, add chicken pieces. Bake uncovered in moderate oven, Mark 4, 350°F., 45 minutes to 1 hour, basting frequently.

Serve with chopped onion and lemon wedges.

Canneloni—pancakes filled with a savoury mixture, topped with sauces, baked until piping hot.

Fruit Taj

2 large oranges
2 large bananas
lemon juice
¼ pint (½ cup) softened
   vanilla ice-cream

1 egg-yolk
¼ pint (½ cup) whipped
   cream
½ to 1 tablespoon rum
1 tablespoon slivered
   dates

Peel and section oranges; arrange sections in serving bowls or glasses. Peel and slice bananas and place over oranges, sprinkle with lemon juice. Stir together softened ice-cream, beaten egg-yolk, whipped cream and rum; spoon over fruit, garnish with dates.

Indonesia

Spices are an integral part of Indonesian cookery, for these are the Spice Islands of history. Many countries have had an effect on the history of Indonesia—India, China, Arabia, Portugal, Holland; the influence of these countries is reflected in Indonesian recipes.

Sambel Oelek, mentioned in some of the recipes on this page, is obtainable in jars from most large food stores; it is made up of finely minced red chillies, seasoned with salt. If unobtainable, use same amount of finely crushed chillies; season well with salt.

See page 94 for Nasi Goreng—Indonesia's famous version of Fried Rice.

Saté Kambing

Cut 1½ lb. lean lamb into ¾ in. cubes, thread on to thin bamboo skewers. Place 4 or 6 cubes on each skewer. There should be enough meat cubes for about 15 skewers. Grill until meat is done, turning several times. Serve hot with either of these Saté sauces.

Soy Sauce

4 tablespoons soy
   sauce
3 chives or spring
   onions (scallions)

1 teaspoon sambal
   oelek
2 tablespoons lemon
   juice

Slice chives thinly crosswise; combine with remaining ingredients in oblong dish. This shape makes it easy to dip the saté sticks.

Peanut Sauce

1 small onion
2 cloves garlic
1 tablespoon butter
1 teaspoon sambal
   oelek
½ pint (1 cup) water

2 oz. (¼ cup) peanut
1½ tablespoons soy
   sauce
½ teaspoon sugar
1 tablespoon lemon
   juice

Thinly slice onion. Sauté onion and garlic in butter until transparent, add sambal oelek. Reduce heat, stir well. Add water, then peanut butter, bring slowly to boil. Continue stirring until mixture becomes smooth. Season with soy sauce, sugar and lemon. Taste; add a little salt if necessary.

Serundeng

½ lb. (1⅛ cups) raw
   peanuts
½ pint (1 cup) oil
1 beef stock cube
4 tablespoons hot
   water
½ lb. (1⅓ cups) desic-
   cated coconut

1 teaspoon sugar
1 medium onion
2 cloves garlic
2 teaspoons coriander
1 bayleaf
salt, pepper

Wash and dry peanuts, deep-fry in hot oil until crisp. Dissolve beef stock cube in hot water, pour over coconut, season with sugar. Add grated onion, grated garlic, coriander and bayleaf, all of which have been sautéed in little hot butter. Add salt and pepper to taste. Mix thoroughly by hand so all spices blend with the coconut.

Put into small baking dish or ovenproof dish. Pour over the oil. Cook in moderately slow oven, Mark 3, 325°F., 30 minutes, stirring occasionally to keep from burning. Reduce heat to low, cook until coconut is golden brown. Remove from oven, stir in peanuts. Put in colander to drain and cool.

NOTE: Serundeng will keep in airtight jar about 2 weeks. It is very tasty if sprinkled on individual helpings of vegetables.

Gado-Gado

3 medium potatoes
½ lb. green beans
2 to 3 carrots
¼ cabbage
1 lettuce
2 medium tomatoes

3 to 4 hard boiled eggs
1 tablespoon crisp fried
   onion flakes
peanut sauce (see
   page 132)

Boil potatoes in their jackets; skin and dice. Cut beans into thin, diagonal slices; boil and drain. Scrape carrots, cut into matchstick-sized strips; boil and drain. Shred cabbage very finely. Put into boiling water, bring to boil again (don't over-cook); drain. Arrange vegetables on a platter as follows:

First, the washed, well-crisped lettuce, then potatoes, cabbage, beans, carrots, sliced or quartered tomatoes, sliced or quartered eggs. This gives a nice contrast of colours.

Pour over the Peanut Sauce just before serving; sprinkle with onion flakes, see Goreng Bawang.

This goes very well with a grill, or serve it as a barbecue salad. For a quick, tasty salad, pour the sauce over hard boiled eggs, lettuce and tomatoes.

The peanut sauce is nice to serve hot in winter and at room temperature in summer.

Goreng Bawang

These fried onion flakes are widely used as a garnish for Indonesian dishes. They also give an interesting flavour when sprinkled over European-style soups just before serving; nice with chicken, beef or vegetable soups.

Skin, wash and slice onions; cut them into very thin and even slices. Heat a little oil in fry-pan fry the onions, stirring evenly. When partly cooked, reduce heat to very low; turn onions frequently so they become evenly browned without burning. If it seems they might burn, remove from heat before they are fully browned and keep stirring. The heat of the oil should be sufficient to complete the cooking.

When cooked pour onions and oil quickly into strainer over basin. This is to avoid some of the flakes becoming over-brown and ensures the onion flakes will be left crisp and dry.

Sambal Goreng Udang

1 to 2 tablespoons
   butter
1 onion, chopped
2 cloves garlic, crushed
2 pints prawns
   (shrimps)
2 teaspoons sambal
   oelek (or 4 or 5
   chillies)

3 or 4 pieces green
   ginger, about 1 in.
   thick
1 lb. green beans
1 pint (2 cups)
   coconut milk (see
   page 58)
1 firm tomato
3 to 4 spring onions
   (scallions)

Heat butter, fry onion and garlic until they change colour. Add shelled, deveined prawns (shrimps), sambal oelek, ginger and beans, which have been sliced diagonally, thinly and evenly. Cook about 3 minutes; add coconut milk. Stir continually to avoid curdling; bring to boil. Add peeled, chopped tomato, spring onions (scallions) cut into 2 in. length, including green tops. Stir constantly. When beans are tender, remove from heat.

This dish goes very well with Serundeng.

Telur Balado

1 medium onion
4 to 5 tablespoons oil
2 tablespoons sambal
   oelek

2 tomatoes
1 chicken stock cube
salt to taste
6 hard boiled eggs

Fry thinly sliced onion in hot oil. When onion changes colour, reduce heat to low. Add sambal oelek, peeled, chopped tomatoes, crumbled chicken cube, salt to taste; simmer 5 minutes, stirring continuously. Add shelled eggs, simmer another 5 minutes. Turn eggs occasionally. Remove pan from heat.

Cut the eggs neatly in halves with sharp knife, arrange on platter, pour over the chilli sauce.

Barbecues

It is pleasant to be able to take advantage of a good fine day and cook and eat out of doors. The recipes below are simple and do not require lengthy preparation.

Barbecued Sausage

2 lb. pork sausages	1 dessertspoon light
butter	brown sugar
3 to 4 sticks chopped	1 dessertspoon
celery	prepared mustard
2 large onions	1 teaspoon
3 to 4 tablespoons	Worcestershire sauce
vinegar	
1½ gills (⅔ cup) tomato	
sauce	
3 to 4 tablespoons	
water	

Cook sausages until well browned, pricking several times. (This can be done in pan over barbecue.) Melt a little butter in saucepan, add celery and chopped onions, sauté until tender. Add remaining ingredients, stir well; add sausages. Simmer 10 to 15 minutes.

Serves 4 to 6.

NOTE: To hasten cooking time, put sausages into saucepan of cold water, bring slowly to boil, simmer 5 minutes; drain. This can be done some hours beforehand. Then brown or barbecue, and add to sauce, as above.

Barbecued Corn

Remove husk and silk from corn. Spread cobs generously with softened butter, season well with salt and pepper. Wrap each cob in double thickness of aluminium foil, twisting or folding ends to make a seal. Place on grill of barbecue over hot coals. Cook, turning often, 15 to 20 minutes, depending on heat of fire. Or cobs can be boiled for 10 minutes, removed from water, and brushed generously with melted butter, then barbecued on grill over hot coals for 10 minutes, brushing occasionally with melted butter.

NOTE: Quick-frozen corn can be used in either of the above ways, too; because it has gone through preliminary processing, cooking time is much shorter. Specific cooking times are given on packet.

Barbecued Chicken

1 small chicken	salt, pepper
oil	

NOTE: This quantity makes 2 servings.

Split chicken in half lengthwise. Break drumstick, wing joints and thigh so chicken stays flat during cooking. Brush joints with oil and season well with salt and pepper. Place on grill with bone side nearest fire. When one side is well browned, turn and brown skin side, brushing with oil.

Salad Kebabs

8 oz. processed cheese	lettuce
4 oz. grapes or pitted	1 small cucumber
black olives	French dressing (see
1 bunch radishes	page 121)
2 slices pineapple	

Cut cheese into 1 in. cubes. Wash grapes and radishes, and cut pineapple into pieces. Wash lettuce and place in plastic container in refrigerator until crisp: tear into neat pieces. Cut thick slices of cucumber in half. Thread pieces of cheese alternately with the other ingredients on to individual skewers with lettuce between. Dip each skewer into dressing before serving or serve dressing separately.

Makes 4 to 6.

Foil Baked Potatoes

potatoes	salt
oil	

Scrub potatoes well, dry. Brush generously with oil, sprinkle with salt; wrap in foil. Roast in the coals about 1 hour. Or place on barbecue grill; allow about 1¼ hours for cooking, turning frequently. Split open, top with butter or sour cream.

Well-chilled melon slices make a wonderful dessert at the barbecue.

Seekh Kabab

2 lb. lean minced (ground) lamb or beef
1 small onion
2 tablespoons finely chopped spinach
pinch chilli powder
½ teaspoon salt
½ teaspoon cardamom
½ teaspoon cinnamon
½ teaspoon ground cloves

Pound the meat well in a basin and mix it thoroughly with grated onion, spinach, chilli powder and spices. Let stand for 10 minutes. Then lightly grease skewers and form meat firmly around skewers in 3½ in. long kebabs. Cook over the barbecue until brown, turning occasionally.
Serves 4 to 6.

Hamburgers

3 lb. minced (ground) steak
1 oz. (½ cup) chopped parsley
1 tablespoon Worcestershire sauce
1 teaspoon allspice
1 small onion, finely chopped
salt, pepper

Blend all ingredients together as lightly as possible. Form into flat cakes. The less handling the uncooked mixture receives, the more tender the hamburgers will be. Grill slowly, allowing 5 to 10 minutes for each side.
Makes approx. 1 dozen large hamburgers.

Red Cabbage Salad

½ pint (1 cup) white vinegar
3 oz. (⅜ cup) sugar
1 clove garlic
2 bayleaves
1 tablespoon salt
12 peppercorns
1 small red cabbage
2 red apples

Place vinegar, sugar, crushed garlic, bayleaves, salt and peppercorns into saucepan, slowly bring to boil, simmer 5 minutes. In bowl, mix together finely shredded cabbage and unpeeled, grated apples, strain over hot liquid; stir, refrigerate. Can be bottled in sterilised jars and kept 1 to 2 weeks in refrigerator.

Parsley Salad

1 very big bunch parsley
4 spring onions (scallions)
1 lb. tomatoes
leaves from 5 or 6 mint sprigs
1 cucumber
½ lb. bourghol (cracked wheat)
juice 6 large lemons
1½ gills (⅔ cup) oil
pinch chilli powder
salt

Wash parsley, spring onions, tomatoes and mint; dry. Chop parsley, spring onions (including green tops) and mint very finely. Peel and chop tomatoes and cucumber very finely. Combine prepared vegetables, bourghol, lemon juice, oil, chilli powder and salt in bowl; mix well.

Serve garnished with slices of lemon, cucumber and tomato. A bowl of crisp lettuce leaves is the correct accompaniment to this salad. Some of the salad is spooned into the centre of lettuce leaf, which is rolled round filling and eaten in this way. The crispness of the lettuce makes a good contrast with the flavour of this wonderful salad.
NOTE: Cracked wheat is available at some health-food shops, or at Continental food stores or delicatessens.

Barbecued Fish

1 small whole fish per person (mullet, trout, herring)
salt, pepper
butter
lemon juice

Mullet, barbecued this way, is delicious. Clean and scale fish; if using mullet, make sure all black lining of fish is removed. Sprinkle inside of fish with salt and pepper and squeeze of lemon juice. Arrange each fish on square of well-greased aluminium foil, sprinkle top of fish with salt and pepper, add small knob of butter. Wrap fish neatly and securely in foil. Place on barbecue; cook, turning occasionally, approximately 20 minutes.
Serve in the foil. Serve with chopped parsley and lemon wedges.

Barbecue Sauce

1 tablespoon oil
1 onion
¼ pint (½ cup) tomato purée
1½ gills (⅔ cup) water
2 tablespoons vinegar
1 tablespoon Worcestershire sauce
1 teaspoon salt
1 teaspoon paprika
¼ teaspoon black pepper
1 teaspoon curry powder
1 tablespoon brown sugar

Heat oil in saucepan, add finely chopped onion and cook until brown. Add remaining ingredients and simmer, stirring for 5 minutes. Strain through fine strainer. Serve with chops, steaks or sausages.

Makes approx. ¾ pint.

Garlic Bread

1 long loaf crusty French bread
4 oz. (½ cup or 1 stick) butter
salt, pepper
2 cloves garlic

Slice loaf, cutting just to bottom crust but not right through. Melt butter and add salt, pepper and crushed garlic. Fan slices of bread apart, and pour a little garlic butter between each slice. Brush top with any remaining butter. Wrap in aluminium foil, heat on barbecue.

Or salt, pepper and garlic can be blended into softened butter and spread on the cut slices. Spread any remaining butter over top of loaf before wrapping in foil.

NOTE: If desired, some chopped parsley and chopped chives, can be added to softened butter and crushed garlic, then spread on both sides of each slice.

Cabbage Relish

1 small cabbage
3 carrots
1 lb. white onions
4 green peppers
1 to 2 tablespoons salt
1 lb. (2 cups) sugar
1½ dessertspoons mustard seeds
pinch cayenne pepper
2 pints (4 cups) white vinegar
1½ dessertspoons celery seeds
bayleaves

Wash cabbage and shred finely; slice carrots thinly; chop onion and peppers into small dice. Place all vegetables into large earthenware bowl, sprinkle salt over, mix well. Cover, stand overnight.

Next day, drain vegetables well, discard liquid. Pack vegetables firmly into hot, sterilised jars, placing a bayleaf in each jar. Combine all remaining ingredients in saucepan, stir over heat until sugar dissolves. Bring to boil, reduce heat, simmer 5 minutes. Cover vegetables with hot vinegar. Seal when cold.

Makes approx. 6 pints.

Delicious with any hot or cold meats served at the barbecue.

Barbecued Mushrooms and Bacon

chicken livers
mushrooms
bacon rashers

Wash, trim and dry chicken livers; cut in half. Cut mushrooms in half or leave button mushrooms whole. Cut bacon rashers into three if large, or two pieces if small. Roll half a mushroom and half a chicken liver into each piece of bacon. Thread bacon rolls on to skewers. Place on barbecue until bacon is crisp, turning occasionally.

Grilled Pineapple

1 large ripe pineapple
melted butter

Cut unpeeled pineapple into 6 or 8 wedges. Remove core from each wedge. Brush generously with melted butter, grill on barbecue until lightly browned. Serve as is, warm, with cream. The skin will come away easily as the slices are eaten.

Melons

On a hot day, there's nothing nicer to serve for a barbecue dessert than a slice of well-chilled melon. Or, for a more formal type of dessert, melons can be cut into balls or dice and refrigerated. At serving time, spoon into individual glasses or serving dishes, spoon over a little well-chilled sweet white wine.

A ripe melon can be made into a basket to hold fresh fruit salad. Choose a large melon, cut 2 sections from the upper half to leave an arched piece resembling handle of a basket. Carefully cut away melon flesh from under handle and from inside of basket; cut into cubes, drain, removing seeds, then refrigerate. Pile the melon back into the shell, together with any other fresh fruit, cut to similar size. Sprinkle with sugar, a little lemon juice and, if desired, some sweet white wine. Decorate basket with grape or other leaves.

Barbecued Bananas

Choose firm, ripe bananas. Place on barbecue, cook until skins turn black, turning occasionally. Remove from heat with tongs, peel back top layer of skin. If serving as an accompaniment to savoury dishes, season with salt and pepper; if serving as a dessert, sprinkle with equal amounts of cinnamon and sugar, serve with whipped cream.

A dictionary of
Herbs and Spices

The correct use of herbs, spices and aromatic seeds gives flavour and appetizing fragrance to even the most simple foods. The herbs and spices listed here are those most commonly used in cookery; many are easy to grow in the home garden.

Herbs

Fresh herbs from the home garden or dried herbs bought at a food store add new flavour interest to familiar dishes; if substituting dried herbs for fresh in a recipe, use less of the dried variety.

Herbs should enhance, not dominate, the food's natural flavour.

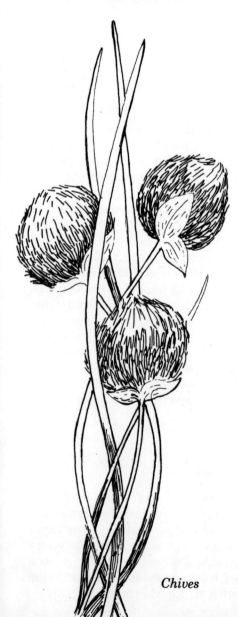

Chives

Balm

Balm, or lemon balm as it is frequently called, is not widely used in the kitchen, although it can be added to salads, mushroom dishes and sweet jellies. The crushed leaves give off a pleasant lemon scent, and a few, added to a teapot with tealeaves, will produce a refreshing drink. Balm is an important ingredient in potpourri, where its tang helps to offset the sweetness of the flower scents.

Variegated balm is another variety of the plant, but is grown more for ornamental than practical purposes.

Basil

There are more than 40 varieties of this sharp, piquant herb, but the best known are the sweet, bush and purple basils. Purple basil has deep purple-greenish leaves; its flavour is inferior to the bush and sweet types. Sweet basil is particularly suitable for drying and therefore the easiest to obtain in dried form.

Basil is traditionally teamed with tomatoes, but its flavour also adds interest to pasta dishes, and combines well with rice, liver, kidneys and fish. Try a little in omelets and with scrambled eggs; if available, use the chopped fresh leaves sprinkled on a green salad. Generally, $\frac{1}{4}$ teaspoon of dried basil with eggs, and $\frac{1}{2}$ teaspoon in a meat recipe is quite sufficient.

Bayleaves

The bay tree is a member of the laurel family. Planted in a pot and clipped to a pleasing shape, this tree can be both attractive and useful. Bayleaves are always an ingredient of bouquet garni; they can also be used by themselves to enhance the flavour of soups, stews, stock, fish, meat and poultry. Whether used fresh or dried, bayleaves are strong, and $\frac{1}{2}$ to 1 leaf is ample in most recipes.

Bouquet Garni

A bouquet garni, or faggot as it is sometimes called, generally consists of a bayleaf, a sprig of fresh thyme, and several parsley sprigs. These are tied together at the stems with cotton or thin string to make removal easier at the end of cooking time. When dried herbs are used it is best to tie them in a piece of muslin.

Use a bouquet garni to flavour stock, soups, stews and fish dishes.

Chervil

Chervil has a serrated and fernlike leaf, with a flavour reminiscent of aniseed. It is sometimes difficult to obtain fresh, but fortunately chervil dries most successfully, retaining both its colour and aroma.

Use dried chervil with discretion in soups, stews, sauces, gravies and with fish and meat. Fresh, the leaves can be chopped and sprinkled fairly liberally on salads and cooked vegetables.

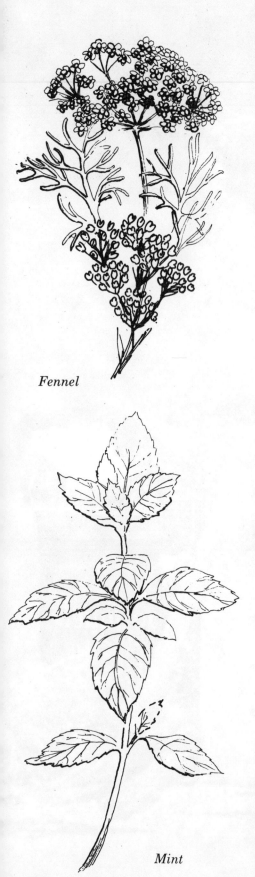

Fennel

Mint

Chives

Chives are easy to grow. Stemming from a small bulb, this member of the lily family seems to thrive in the garden or in a pot; however, if it is impossible to grow your own, bunches can usually be bought. The onion-like leaves, believed to stimulate the appetite, have a mild onion flavour.

Chopped chives add interest to cream cheese, scrambled egg and mashed potato. Try them as a garnish for some soups or sprinkled over a green salad.

Dill

Dill—a favourite herb in Scandinavian and Russian cooking—has a flavour reminiscent of fennel, but milder. Either chopped, fresh leaves or seeds can be used.

In dill pickles the herb helps to make the cucumber more digestible. Flavours of fish and dill combine well—add a few dill seeds to the poaching liquid. Try the chopped, fresh leaves in salads, dressings, sauces or with coleslaw. If fresh dill is difficult to obtain, the dried and powdered variety can be used in recipes where the herb is cooked with other ingredients.

Fennel

Perennial fennel and annual Florence fennel are the two best-known varieties. Seeds of both can be used in cooking, but leaves and stems of Florence fennel have a more pleasant flavour than those of the perennial; leaves, stems, roots and seeds all have an aniseed taste.

Try the raw stems stuffed with cream cheese and cut into 1 in. slices or use to make a delicious salad. Cook the seeds with fish or add to bread and pastries; for a change, use them as a flavouring with apple. Chop the fresh leaves and add to soups and sauces.

Fenugreek

Fenugreek is grown extensively in India, where the leaves are used for fodder. The seeds, which form in long, thin pods, are sold in ground form and are a component of curry powder. Fenugreek can be used in some pickles and with dried beans; also in soups and casseroles.

Fines Herbes

The 'fines herbes' are a combination of parsley, chervil, chives and tarragon. Finely chopped, their most frequent use is in Omelet Fines Herbes, but this combination is also called for in some French recipes for meat, chicken and fish.

Garlic

Garlic is the bulb of a plant belonging to the lily family. In appearance it resembles an irregular-shaped white onion. This is composed of several 'cloves' or segments, each one encased in flaky, white skin. Generally a recipe incorporating garlic will specify one clove to be used, but the strength will depend on the age of the root (young garlic is less pungent than an older bulb) and also the method of cooking.

Garlic is used extensively in Spanish, Italian, and French cooking. It can be added to very many savoury dishes, including soups, stews, roasts, poultry, steaks, stuffings, salad dressings and salads, pickles chutneys.

Before being added to a dish, the garlic clove is peeled, then chopped or crushed. To peel and crush, bring down the flat side of a knife blade sharply on to the clove—the skin can be lifted off quite easily. Add a little salt to the garlic and mash, again using the flat of a knife. Alternatively, peel garlic and crush in a garlic crusher.

Marjoram

There are many varieties of marjoram. In addition to oregano (wild marjoram), knotted (or sweet) is the type most widely used in cooking. The plant grows to about 2 ft. in height and its grey green leaves have a spicy, mint flavour. This herb is sometimes included in a bouquet garni.

Use marjoram mixed with other herbs in stuffings, but try it by itself with eggs, beef, pork, lamb, mutton and in soups, sauces, cheese and fish dishes. Available in powdered form.

Mint

Fresh mint can usually be bought, but it is easy to grow in the home garden; it prefers a sunny position. The most common variety, also best for drying, is spearmint, but there are many others.

Cook several sprigs of fresh mint, or a teaspoon of dried mint, with vegetables, especially peas and new potatoes. Serve some in iced tea and summer fruit drinks. Mint sauce or mint jelly is, of course, the traditional accompaniment to roast mutton or lamb.

Oregano

Oregano, the wild marjoram of Italy and Spain, is prominent in the cooking of these two countries. Available in powdered form, oregano has a strong, pungent flavour and is one of the ingredients in chilli powder.

This herb gives a piquant flavour to such dishes as pizza and chilli con carne, and combines well with tomatoes. Try a little in scrambled eggs and omelets or with pork, veal, beef and fish dishes; add a pinch to French dressing.

Parsley

One of the most widely used and versatile of all herbs, parsley is rich in vitamin C and also contains iron, calcium and vitamin A.

Unlike other herbs, which should be used with discretion, a liberal amount of chopped parsley can be added to many kinds of dishes. Use fresh or fried sprigs as a garnish; add chopped or dried parsley to soups, stews, mashed potatoes, egg dishes, dumplings, sauces.

Peppermint

A herb of the mint family, used for flavouring candies and in liqueurs. The variety known as Black peppermint may be dried for winter use or the fresh leaves may be infused. It has excellent digestive properties.

Rosemary

The variety of rosemary generally cultivated today grows to about 3 ft. in height and is a straight-branched bush with grey-green spiny leaves. It is the leaves that are used in cooking—either fresh or dried and crumbled.

Rosemary has a slight pine flavour that is particularly good with lamb, but it can also be combined with chicken, veal and pork, in soups,

sauces, stuffings or chopped and scattered on salads. Try a little in minestrone or pea soup. Rosemary can often be substituted for thyme in a recipe.

Sage

There are many varieties of this particularly pungent herb, but the grey-leafed type with purple flowers is the most popular and is available whole, crushed or ground.

Use as a seasoning for rissoles, meat loaves, cheese and egg dishes or with fish—and, of course, in sage and onion stuffing. Try rubbing a joint with sage before roasting—but remember its strength, so use sparingly.

Savory

The two best known types of savory are the annual summer and perennial winter varieties—they are similar in flavour and resemble a mild form of sage. Winter savory makes an attractive hedge to a herb garden.

Traditionally associated with beans, savory can be used also with lamb, pork and veal, or combined with other herbs in stuffings, omelets and salads. It is available in dried, powdered form.

Tarragon

There are two varieties of tarragon —French and Russian—but the French, with its superior flavour, is used most in cooking.

Tarragon is an essential ingredient in bearnaise sauce. Its sharp taste blends well with fish and shellfish; for an interesting result, try a little in a chicken stuffing. Mayonnaise, hollandaise sauce and French dressing benefit from a pinch of tarragon and, fresh and chopped, it is delicious sprinkled over salads.

Thyme

Of the many varieties of thyme, lemon-scented and garden thyme are the best known and most often used in the kitchen—both are available in dried-leaf form.

A sprig of thyme is one of the bouquet garni ingredients. Use it also to season meats, soups, stuffings and forcemeat, and vegetables—especially aubergines (eggplants), mushrooms, onions, beetroot, zucchini and marrows.

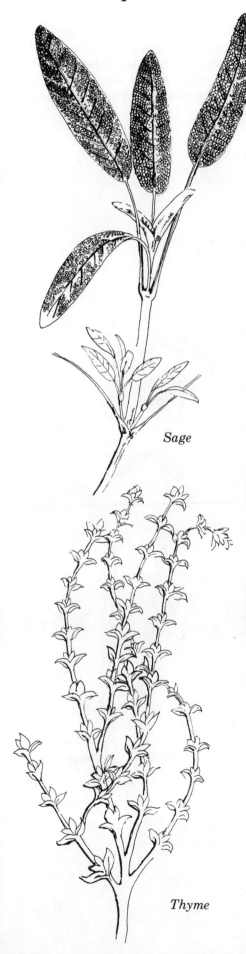

Sage

Thyme

Spices

Spices have little or no food value, but the volatile oils which give them their aroma and distinctive flavour help to make simple foods appetising and interesting.

Most spices are imported and therefore are relatively expensive. For home use buy in small quantities and retain maximum freshness and flavour by storing in airtight containers in a dark, dry, cool place.

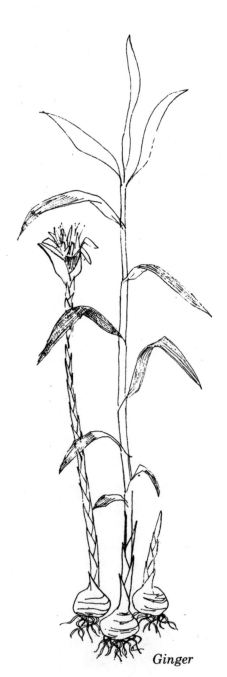

Ginger

Allspice

Allspice (also known as Jamaican Pepper) is the dried fruit of the pimento tree—and no relation to the pepper of that name. It is so named because of its resemblance to the combined flavours of nutmeg, cloves and cinnamon.

Available whole or ground, allspice is used for pickling, fruit preserving, soups, gravies, cakes, puddings, boiled meats.

Cayenne

Cayenne pepper is made from the ground, brilliant red, whole pods of the chilli or capsicum. The plant is ornamental, and is grown in many parts of the world, but chiefly in the East Indies and Africa. Depending on its country of origin, cayenne varies in pungency, but all types are very hot and should be used with discretion. It is an important ingredient in curry powder.

Add a little cayenne to meat, fish and egg dishes, to savory batters, sauces and salad dressings, in cheese dishes and with shellfish.

Cinnamon

The cinnamon tree is an evergreen laurel. The thin bark is peeled from the tree and rolled into sticks as it dries, forming stick cinnamon. True cinnamon grows in Ceylon and India; cassia, a member of the same family comes from South-East Asia, and is almost identical in flavour. The Saigon variety is recognised as being the best-quality ground cinnamon.

Cinnamon has a mellow, slightly sweet flavour that blends with both sweet and savoury foods. When a recipe calls for stick cinnamon, it will usually give the amount to be used in inches, for example, 'a 2 in. stick cinnamon'.

Use ground cinnamon in cakes, milk and fruit puddings or with grilled or stewed meats. Add a cinnamon stick to hot drinks such as mulled wine, use in pickles and with boiled meats and when stewing fruits.

Cloves

Cloves are the buds of an evergreen tree. Used extensively in cookery, they are available whole or ground. Their penetrating, aromatic flavour makes careful use essential—2 or 3 cloves are generally sufficient for most dishes.

Use cloves in some soups, with eggs, fish, meat, stuffings, sauces and gravies, pickles and chutneys. Try a clove-studded orange added to boiling ham or bacon, and an onion stuck with cloves, cooked with boiled chicken. A traditional use is in apple pie; ground cloves are added to cakes and biscuits.

Ginger

Ginger, the root of the plant, can be obtained in four different forms—green (fresh root); ground (dried and powdered root); preserved (cooked in syrup and bottled); crystallized cooked, drained and rolled in sugar).

Green ginger is used with savoury foods (if substituting ground ginger, use only $\frac{1}{4}$ amount specified for green ginger in recipe). Ground ginger is used in savoury and sweet recipes. Preserved and crystallized gingers are interchangeable in recipes, but if no sugar is used in the recipe, rinse sugar coating off the crystallized ginger.

Mace

Mace, the fleshy covering of nutmeg, with a similar but stronger flavour, is available in 'blade' and powdered form, although blade mace is more difficult to obtain. Use it in preserving, flavouring fish, fish sauces and stuffings. Try a pinch of mace on grilled lamb or veal chops. A little added to whipped cream makes an interesting variation—so does a pinch in pie pastry.

Mixed Spice

Mixed spice, as the name implies, is a blend of certain spices in finely ground form. Generally these will be caraway, allspice, coriander, cumin, nutmeg and ginger, but other spices, such as cinnamon, may be included.

Mixed spice is used in cakes, puddings and with fruit.

Nutmeg

From the same tree as mace, nutmeg is the kernel of the fruit; available in whole nut and ground form, the nuts should be grated before use. One nutmeg will generally produce 3 teaspoonfuls when grated, but, for full flavour, prepare only as much as needed at the time, then store remainder of nut until required again.

Although generally included in sweet recipes, nutmeg is also used with meats and poultry, such as chicken, and in sauces.

Paprika

Best quality paprika is made from the dried, ground pods of a variety of sweet red pepper or capsicum imported from Hungary. Has a mild, slightly sweet flavour.

Paprika brightens otherwise insipid-looking dishes when used as a garnish. It can be mixed with breadcrumbs to use as topping for dishes such as macaroni au gratin, or used with breadcrumbs for coating chicken joints for frying.

Pepper

Black and white pepper both come from the berry of a perennial vine. Black pepper is the whole peppercorn, white the inner seed with black outer covering removed. Whole peppercorns keep their flavour better than ground pepper; grind in a peppermill as needed.

Pepper is almost indispensable in savoury cooking. Usually, black is preferable, although it is better to use white in pale coloured foods or cream sauces.

Saffron

Saffron is obtained from the dried stigmas of a type of crocus grown in Europe, mostly in Spain. Since it takes 225,000 stigmas to make 1 lb. of saffron, and each one is hand picked, it is not surprising that this is the world's most expensive spice.

Saffron is used widely in Spanish cooking to impart yellow colour and subtle flavour; available in stigma or powdered form, it should be used very sparingly.

Steep saffron in a little warm water before use. Meat and poultry dishes generally incorporating rice, fish soups such as bouillabaisse, and some traditional breads and cakes include this spice.

Turmeric

Turmeric is the root of a plant of the ginger family. It originated in China and Indonesia, is now produced in India, Haiti and Jamaica.

Deep yellow in colour, it is often a curry ingredient and is used commercially in mustard, curry powder and some pickles. At home, use it in sauces and dressings, marinades for chicken and shellfish and in some pickles and chutneys.

Saffron

Aromatic seeds

The seeds listed below can be used in sweet or savoury dishes; most can be obtained in whole seed or ground form.

Anise

Anise is an annual plant growing to 18 in. in height and producing flat-topped bunches of white flowers. The seeds and fresh leaves are used in cooking, and its sharp, distinctive aroma is unmistakable in the liqueur Anisette.

If you have anise in the garden, chop the fresh leaves and sprinkle them over salads. Use the seeds as a flavouring with shellfish, meat and stuffings. In scones, rolls, bread and biscuits the seeds can be included in the dough or sprinkled on top.

Caraway

Caraway is the aromatic seed of a biennial member of the parsley family.

Most widely used in seed cake and bread, caraway can be cooked with meat, some vegetables and cheese. Add a pinch to stews and marinades, sprinkle a little on pork before roasting; use as a flavouring in cheese dishes or crushed with cottage cheese.

Anise

Cardamom

Cardamom is an Indian native plant extensively in Indian cookery. Cardamom pods or the whole or ground seeds can be bought. The off-white pods are about ½ in. in length and contain about 12 to 18 seeds. The seeds are very hard, so they should be crushed before use to release their pungent flavour.

Whole cardamom seeds are used in fruit punches, pickles and marinades. In their ground form they are included in bread and cakes, meatballs and roast pork. The flavour of cardamom combines very well with coffee and, in its ground form, is a component of curry powder.

Celery Seed

Celery seeds do not come from the well-known vegetable, but from a plant related to the parsley family. They are available whole or ground. Sprinkle whole seeds on herb breads or include in the dough; scatter on canapés; add to marinades for beef or sprinkle on roast veal; include in pickles.

Use ground celery seeds with eggs, cheese, in salads and salad dressings and with vegetables such as potatoes, aubergines, tomatoes, peppers.

Coriander

Coriander is available in whole seed or ground form. It is a comparatively mild spice, has a flavour similar to nutmeg. The longer the seeds are kept (they should be stored in a dry place) the more pronounced the flavour becomes. Seeds can be left whole in cooking but it is usual to crush them first.

Use with dried pea and bean soups, spicy sauces, roast or stewed meat, some fish dishes, omelets, baked eggs and some cakes and pies such as coffee cake, Danish pastries and apple pie. When using coriander to flavour custards or milk puddings, include a small piece of lemon or orange rind; the two flavours blend well.

Cumin Seed

Cumin, a low-growing annual from the Mediterranean, is used in Near and Middle Eastern cookery, and is a basic ingredient of curries. The dried ripe fruit of the plant forms the spice. With its pungent aroma, cumin is used by the Dutch and Swiss to flavour cheese, by the Germans in sauerkraut and by the Hebrews in unleavened bread. It is available ground or in whole seed form.

Use cumin in rye bread, pickles, chutney, rice cabbage and bean dishes with pork and lamb.

Mustard

The hardy annual mustard plant will grow in almost any temperate area of the world. There are two main varieties, both native to Europe and producing seeds that vary in strength and flavour. Ready-mixed mustards are becoming more and more popular.

Use mustard seed in casseroles, pickles, salads, dressings and vegetable dishes. Prepared mustards, traditional accompaniment of beef, steak and ham, can be added to cheese dishes, sauces and dressings.

Poppy Seeds

Grown mainly in Holland, poppy seeds are the non-narcotic seeds of the poppy. They can be used whole or ground. For best flavour bake in moderate oven, Mark 4, 350°F., approximately 10 minutes, or toast in dry frying pan over low heat. Sprinkle whole on breads, pastries, salads, pasta, baked or grilled fish, buttered new potatoes and cauliflower. Use ground in cakes or strudel fillings. Purists, however, believe in using poppy seeds only in sweet foods.

Sesame Seeds

Sesame seeds are small, flat and round—and light brown, high in mineral and protein content. In many parts of the world, oil extracted from the seeds is used for cooking. The faintly nutty flavour of the seeds is brought out by baking 20 minutes in moderate oven, Mark 4, 350°F.

Sesame seeds are sprinkled on breads, buns, cakes and pastries. They can also be added to cheese mixtures and fish dishes, sprinkled on canapés, added to salad dressings.

Miscellaneous

Below we list a variety of ingredients which add zest to your cooking.

Capers

The floral bud of the caper bush, that grows along the Mediterranean shores of southern Europe. Once picked, the buds are dried and pickled in vinegar.

Capers add a sharp and piquant flavour to sauces accompanying boiled meat and fish, particularly caper sauce served with boiled mutton. Try them also in salads, or as a garnish.

Curry Powder

Curry powder is a blend of at least 6 spices which may include cumin, coriander, fenugreek, turmeric, ginger, pepper, mace, cardomom and cloves.

In addition to curries, use curry powder with eggs, in marinades, sprinkled on grilled fish, or to flavour sauces and butters. Amount used will vary according to the brand of curry powder and strength desired. Curry powder should be fried at start of making a curry—this releases its full flavour and also cooks the spices.

Garam Masala

Garam Masala is the mixed spice of India; it is a combination of ground coriander seeds, cumin seeds, cloves, cinnamon, peppercorns, nutmeg and cardamom seeds. Unlike curry powder, it should be added to a dish at the end of cooking time so its delicate flavour is retained. The spices included in the mixture and quantities used are variable. Garam Masala is used extensively in Indian cooking.

Horseradish

Horseradish is the root of a perennial plant, a member of the mustard family. It can be bought in jars, blended in a creamy sauce.

Horseradish, the traditional accompaniment to roast beef, can be combined with mayonnaise to give a sharp and piquant dressing. The young and tender leaves of the plant can be chopped and used in salads.

Monosodium Glutamate

Monosodium Glutamate or MSG, as it is commonly known, is widely used in Chinese cookery. It is the sodium salt of glutamic acid present in nearly all animal and vegetable protein, and is used in cookery to give accent to flavour.

It is used in some savoury foods only and should not be added to sweet foods, fruits or dairy products.

Salt

Salt, or sodium chloride as it is scientifically known, is a mineral mined in many parts of the world; it is also contained naturally in most foods. Salt added to food during cooking will help to bring out the flavour, and will also stimulate the appetite. A certain amount of salt in the diet is essential for health, while too much can be harmful. Salt also acts as a preservative.

Vanilla

The vanilla bean is the seed pod of a yellow-flowered orchid native to Central America; the pods are odourless and flavourless. Over a period of 6 months, they are subjected to alternate heat and darkness to induce fermentation. When almost black in colour, the vanilla bean, as we know it, emerges.

Vanilla extract is produced by steeping the cured pods in a mixture of alcohol and water.

Keep a vanilla bean in a jar containing sugar—the flavour is imparted to the sugar to be used in cakes and custards. Heat the whole pod, or a small piece, in milk for any sweet dish requiring these two ingredients. The bean can be washed and dried afterwards to be stored and used again. An alternative method is to split the bean and remove the seeds. Store the bean in a sugar jar and use the seeds—the part with the strongest flavour—for heating with milk.

Vanilla flavour is popular for many sweet recipes, including custards, ice-cream, cakes, puddings, confectionery.

Nutmeg

Sauces

Basically, there are two types of savoury sauces—brown and white; nearly all sauces are variations of these. In addition, there are the butter sauces—Hollandaise and Bearnaise, and the compound sauces, Mayonnaise (see page 121) and its variations. All the favourite savoury sauce recipes are given here. See Desserts section, page 222, for a selection of delicious dessert sauces.

Basic White Sauce

1 oz. (2 tablespoons) butter	1 pint (2 cups) hot milk
2 tablespoons flour	salt, pepper

Melt butter over low heat, remove from heat, stir in flour, working until smooth. Return to heat, cook few minutes, remove from heat. Gradually stir in heated milk, return to heat; cook, stirring constantly until boiling point is reached. Reduce heat, simmer further 3 minutes, season to taste.

The amount of flour and butter used in sauces depends on the consistency desired.

Thin Sauce Use 1 oz. (2 tablespoons) butter and 2 tablespoons (approximately 1 oz.) flour to 1 pint (2 cups) liquid.

Medium Sauce Use 1½ oz. (3 tablespoons) butter and 3 tablespoons (approximately 1½ oz.) to 1 pint (2 cups) liquid.

Thick Sauce Use 2 oz. (¼ cup) butter and 4 tablespoons (approximately 2 oz.) flour to 1 pint (2 cups) liquid.

Parsley Sauce Stir 2 to 3 tablespoons finely chopped parsley and a squeeze of lemon juice into 1 pint (2 cups) medium-thickness white sauce.

Onion Sauce Chop 2 onions finely, cook in boiling salted water until tender, drain. Add onions, a squeeze of lemon juice and 1 teaspoon finely chopped parsley to 1 pint (2 cups) medium-thickness white sauce. (Cooking liquid from onions can be used as part of liquid in making the white sauce).

Mornay Sauce Make up thick white sauce, remove from heat, stir in 4 oz. (1 cup) grated cheese; add a sprinkling of nutmeg. Stir, off heat, until cheese melts completely.

Mushroom Cream Sauce

½ lb. mushrooms	1 gill (½ cup) medium white sauce
1 oz. (2 tablespoons) butter	salt, pepper
1½ gills (⅔ cup) medium cream	

Chop mushrooms very finely, sauté in hot butter until lightly browned. Add cream, cook over low heat 5 minutes. Stir in white sauce, season to taste; heat through gently.

Béchamel Sauce

bayleaf	½ pint (1 cup) milk
parsley stalks	½ oz. (1 tablespoon) butter
slice of onion	butter
4 peppercorns	1 tablespoon flour
sprig thyme	salt, pepper

Place bayleaf, parsley stalks, onion slice, peppercorns and thyme into milk in small saucepan over low heat. Gradually bring to boiling point, remove from heat, let stand 5 minutes. Melt butter in saucepan, add flour, stir until smooth; remove pan from heat, gradually add the strained milk, stirring constantly. When thoroughly blended, return to heat and stir until sauce boils and thickens. Season to taste with salt and pepper.

Brown Sauce

1 carrot	1 pint (2 cups) boiling water
1 medium onion	water
1 stick celery	1 tablespoon tomato purée
1 clove garlic	purée
3 tablespoons oil	bayleaf
2 tablespoons flour	parsley stalks
2 beef stock cubes	sprig of thyme

Coarsley chop carrot, onion and celery; crush garlic. Heat oil in saucepan. Sauté carrot, onion, celery and garlic until lightly browned. Stir in flour and cook until well browned; do not allow to burn. Dissolve stock cubes in boiling water. Add to pan with tomato purée and herbs. Simmer, uncovered, 30 minutes. Strain, adjust seasoning.

A well-flavoured sauce can transform simple grilled or roasted meats into gourmet dishes.

Quick Sauce Bordelaise

2 small onions	1½ gills (⅔ cup) stock
6 mushrooms	1 tablespoon tomato
butter	purée or paste
1½ gills (⅔ cup) dry	salt, pepper
white wine	

Chop onions very finely, slice mushrooms. Sauté in a little butter until lightly browned. Add wine and stock and simmer until reduced to ½ pint (1 cup) of liquid. Stir in tomato purée or paste; season to taste.

Oyster Sauce

½ pint (1 cup) milk	2 tablespoons flour
¼ pint (½ cup) water	1 dessertspoon lemon
½ carrot	juice
1 slice of onion	salt, pepper
few peppercorns	1 bottle or can of
parsley sprig	oysters (10 to 12
1 small bayleaf	oysters)
1 oz. (2 tablespoons)	3 to 4 tablespoons
butter	heavy cream

Place milk, water, diced carrot, onion slice, peppercorns, parsley and bayleaf in saucepan. Bring to boil; reduce heat, simmer very slowly, uncovered, 5 minutes. Strain, reserve stock. Melt butter in saucepan, stir in flour, cook 1 minute, remove from heat. Gradually add strained stock. Return to heat, simmer until smooth and thickened, stirring constantly.

Add lemon juice, season to taste. Add drained, chopped oysters, simmer very slowly further 5 minutes. Stir in cream. Reheat gently, do not boil. Serve over grilled (broiled) steaks or steamed or poached fish.

Sauce Bercy

1 tablespoon finely	juice of ½ lemon
chopped shallots	1 dessertspoon chopped
½ oz. (1 tablespoon)	parsley
butter	½ oz. (1 tablespoon)
1 wineglass white wine	butter
2 wineglasses white	½ oz. (1 tablespoon)
stock	flour
salt, pepper	

Sauté the shallots in butter. Add wine and reduce by half. Add stock, seasoning, lemon juice and parsley, bring to the boil.

Mix flour and butter smoothly, add to the pan in small pieces, stirring well. Boil for 1 minute, adjust seasoning.

Mustard Sauce

1 oz. (2 tablespoons)	1 teaspoon dry mustard
butter	½ teaspoon vinegar
1½ tablespoons flour	1 tablespoon heavy
½ pint (1 cup) stock	cream
salt, pepper	1 egg-yolk

Melt butter in saucepan. Stir in flour, cook until lightly brown; remove from heat. Gradually add stock, blend well. Return to heat, bring to boil; reduce heat, simmer until smooth and thickened, stirring constantly. Season to taste with salt and pepper.

Blend mustard and vinegar with a little of the sauce until smooth. Add to sauce, blend well. Remove from heat, stir in cream and beaten egg-yolk.

Stroganoff Sauce

1 oz. (2 tablespoons)	½ teaspoon dry mustard
butter	salt, pepper
1 large onion	½ pint (1 cup) sour
½ lb. mushrooms	cream

Melt butter in pan, add finely chopped onion, sauté gently until onion is tender. Add sliced mushrooms, cook until mushrooms are well softened. Add mustard, salt, pepper to taste, then stir in sour cream; heat together gently, simmer 5 minutes.

This sauce is equally good spooned over grilled (broiled) or pan-fried steaks, or over thick slices of roasted beef fillet.

Madeira Sauce

½ oz. (1 tablespoon)	¾ pint (1½ cups) boiling
butter	water
1 rasher bacon	2 beef stock cubes
2 shallots	salt, pepper
1 dessertspoon flour	pinch mixed herbs
1 teaspoon tomato	¼ pint (½ cup) madeira
paste	
4 mushrooms	

Heat butter in pan, add finely chopped bacon and shallots, cook over low heat until lightly browned. Stir in flour, add paste, finely chopped mushrooms. Gradually stir in boiling water, in which stock cubes have been dissolved. Season, bring to boil. Reduce heat, simmer 20 minutes. Add herbs, bring to boil again further 5 minutes; strain.

Let sauce simmer over low heat until reduced to half quantity. Add madeira, reboil gently until sauce thickens.

Mushroom Sauce

½ oz. (1 tablespoon) butter	1 tablespoon cornflour (cornstarch)
1 small onion	½ pint (1 cup) milk
2 oz. mushrooms	salt, pepper
4 tablespoons white wine	1 to 2 tablespoons cream

Melt butter, fry the chopped onion and sliced mushrooms, but do not brown. Add wine, cook gently for 1 minute. Blend the cornflour (cornstarch) with the milk, add to pan. Bring to boil, stirring continually, and cook 1 minute. Remove from heat, season to taste, stir in the cream.

Chinese Plum Sauce

3 oz. (⅜ cup) butter	1 tablespoon wine vinegar
1 onion	½ teaspoon ginger
½ lb. (1 cup) plum jam	¼ teaspoon dry mustard
2 tablespoons soy sauce	

Melt butter in saucepan and sauté chopped onion until tender. Remove pan from heat, add remaining ingredients; heat gently, stirring, until well combined.

Serve with pork or veal.

Bearnaise Sauce

4 tablespoons tarragon	3 egg-yolks
6 peppercorns, crushed	4 oz. (½ cup or 1 stick) butter
1 shallot	salt, pepper
1 bayleaf	

Boil vinegar, peppercorns, chopped shallot and bayleaf together until liquid is reduced to 2 tablespoons, strain. Beat egg-yolks lightly in top of double boiler and stir in strained liquid. Gradually beat in cooled melted butter and stir continuously over simmering water until thickened. Season with salt and pepper.

Tartare Sauce

1½ gills (⅔ cup) mayonnaise (see page 121)	½ teaspoon chopped chives
2 tablespoons capers	1 tablespoon chopped parsley
2 tablespoons chopped gherkins	

In bowl combine mayonnaise, finely chopped capers, gherkins, chives and parsley. Serve with fish.

Hollandaise Sauce

3 tablespoons wine vinegar	2 egg-yolks
6 peppercorns	salt, pepper
½ bayleaf	few drops lemon juice
4 oz. (½ cup or 1 stick) butter	

Simmer vinegar, peppercorns and bayleaf gently together until liquid is reduced to half the quantity, strain. Work butter until slightly soft. Cream egg-yolks with a little of the butter and a pinch of salt in the top of a double saucepan; stir in strained liquid. Stir over gentle heat until just beginning to thicken. Add remaining butter in small pieces, stirring continually. When all the butter has been added, add lemon juice to taste.

Sauce Remoulade

½ pint (1 cup) mayonnaise (see page 121)	1 dessertspoon finely chopped parsley
2 tablespoons finely chopped dill pickle or gherkin	dash of Worcestershire or anchovy sauce
1 dessertspoon finely chopped capers	2 tablespoons whipped cream
1 teaspoon prepared mustard	

Combine all ingredients except cream, mix well. Stir in cream. Serve with any seafood.

Caper Sauce

¼ pint (½ cup) mayonnaise (see page 121)	1 teaspoon vinegar from capers
1 tablespoon chopped, drained capers	1 tablespoon finely chopped parsley

Combine all ingredients, mix well to blend.

Cucumber-Mayonnaise Sauce

1 large cucumber	1½ tablespoons milk
4 stuffed olives	1½ tablespoons chopped parsley
¼ pint (½ cup) mayonnaise (see page 121)	1 tablespoon lemon juice
4 tablespoons sour cream	salt

Peel, seed, grate and drain cucumber, chop olives. Heat mayonnaise and cucumber in small saucepan over low heat. Combine remaining ingredients in bowl, stir into cucumber mixture. Keep over low heat a few seconds, stirring constantly. Serve with fish.

Cakes

Tea cakes, coffee cakes, small cakes, butter cakes, fruit cakes, slices, a superb torte and gateau—there's an irresistible selection of cakes to choose from, for every occasion.

Butterscotch Teacake

4 oz. (½ cup or 1 stick) butter	8 oz. (2 cups) plain flour
6 oz. (1 cup) brown sugar	3 teaspoons baking powder
1 large egg	¼ pint (½ cup) milk

Butterscotch Icing

4½ (⅔ cup) dark brown sugar	1 oz. (2 tablespoons) butter
4 dessertspoons milk	3 to 4 oz. (about ¾ cup) icing (confectioners') sugar
pinch salt	chopped almonds

Cream butter and sugar until light and fluffy. Add egg, beat well. Fold in sifted flour and baking powder alternately with the milk. Turn mixture into greased 8 in. sandwich tin. Bake in moderate oven, Mark 4, 350°F., 40 to 45 minutes, or until cake is cooked. Turn cake on to a wire tray. When cold, top with Butterscotch Icing.
Icing Place all ingredients except icing sugar and almonds in a saucepan and cook, stirring constantly, until mixture begins to boil. Boil steadily, without stirring, 4 to 5 minutes. Allow to cool until warm, beat in sifted icing sugar, adding more icing sugar, if necessary, to give a spreading consistency. Spread over cake, sprinkle with chopped almonds.

Apple Teacake

1 to 2 apples	6 oz. (1½ cups) self raising (all purpose) flour
2 oz. (¼ cup) butter	
4 oz. (½ cup) castor (superfine) sugar	pinch salt
1 egg	8 tablespoons milk
	2 teaspoons cinnamon
	extra sugar

Peel and core apples, cut into thin slices, cut each slice in half.
    Cream butter, add sugar and beat until light and fluffy; beat in egg. Fold in sifted flour and salt alternately with milk, mix well. Spread mixture into well-greased 8 in. sandwich tin, arrange a whirl of apple slices on top, sprinkle with combined cinnamon and extra sugar. Bake in moderate oven, Mark 4, 350°F., approximately 45 minutes.

Streusel Coffee Cake

6 oz. (¾ cup) butter	5 oz. (1¼ cups) self raising (all purpose) flour
8 oz. (1 cup) sugar	
1 teaspoon vanilla	
3 eggs	3 oz. (¾ cup) plain flour
	3 tablespoons milk

Topping

4 oz. (1 cup) plain flour	3 oz. (½ cup) dark brown sugar
1 tablespoon cinnamon	
	3 oz. (⅜ cup) butter

Cream together butter and sugar until light and fluffy, add vanilla. Add eggs one at a time, beating well after each addition. Sift flours, add alternately with milk, mix thoroughly. Spread into greased 9 in. square cake tin. Sprinkle topping over cake. Bake in moderately hot oven, Mark 5, 375°F., 35 to 40 minutes, or until cooked when tested with a skewer.
Topping Sift together dry ingredients. Rub in butter thoroughly, roll into a ball. Refrigerate until firm.

Butterscotch Teacake, Chelsea Butter Bun and Almond Meringue Cake—full-of-flavour cakes that go equally well with tea or coffee.

Orange Loaf Cake

4 oz. (½ cup) castor (superfine) sugar	1 dessertspoon grated orange rind
8 tablespoons milk	2 eggs
4 oz. (½ cup or 1 stick) butter	8 oz. (2 cups) self raising (all purpose) flour

Dissolve sugar in 4 tablespoons of milk in a small mixing bowl. Add butter and orange rind and cream well. Add beaten eggs a little at a time. Sift flour, fold in alternately with remaining milk. Spoon mixture into greased and lined 9 in. × 5 in. loaf tin. Bake in moderate oven, Mark 4, 350°F., 40 minutes.

Patty Cakes

4 oz. (½ cup or 1 stick) butter	little milk
4 oz. (½ cup) castor (superfine) sugar	½ teaspoon vanilla
2 eggs	8 oz. (2 cups) self raising (all purpose) flour

Cream butter and sugar together until light and fluffy. Add vanilla, then gradually beat in the lightly beaten eggs. Fold in the sifted flour, adding a little milk if necessary, mix well. Drop dessertspoonfuls of mixture into well greased, deep patty tins. Bake in moderately hot oven, Mark 5, 375°F., 10 to 15 minutes.
Makes 2 dozen.

Butterfly Cakes Cut a slice from top of cooled patty cake, then cut this slice in half to form two wings. Pipe or spoon whipped cream across top of cake, set the wings in position. Dust with sifted icing (confectioners') sugar; top, if desired, with a halved strawberry.

Ginger Cake

1 lb. (4 cups) plain flour	12 oz. (1 cup) treacle
½ teaspoon salt	6 oz. (¾ cup) butter
2 dessertspoons baking powder	12 oz. (2 cups) light brown sugar
3 dessertspoons ground ginger	1 egg
1 teaspoon bicarbonate of soda	½ pint (1 cup) milk

Lemon Icing

12 oz. (2 cups approx.) icing (confectioners') sugar	½ oz. (1 tablespoon) butter
	lemon juice

Sift flour, salt, baking powder, ginger and bicarbonate of soda into a basin. Place treacle, butter and brown sugar into a saucepan, stir over a low heat until sugar dissolves. Cool. Add to dry ingredients; mix in egg and warmed milk. Pour into greased and paper-lined 10 in. square or large oblong cake tin.

Bake in moderately hot oven, Mark 5, 375°F., 1 hour. Cool slightly before turning out on to a wire tray. When cold, top with lemon icing.
Lemon Icing Sift icing sugar. Soften butter with a wooden spoon, then gradually add icing sugar, working well in, until the mixture is crumbly. Add sufficient lemon juice, a little at a time, to make a smooth spreading consistency.

Basic Butter Cake

4 oz. (½ cup or 1 stick) butter	8 oz. (2 cups) self raising (all purpose) flour
6 oz. (¾ cup) castor (superfine) sugar	pinch salt
1 teaspoon vanilla	3 to 4 tablespoons milk
2 eggs	

Cream butter, sugar and vanilla together until light and fluffy. Add eggs one at a time, beat well. Fold in sifted dry ingredients alternately with the milk. Spoon into a greased and lined 7 in. or 8 in. cake tin. Bake in a moderate oven, Mark 4, 350°F., 50 to 60 minutes.

Variations

Light Fruit Cake
Add 6 oz. (1 cup) mixed fruit and ½ teaspoons mixed spice, nutmeg and grated lemon or orange rind.

Marble Cake
Divide mixture into three portions. Colour one portion pink; to second portion add 3 dessertspoons cocoa blended smoothly with 3 dessertspoons warm milk; leave third portion plain. Spoon mixtures into tin in alternate spoonfuls. Cut through two or three times with knife blade or skewer, to give pattern.

Lamingtons
Pour cake mixture into a well-greased 7 in. × 11 in. tin. Bake in moderate oven, Mark 4, 350°F., 30 to 40 minutes. Allow to stand in the tin for a few minutes before turning out on to wire tray.

It is best to make the cake the day before you want to cut and ice the lamingtons, as fresh cake will usually crumble.

Cut cake into squares. Dip in chocolate icing, then toss in coconut.
Chocolate Icing for Lamingtons Sift 1 lb. (3 cups) icing (confectioners') sugar and 4 dessertspoons cocoa into a basin. Add 1 dessertspoon melted butter to 6 to 8 tablespoons warmed milk. Add sufficient milk mixture to icing sugar mixture to make a smooth coating consistency; beat well.

One-Egg Butter Cake

8 oz. (2 cups) plain
   flour
pinch salt
2½ teaspoons baking
   powder
3 oz. (⅜ cup) butter

8 oz. (1 cup) castor
   (superfine) sugar
1 egg
1 teaspoon vanilla
4 to 5 tablespoons milk

Sift together flour, salt and baking powder. Cream butter until soft, gradually add sugar and beaten egg, beat well until light and fluffy; add vanilla. Add dry ingredients alternately with the milk. Spoon into a well-greased 7 in. cake tin. Bake in moderate oven, Mark 4, 350°F., approximately 55 minutes.

Two-Egg Butter Cake

4 oz. (½ cup or 1 stick)
   butter
8 oz. (1 cup) castor
   (superfine) sugar
2 large eggs, or 3
   smaller eggs
12 oz. (3 cups) plain
   flour

4 teaspoons baking
   powder
pinch salt
about ¼ pint (½ cup)
   milk
1 teaspoon vanilla

Cream butter, add sugar and 1 egg; beat until light and fluffy. Add remaining egg, beat well. Sift together dry ingredients; add alternately with milk to creamed mixture; add vanilla. Pour into well-greased 8 in. cake tin.

Bake in moderately slow oven, Mark 3, 325°F., approximately 1¼ to 1½ hours. Let cake cool in tin 5 to 10 minutes before turning out.

Cherry Cake

4 oz. (½ cup) glacé
   cherries
6 oz. (¾ cup) butter
6 oz. (¾ cup) castor
   (superfine) sugar
3 eggs

3 oz. (¾ cup) plain flour
3 oz. (¾ cup) self
   raising (all purpose)
   flour
3 dessertspoons milk

Snow Glaze

10 oz. (2 cups) icing
   (confectioners')
   sugar
1 teaspoon softened
   butter

¼ teaspoon vanilla
1 to 2 dessertspoons
   milk

Cut cherries into thirds. Cream butter and sugar until light and fluffy. Gradually add well-beaten eggs. Fold in sifted flours alternately with milk; lastly fold in cut cherries. Place mixture into a large, well-greased baba mould, or greased 8 in. round cake tin.

Bake in moderate oven, Mark 4, 350°F., approximately 1 hour, or until golden brown and cooked when tested with skewer. Allow to stand 10 minutes before turning out; cool.

When cold, ice with Snow Glaze and decorate with glacé cherry halves, if desired.

Snow Glaze   Combine sifted icing (confectioners') sugar, butter and vanilla in small basin. Gradually beat in milk until mixture is smooth and of a coating consistency; a little more milk may be necessary. Spread over cake; or warm over low heat and allow to trickle over top of cake and down the sides.

Madeira Cake

6 oz. (¾ cup) butter
5 oz. (⅝ cup) castor
   (superfine) sugar
grated rind medium
   size lemon

3 large eggs
8 oz. (2 cups) plain flour
2 teaspoons baking
   powder
candied peel

Cream butter until light and fluffy, gradually beat in sugar. Add grated lemon rind, mix well. Beat eggs lightly, add gradually to mixture, beat well. Sift flour with baking powder; lightly fold into beaten mixture. No extra liquid should be added. Turn mixture into greased, lined 7 in. cake tin. Bake in moderate oven, Mark 4, 350°F., approximately 1 hour. Place small pieces of candied peel on top, decoratively, after ¾ hour of cooking time.

Apple Shortcake

4 oz. (½ cup or 1 stick)
   butter
4 oz. (½ cup) castor
   (superfine) sugar
1 egg
4 oz. (1 cup) self
   raising (all purpose)
   flour
4 oz. (1 cup) plain flour

¼ teaspoon salt
1 tablespoon
   marmalade
3 peeled, coarsely
   grated apples
grated rind and juice
   ½ lemon
extra sugar

Cream butter and sugar lightly, add egg, beat well; mix in sifted flours and salt. Divide mixture into two, roll each piece into a round; place one round in base of 8 in. greased sandwich tin, cover with grated apple and marmalade. Sprinkle with grated lemon rind and juice, then with 1 tablespoon extra sugar. Cover with second round of dough, pressing well at sides. Brush with water, sprinkle evenly with extra castor sugar. Bake in moderate oven, Mark 4, 350°F., 35 to 40 minutes.

Chelsea Butter Bun

12 oz. (3 cups) self raising (all purpose) flour	1½ oz. (3 tablespoons) butter
½ teaspoon salt	¼ to ½ pint (½ to 1 cup) milk

Filling

2 oz. (¼ cup) butter	2 oz. (¼ cup) chopped glacé cherries
2 oz. (⅓ cup) light brown sugar	2 oz. (⅓ cup) mixed peel
2 oz. (⅓ cup) sultanas	1 teaspoon cinnamon
2 oz. (⅓ cup) currants	

Glaze

2 dessertspoons water	1 teaspoon gelatine
2 dessertspoons sugar	

Sift flour and salt into a basin, rub in butter lightly. Mix to a firm dough with milk. Roll dough into oblong shape, ¼ in. in thickness.

Filling Cream butter and brown sugar together. Spread over dough; sprinkle with fruit and cinnamon. Roll up lengthwise; cut roll into 14 thick slices. Pack into a greased 8 in. sandwich tin, cut side down. Bake in a moderate oven, Mark 4, 350°F., 25 to 30 minutes.

Brush bun with glaze, while still hot.

Glaze Place ingredients into a small bowl, stir over hot water until gelatine and sugar dissolve.

Christmas Cake

10 oz. (1¼ cups) butter	½ teaspoon nutmeg
10 oz. (1⅔ cups) dark brown sugar	½ teaspoon mixed spice
1 tablespoon black treacle	1¼ lb. (3⅔ cups) currants
grated rind of 1 lemon	12 oz. (2 cups) sultanas
grated rind of 1 orange	8 oz. (1½ cups) raisins
5 large eggs	4 oz. (¾ cup) prunes
2 tablespoons brandy	4 oz. (¾ cup) dates
12 oz. (3 cups) plain flour	4 oz. (1 cup) almonds
½ teaspoon cinnamon	4 oz. (¾ cup) candied peel
	4 oz. (½ cup) glacé cherries

Prepare a 9 in. round tin at least 3 in. deep. Line the sides and bottom with a double layer of greased grease-proof paper and tie a deep band of brown paper round the outside of the tin, standing 1 to 2 in. above the top of the tin.

Beat the butter, sugar, treacle, lemon and orange rind together until very soft and creamy. Gradually add the beaten eggs and brandy, adding a little sifted flour if the mixture shows signs of curdling. Sieve flour and spices together. Mix all the fruit—the last six ingredients should be chopped. Stir the flour and fruit into the creamed mixture, mix well but do not over beat. Put into the prepared tin and bake in the centre of a very moderate oven, Mark 3, 325°F., for 1½ hours, then reduce heat to Mark 2, 300°F., for a further 3 hours. Allow to cool in the tin, and when quite cold, wrap securely in foil and store till required.

Chocolate Fruit Cake

1 lb. (2⅔ cups) sultanas	1 teaspoon grated orange rind
8 oz. (1½ cups) raisins	1 teaspoon grated lemon rind
4 oz. (⅔ cup) currants	1 teaspoon vanilla
4 oz. (1½ cups) glacé cherries	¼ teaspoon almond essence
3 oz. (½ cup) mixed peel	2 tablespoons marmalade
2 oz. (⅓ cup) glacé pineapple	4 oz. (4 squares) plain chocolate
2 oz. (⅓ cup) glacé apricots	4 eggs
2 oz. (⅜ cup) prunes or dates	10 oz. (2½ cups) plain flour
1 oz. (⅜ cup) dried apricots	1 teaspoon mixed spice
6 tablespoons brandy	¼ teaspoon nutmeg
8 oz. (1 cup) butter	1 teaspoon cinnamon
9 oz. (1½ cups) dark brown sugar	pinch salt

Chop fruit and place in a basin, pour over brandy, mix well, cover and stand overnight. Cream butter with sugar, add grated fruit rinds, essences, marmalade and melted chocolate; mix thoroughly. Drop in the eggs one at a time, beating well after each addition. Fold in sifted dry ingredients alternately with the prepared fruits; mix well. Place mixture into deep 9 in. cake tin, which has been lined with 1 thickness white paper and 2 thicknesses brown paper. Bake in slow oven, Mark 1, 275°F., approximately 4 hours, or until cooked, when a skewer, inserted, comes out clean. Allow to cool completely in tin. Then remove from tin, peel off brown paper layers. Wrap in clean towel or aluminium foil, store in a reasonably cool place until required.

At top, from left. Madeira Cake, Chocolate Fruit Cake, topped with Marzipan Fruits, Cherry Cake; below, Ginger Cake, Patty Cakes, Easy Dundee Cake.

Easy Dundee Cake

2 oz. (⅓ cup) mixed peel
8 oz. (1½ cups) raisins
10 oz. (2½ cups) plain flour
1 teaspoon baking powder
½ teaspoon mixed spice
6 oz. (¾ cup) castor (superfine) sugar

6 oz. (¾ cup) softened butter
8 oz. (1⅓ cups) currants
8 oz. (1⅓ cups) sultanas
2 oz. (¼ cup) cherries
5 eggs
little milk if required
1 oz. (¼ cup) blanched almonds

Chop peel and raisins, sift dry ingredients. Place softened butter in a large bowl, add all remaining ingredients with the exception of the almonds; beat together until smooth and thoroughly mixed (this is best done in an electric mixer). Place in an 8 in. round deep cake tin that has been lined with 2 layers of greaseproof paper. Decorate top with almonds and, if desired, glacé cherries.

Bake in a moderately slow oven, Mark 3, 325°F., 2 to 2½ hours.

When cake is cooked, cover with a clean tea-towel and leave to cool in tin.

Strawberry Hazelnut Gateau

4 egg whites
pinch salt
10 oz. (1¼ cups) castor (superfine) sugar
4½ oz. (1 cup) ground hazelnuts

1 teaspoon vinegar
½ teaspoon vanilla
4 dessertspoons black coffee

Filling

1 lb. strawberries
1 pint (2 cups) whipped cream

6 oz. (6 squares) plain chocolate
water

Beat egg-whites with salt until stiff; gradually add sugar; beat until mixture is of meringue consistency. Fold in remaining ingredients. Spread in 2 greased and floured 8 in. springform pans. Bake in moderate oven, Mark 4, 350°F., approximately 35 minutes; release sides of pans. Cool on base of pan.

Remove from base, place a layer of meringue on serving plate. Spread with thin layer of chocolate, which has been melted with the water. Spread ¾ in. layer of cream over chocolate. Top with layer of sliced strawberries; reserve remainder for decoration.

Spread second layer of meringue with remaining chocolate mixture, place on strawberry layer, chocolate-side up. Cover and top with remaining cream.

Refrigerate several hours, or preferably overnight. Serve decorated with reserved strawberries.

Sultana Cake

1½ lb. (3⅔ cups) sultanas
8 oz. (1 cup) butter
8 oz. (1 cup) castor (superfine) sugar
5 eggs
10 oz. (2½ cups) plain flour

1 oz. (¼ cup) self raising (all purpose) flour
pinch salt
4 oz. (1 cup) blanched almonds
2 to 3 tablespoons brandy
½ teaspoon vanilla

Cover sultanas with warm water, soak for 2 hours. Drain, let dry at least 24 hours.

Cream butter and sugar together until light and fluffy. Add eggs one at a time, beating well after each addition. If necessary, add a little flour towards the end of the egg additions, to prevent curdling. Add sifted flours and salt alternately with the sultanas, then add chopped almonds, reserving a few to decorate the top of cake. Fold in brandy and vanilla. Place mixture into a greased and paper lined 8 in. or 9 in. square cake tin. Bake in moderately slow oven, Mark 3, 325°F., approximately 1¾ hours.

Devil's Food Cake

2 oz. (¼ cup) butter
8 oz. (1 cup) sugar
2 eggs
6 oz. (1¼ cups) self raising (all purpose) flour
4 tablespoons sour milk

6 tablespoons black coffee
2 oz. (2 squares) plain chocolate
1 teaspoon bicarbonate of soda
1 teaspoon vanilla essence

Frosting

1 egg white
3 dessertspoons cold water
7 oz. (⅞ cup) sugar

¼ teaspoon cream of tartar
½ teaspoon vanilla
little melted chocolate

Grease two 9 in. sandwich tins.

Cream butter and sugar until light and fluffy. Beat in eggs gradually. Add flour and sour milk alternately. Pour boiling coffee on to melted choclate and add bicarbonate. Cool a little, add to mixture with vanilla. Bake in a moderate oven, Mark 5, 375°F., for 25 minutes. When cold, fill and spread with frosting.

To make frosting Whisk all ingredients except vanilla in a basin over hot water for about 7 minutes until mixture stands in peaks then add vanilla.

Dribble a little melted chocolate over the top.

Dark Chocolate Cake

1½ gills (⅔ cup) hot coffee	1 teaspoon bicarbonate of soda
2 oz. (½ cup) cocoa	¼ pint (½ cup) sour cream
10 oz. (1¼ cups) sugar	
4 oz. (½ cup or 1 stick) butter	8 oz. (2 cups) plain flour
3 eggs, separated	4 oz. (½ cup) sugar, extra
1 teaspoon salt	
1 teaspoon vanilla	whipped cream

Sour Cream Frosting

4 oz. (4 squares) plain chocolate	pinch salt
¼ pint (½ cup) sour cream	4 dessertspoons icing (confectioners') sugar

Stir hot coffee gradually into cocoa. Combine sugar with butter, egg-yolks, salt, vanilla and half the cocoa mixture. Beat until light and creamy. Mix bicarbonate of soda and sour cream together. To butter and sugar mixture add sour cream and cocoa-coffee alternately with sifted flour. Beat egg-whites until stiff, gradually add the extra 4 oz. (½ cup) sugar, beat until meringue stands in stiff peaks. Fold into chocolate mixture. Pour into 9 in. or 10 in. greased and paper-lined deep cake tin. Bake in moderate oven, Mark 4, 350°F., 1 to 1¼ hours.

Cool completely on wire tray, then cut into 2 layers and join with whipped cream. Spread frosting in a thin layer over top and sides of cake, decorate with walnut halves and cherries if desired.

Refrigerate until Sour Cream Frosting is firm.
Sour Cream Frosting Melt chopped chocolate over hot water. Remove from heat, allow to cool slightly, then stir in sour cream and salt. Add sifted icing sugar and beat until a spreading consistency.

Date and Walnut Loaf

4 oz. (1 cup) self raising (all purpose) flour	2 oz. (⅜ cup) chopped dates
4 oz. (½ cup) sugar	2 oz. (½ cup) chopped walnuts
½ teaspoon bicarbonate of soda	1 oz. (2 tablespoons) butter
2 teaspoons cinnamon	¼ pint (½ cup) water

Sift flour, sugar, bicarbonate of soda and cinnamon into a basin. Add the chopped dates and walnuts, mix well. Heat butter and water in a saucepan until water just comes to the boil. Make a well in the centre of the dry ingredients, add hot liquid and mix thoroughly. Spoon into greased 10 in. × 3 in. tin. Bake in a moderate oven, Mark 4, 350°F., approximately 40 minutes. Serve with butter.

Mocha Torte

6 eggs, separated	1 teaspoon instant coffee powder
4 oz. (½ cup) castor (superfine) sugar	4 dessertspoons water
4 oz. (4 squares) plain chocolate	2 dessertspoons plain flour

Coffee Cream

1 dessertspoon instant coffee powder	2 oz. (¼ cup) castor (superfine) sugar
½ pint (1 cup) cream	

Beat egg-yolks and sugar until pale and creamy. Melt chopped chocolate over hot water, allow to cool slightly; add to egg-yolk mixture, mixing well. Stir coffee into water, add to chocolate mixture. Gently fold in sifted flour and lightly beaten egg-whites. It is important not to overmix.

Pour mixture into 3 greased and lined 8 in. sandwich tins, bake in moderately slow oven, Mark 3, 325°F., 30 to 35 minutes; cool on wire rack.

When cold, join together with Coffee Cream. Cover top and sides of cake with remaining Coffee Cream, decorate with toasted almonds; drizzle a little melted chocolate over, if desired. Refrigerate.
Coffee Cream Combine all ingredients in mixing bowl, refrigerate at least 1 hour. When ready to use beat until thick.

Orange Date Cake

¼ pint (½ cup) orange juice	1 lb. (2 cups) castor (superfine) sugar
1 lb. (2½ cups) dates	3 oz. (½ cup) mixed peel
1 lb. 2 oz. (4½ cups) self raising (all purpose) flour	3 eggs
pinch salt	½ to ¾ pint (1 to 1½ cups) warm milk
8 oz. (½ cup) butter	½ teaspoon vanilla

Pour orange juice over chopped dates, cover, leave overnight.

Next day sift flour and salt into bowl. Rub in butter until mixture resembles fine breadcrumbs; mix in castor sugar. Add mixed peel, dates and orange juice, rub through lightly, separating the pieces. Make well in centre of dry ingredients. Add beaten eggs alternately with milk to which vanilla has been added, stirring until all dry ingredients are well mixed. Place mixture into greased and paper lined 10 in. square cake tin. Bake in moderate oven, Mark 4, 350°F. 30 minutes, reduce heat to moderately slow, Mark 2, 300°F., and continue cooking further 1½ hours. Leave in tin to cool.

Chocolate Orange Cake

6 oz. (¾ cup) butter
6 oz. (¾ cup) castor (superfine) sugar
3 eggs

6 oz. (1½ cups) self raising (all purpose) flour
2 tablespoons milk
grated rind 2 oranges

Chocolate Icing

6 oz. (1 cup) icing (confectioners') sugar

1 tablespoon cocoa
½ teaspoon butter
water to mix

Cream butter and sugar until light and fluffy, beat in eggs one at a time, beating well after each addition. Sift flour, fold in alternately with milk; add grated orange rind. Place mixture in greased and paper lined 9 in. × 5 in. loaf tin. Bake in moderate oven, Mark 4, 350°F., approximately 1 hour or until skewer inserted in centre comes out clean. Leave in tin a few minutes before turning out on to wire tray. When cold, top with chocolate icing.
Chocolate Icing Sift icing sugar and cocoa into bowl, add butter, then mix to a stiff consistency with a little cold water. Place over hot water and stir until a pouring consistency; this will take only a minute or two. Pour on top of cake and spread with spatula, swirling icing with tip of spatula.

Almond Meringue Cake

4 oz. (½ cup or 1 stick) butter
4 oz. (½ cup) castor (superfine) sugar
4 egg-yolks

1 teaspoon vanilla
4 oz. (1 cup) self raising (all purpose) flour
pinch salt
4 to 5 tablespoons milk

Topping

4 egg-whites
6 oz. (¾ cup) castor (superfine) sugar
2 dessertspoons sugar, extra

½ teaspoon cinnamon
1 oz. (⅛ cup) blanched, slivered almonds

Cream butter and sugar until light and fluffy. Beat in yolks and vanilla. Sift flour and salt; add alternately with milk. Spread mixture into a greased 8 in. springform pan.
Topping Beat egg-whites until stiff, gradually add sugar, beating well. Spread this meringue over mixture in pan. Mix together the extra sugar and cinnamon, sprinkle over meringue. Sprinkle with almonds. Bake in moderate oven, Mark 4, 350°F., 60 to 65 minutes, or until cake is cooked when tested with a skewer. Leave in pan 10 minutes before turning out.

Pineapple Fruit Cake

8 oz. (1 cup) sugar
15 oz. can crushed pineapple
1 lb. (2¾ cups) mixed fruit
1 teaspoon bicarbonate of soda

1 teaspoon mixed spice
4 oz. (½ cup or 1 stick) butter
4 oz. (1 cup) plain flour
4 oz. (1 cup) self raising (all purpose) flour
2 eggs

Place sugar, contents of can of pineapple, chopped mixed fruit, bicarbonate of soda, spice and butter into a saucepan. Bring to boil, boil 3 minutes; remove from heat, cool completely.
Sift flours together, mix into cold fruit mixture with well-beaten eggs. Place mixture into greased and lined 8 in. cake tin.
Bake in moderate oven, Mark 4, 350°F., approximately 1½ hours, reduce heat to moderately slow, Mark 2, 300°F., bake further 20 to 30 minutes or until a skewer, inserted, comes out clean.

Pineapple Teacake

15 oz. can crushed pineapple
4 oz. (½ cup or 1 stick) butter
6 oz. (1½ cups) self raising (all purpose) flour
pinch salt

4 oz. (½ cup) sugar
1 egg
scant ¼ pint (7 tablespoons) milk
4 oz. (⅓ cup) honey
1 oz. (¼ cup) coconut

Drain pineapple (the juice is not needed for this recipe). Melt 2 oz. (¼ cup) butter and allow it to cool slightly.
Sift flour and salt, add sugar. Combine beaten egg, milk and melted butter, add to dry ingredients; mix well. Pour into a greased deep 8 in. round cake tin, spread pineapple over the batter. Cream remaining butter and honey well, spoon over pineapple; sprinkle with coconut. Bake in moderately hot oven, Mark 4, 350°F., 35 to 40 minutes.
When cool, sprinkle top with sifted icing sugar.

Index